Library Services to Youth of Hispanic Heritage

Library Services to Youth of Hispanic Heritage

BARBARA IMMROTH *AND*
KATHLEEN DE LA PEÑA MCCOOK, *EDITORS*

Assisted by Catherine Jasper

McFarland & Company, Inc., Publishers
Jefferson, North Carolina, and London

Library of Congress Cataloguing-in-Publication Data

Library services to youth of hispanic heritage / Barbara Immroth and Kathleen de la Peña McCook, editors ; assisted by Catherine Jasper.
p. cm.
Includes bibliographical references and index.
ISBN 0-7864-0790-5 (softcover : 50# alkaline paper) ∞
1. Hispanic Americans and libraries. 2. Hispanic American children — Books and reading. 3. Hispanic American youth — Books and reading. 4. Hispanic American children — Education. 5. Hispanic American youth — Education. 6. Children's libraries — United States. 7. School libraries — United States. 8. Public libraries — Services to Hispanic Americans — United States. I. Immroth, Barbara Froling. II. McCook, Kathleen de la Peña.
Z711.8.L54 2000
027.6'3 — dc21 00-37247

British Library cataloguing data are available

Manufactured in the United States of America

McFarland & Company, Inc., Publishers
Box 611, Jefferson, North Carolina 28640
www.mcfarlandpub.com

CONTENTS

Preface

At this turn of the century, services for the education of Hispanic youth become increasingly important to the entire population of the United States. Practitioners who are active in this field do not generally have the time to report their successful activities so that others can replicate their projects and learn from their experiences, so we are fortunate to have these essays about programs, services, collections and evaluation for Hispanic youth at a number of libraries. Those who desire information about successful programs for youth of Hispanic heritage may learn from them. In addition to the experience-based papers, several in this collection are research-based and provide more information and suggestions about data collection for those who want to establish similar projects in their libraries or for students to learn for their future professional work.

The first essay serves as an introduction for the rest. It is written by Barbara Immroth, professor at the University of Texas at Austin. She is the American Library Association representative to the International Federation of Library Associations Standing Committee on Children's Libraries and a past president of the Association for Library Services to Children.

The next two essays come under **Part I: The Trejo Foster Foundation.**

Kathleen de la Peña McCook, articulates a theoretical context for library service to Hispanic youth in the essay "Concepts of Culture: The Role of the Trejo Foster Foundation." She presents the concept of culture and the complexity of Latin American cultures across four centuries. A brief description of the history and purpose of the Trejo Foster Foundation is also presented.

Dr. Isabel Schon, in the Alice G. Smith Lecture, describes her philosophy ("If you want to know me, know my stories") and her life's work, now carried out at the Center for the Study of Books in Spanish for Children and Adolescents.

Part II: Programs. Programming in libraries around the country, representative, no doubt, of best practice, is described in this section of the book.

Lucía M. González, recipient of the University of South Florida's School of Library and Information Science Jean Kay Gates Distinguished Alumna Award, describes "Developing Culturally Integrated Children's Programs." González says, "My dreams always come true," and she warns us not to settle for one-time or short term programming for special populations. Rather, she advises us to integrate the culture throughout all of the programming, so all of the children are exposed to it. She provides ideas on free and low-cost publicity and describes *La hora de cuentos* and Project Colorin' Colorado, programs at the Miami-Dade Public Library. She tells how she raises the circulation exponentially at her library through meeting the needs of her community.

Rose V. Treviño, in "Buenos Días/ Good Morning: Bilingual Programs for

Children," presents program plans from the San Antonio Public Library that encourage reading. There is hope for the next generation with librarians using these model programs to serve the public. Rose has won the Siddie Joe Johnson Award for outstanding service to children and the John Cotton Dana Award from the American Library Association for the bilingual Born to Read program targeted at Hispanic teen mothers.

Dana Watson describes the process of providing young readers with the materials they need in her essay "Connecting Readers' Advisors and Youth." She outlines strategies for active and passive readers' advisory and tailors these principles to use in Hispanic communities.

Judith Rodriguez is the supervising librarian for the program Connecting Libraries and School Project at the New York Public Library. She tells how she developed "Parents' Workshops" for Latino families and her work in the Washington Heights area introducing Latino parents to children's literature through picture book discussion groups and poetry workshops in Spanish and English.

Catherine Jasper, reference librarian at the Tampa-Hillsborough Public Library and a former ESL teacher, presents her experience as a student at University of South Florida attending a funded summer institute in "Services to Migrant and Seasonal Farmworkers in Florida."

Tim Wadham, author of *Programming with Latino Children's Materials: A How-to-Do-It Manual,* tells about "Bridging Cultures Through Literature," his discovery of Spanish language literature for children and how he uses it in his programming.

Derrie Perez, director of the Tampa Campus Library of the University of South Florida, presents "The Support Role of Community College/Learning Resource Programs in Academic Success," in which she uses her experiences as vice president at Hillsborough Community College Learning Resources as context.

Collection development for Spanish language materials is the topic of several essays in **Part III: Collections.**

Eliza T. Dresang, author of *Radical Change: Books for Youth in a Digital Age,* analyzes recent award-winning literature in "Outstanding Literature: Pura Belpré and Américas Selections with Special Appeal in the Digital Age."

Oralia Garza de Cortés, in "Give Them What They Need," recounts a story about poor library service to Hispanic youth. She presents research supporting ways to improve services, and lists nine needs of Latino children and their families to be addressed by public service librarians.

In a co-authored paper, "Poetry of the African Diaspora: In Search of Common Ground Between Anglo and Latin American," Sonia Ramírez Wohlmuth uses her knowledge of intercultural communications and Latin America Literature and Henrietta M. Smith uses her knowledge of the Coretta Scott King Awards books, for a boundary-crossing exploration of collection development.

In "Collection Development Across the Borders," Haydee C. Hodis presents ways librarians can familiarize themselves with Spanish-language material and describes a core collection for serving youth of Hispanic heritage.

The next section is **Part IV: Planning and Evaluating.** In the category of evaluation, measurement and organization of resources and services are several useful studies for planners of library programs and collections for youth of Hispanic heritage.

James O. Carey, active in implementing the new *Information Power: Building Partnerships for Learning* (ALA, 1998) for school library media centers, presents his paper on "Implementing New Services," a blueprint for a planning process leading to action.

Elaine Yontz writes about "Subject Access to Fiction: A Case Study Based on the Works of Pat Mora." Her suggestions for subject access can easily be implemented in libraries of any size.

Alice Robbin, associate professor at the School of Library and Informative Science at Indiana University, writes about "Hispanic Demographics and Implications for Media Services," an essay generated from her analysis of the political controversy over revising federal statistics policy for classifying racial and ethnic group data.

Milagros Otero Guzman reports on "Services to Young Adults in Puerto Rican Public Libraries," based on her master's research at the University of Puerto Rico, Rio Piedras.

Dean K. Jue investigates the relationship of materials circulation to the value of library service for Hispanics in "Measuring In-Library Usage.

Part V is **Bibliographic Resources**, and two experienced writers have produced useful bibliographies.

Patricia F. Beilke compiled "Planning School Library Media Services K–8: Selected Resources," the result of her years of study on this topic.

Janice Greenberg compiled "Collection Development: An Annotated Bibliography." She previously compiled the bibliography "Leadership and Participative Management for the Third National Institute for Hispanic Library Education."

The final essay in the book comes under **Part VI: For the Future**.

"REFORMITA: A Gang for the New Millennium," by Dr. Arnulfo Trejo, suggests another creative approach to enhancing library services to youth of Hispanic heritage. Dr. Trejo continues his lifelong quest to address the need for systemic changes.

Further information about the writers of these essays may be found at the back of the book just before the index.

All of these papers suggest that the best practices for services and materials for all children of all backgrounds is similar to those practices adapted for outstanding service and collections for youth of Hispanic heritage. While more emphasis is placed on use of Spanish language and Spanish materials and of the necessity for outreach to the underserved population, the established practice of library service to children and youth in the United States forms the basis from which the services and collections described in these papers are derived.

It is the hope of the editors that these papers will provide the knowledge, incentive and enthusiasm for others to develop and expand the network of library services and collections to the exponentially growing population of Hispanic youth — and provide the next generation with a bright future through libraries.

— *The Editors*

A Bright Future for Youth of Hispanic Heritage

Barbara Immroth

The desire to prepare one's children for a happy, productive life is universal. Parents, family members, educators, community leaders, and policy makers all over the world work toward a better future for today's youth.

Librarians, too, share this goal. Worldwide, they strive to establish and provide quality services for the children in their communities. The International Federation of Library Associations and Institutions (IFLA), in its *Guidelines for Children's Services,* takes up the cause of children everywhere, enjoining its members to be

> helpful to librarians serving children in various countries throughout the world. Although the context of services for children and the specifics of how services are delivered differ greatly from one country to another, these services are recognized as an important component of all public library work. It is only by serving children that libraries can truly "contribute to lifelong universal education" (UNESCO Public Library Manifesto) and develop informed citizens who will support and maintain political library and economic prosperity.[1]

In promoting their *Guidelines,* the IFLA Standing Committee on Children's Libraries held a seminar in 1997 on education and training for staff working with children and youth libraries in developed and developing countries. Issues, trends and the status of education for children and youth librarianship were explored in four strands: changing needs of children, the community, society at large, and the world; changing needs in technology; changing needs in financial resources; and changing needs in organizations. The participants from around the world gave numerous examples of change and offered programming, resource and service strategies for meeting these changes.[2]

In the United States, children's librarians have been zealously working toward the goal of a better, more productive future for children over one hundred years. Public librarians throughout the country strive to provide quality resources and services for children and youth. On the national level, for instance, the American Library Association has sponsored and collaborated on numerous projects, such as the Association for Library Service to Children's Born to Read and Between the Lions partnerships and the American Association of School Librarians' ICONnect and Library Power collaborations.

The U.S. National Commission on Libraries and Information Science (NCLIS) has adoped a resolution recognizing the important role libraries play in the lives of American children:

> NCLIS urges that our society — officials and educators at all levels, community leaders, parents and other adult caregivers, confidantes and role models — utilize the vast potential of libraries and support the current and potential abilities and efforts of librarians in assisting adults, youth and children to seek positive outcomes through wise use of information.[3]

The U.S. Department of Commerce, in its *Falling Through the Net: Defining the Digital Divide*, describes the division between the information "haves" and "have nots" and emphasizes that "information tools such as the personal computer and the Internet are increasingly critical to economic success and personal advancement."[4] Where but the public library, that veritable mine of information, can the underprivileged stake their claims to a life of knowledge acquisition?

While the public acknowledges the need for a literate, well-educated population, however, we see growing numbers of illiterate adults, school dropouts and workers unprepared for the latest in workplace technology, which demands a higher level of literacy than ever before. Society, too, has embraced modernity, and with the gadgets of applied science seeming to change as often and as unpredictably as the whims of fashion, the world can be an unfriendly place for information — and literacy — have-nots.

Stephen Krashen, in *The Power of Reading*, points out that literacy is relative, and even those armed with basic skills may be overwhelmed by the mercurial demands of the PC Age:

> Nearly everyone in the United States can read and write. They just don't read and write very well. Although basic literacy has been on the increase for the last century, the demands for literacy have been rising faster. Many people clearly don't read and write well enough to handle the complex literacy demands of modern society.
>
> The cure for this kind of literacy crisis lies, in my opinion, in doing one activity, an activity that is all too often rare in the lives of many people: reading.[5]

Many projects and programs have been developed for libraries to address the problems of illiteracy. The "Prototype of Public Library Services for Young Children and Their Families," for instance, declares the need for experienced children's librarians and child care educators; for more extensive services, better attitudes and skills; and for broader organizational structures and greater resources. The prototype intends public libraries to be agents in the development of children, ensuring for all the opportunity to succeed in school and become lifelong learners.[6]

Within the broader societal and professional context of providing the best possible education for the future of children and youth, it is hardly surprising that librarians who provide services to a specific population, in this case, the youth of Hispanic heritage in the United States, are enthusiastically involved in promoting and providing expanded resources and services for their clients.

As we enter the 21st century, services for the education of Hispanic youth become increasingly important to the entire population of the United States. Librarians active in this field do not often have the time to write about their successful activities so that others can replicate their projects and learn from their experiences. The Trejo Institute provides an unusual opportunity to learn about a rich variety of services for youth at a number of libraries. Librarians who desire information about successful programs for youth of Hispanic heritage may learn from the experiences of those preceding them down this pathway. In addition, research-based information and suggestions about data collection provide a basis for establishing similar projects in other libraries and data for graduate students to apply to their future professional work.

One of the most important investments adults can make to ensure children's education success is to foster in them a love of books and reading. Libraries can serve as a starting point for parents, families, teachers and caregivers who seek enjoyable books to share with children. Librarians can guide boys and girls in their quests to become capable, enthusiastic and avid readers. Librarians embracing these ideals and armed with the ideas and experience of others can enable the youth of Hispanic heritage to take their place as literate, productive lifelong learners.

Notes

1. *Guidelines for Children's Services*, ed. Adele M. Fasick (The Hague International Federation of Library Associations and Institutions), *IFLA Professional Reports*, No. 25 (1991): p. 1.
2. Barbara Immroth, "Quality Library Services to Children and Young Adults for Changing Needs" in *Libraries: Global Reach—Local Touch*, eds. Kathleen de la Peña McCook, Barbara J. Ford and Kate Lippincott (Chicago: American Library Association, 1998): pp. 181–86.
3. Resolved by the U.S. National Commission of Libraries and Information Science at its meeting on June 26, 1998, in Washington, D.C.
4. U.S. Department of Commerce, National Telecommunications and Information Administration, *Falling Through the Net: Defining the Digital Divide*, 1999. http://www.ntia.doc.gov/ntiahome/fttn99/execsummary.html
5. Stephen Krashen, *The Power of Reading: Insights from the Research* (Englewood, Col.: Libraries Unlimited, 1993): pp. ix.
6. *Achieving School Readiness: Public Libraries and National Education Goal No. 1*, eds. Barbara Immroth and Viki Ash-Geisler (Chicago: Amercan Library Association, 1995): pp. 139–146.

Part I : The Trejo Foster Foundation

Concepts of Culture: The Role of the Trejo Foster Foundation

Kathleen de la Peña McCook

Maintaining cultural identity has been an important aspect of life in the United States over the last three decades. Much has been written of the rejection of the idea of the nation as a cultural melting pot with strong admonition given those who had sought to eradicate individual cultures of the newly arrived. Today, schools, libraries and communities celebrate ethnic diversity with events like Black History Month and Hispanic Heritage Month.

To some degree it might be assumed that public celebration of diverse cultures has long been thoroughly integrated in calendars, curricula and the media. However, this is not the case. In librarianship, at least, the widespread recognition of diversity and the incorporation of collection development from diverse cultures in the policies of libraries has been the result of many years of effort by ethnic organizations which have affiliated with national and state associations. The need for such organizations was identified during the 1960s when U.S. librarianship, like so many institutions, sought to focus on the need to expand services to the unserved and on expansion of collections.[1] An overview of the effort to develop outreach services focusing on various ethnic populations by the American Library Association can be found in the projects and publications of the Office for Literacy and Outreach Services.[2]

Concepts of Culture

The word *culture* is generally understood in two ways. The first is the relatively narrow definition that equates culture with aesthetics, especially the fine arts and their institutional settings — museums and orchestras, for instance. This has been extended of late to encompass popular culture and its variations. The other main definition is anthropological, directed at regional or local societies or communities. This makes it possible to examine the ways people interact rather than simply analyze artifacts of their societies. In his essay "The Decline of Cultural Forms," Thomas McFarland differentiates between the shape of culture and the form of culture.[3] Shapes of culture — paintings in a museum, books in a library — become forms of culture when viewed or read in a context of understanding history, artistic styles, or literary precursors.

Thus the work done by librarians may be considered an effort to preserve cultural forms and to some extent celebrate organized characterizations of culture. Yet culture continually shifts. Nuckolls has observed that

American students of anthropology must have the familiar made strange enough to be considered cultural.[4] Because many will not have the opportunity to study anthropology, it must be through universally available cultural centers — notably, public libraries — that culture is preserved and valued in its various forms. While culture can be viewed from different philosophical variations — Marxist, semiotic, functional or hermeneutical — the convergence on autonomy from social structure seems a likely vantage point.[5]

This idea has been manifested in the growing interdisciplinary field of cultural studies which balances the ideas of "grand theory" against the local and idiosyncratic.[6] To define the challenge to librarians and the libraries they manage in terms of preserving culture is difficult, indeed. The task becomes even more complex if an effort is made to link various types of symbolic modes. These might be characterized as primary orality (speech before writing); literacy; and secondary orality (of the late modern electronic media).[7]

But if cultural forms disengage from social structure, on what basis is there focus on services to people characterized by language or national origin? In his essay on cultural pluralism, Bennet M. Berger has observed that focus on subordinate or disadvantaged groups means more differentiation. The reclamation of culture from the elites is an effort to demonstrate that any group can "generate distinctive 'ways of life' — including a language, dialect or argot, and an indigenous set of ideas and customs not shared by outsiders."[8] Taken together these analyses bring a concept of culture not only differentiated and democratized but relativized.[9] Therein we have intellectual justification to match the emotional and spiritual desire to preserve and celebrate differences in culture.

Hispanic Culture and Literature

Applying the "Hispanic" label to cultures from Spain, Latin America and the Caribbean — a label based solely on the shared linguistic base of the Spanish language — is no more legitimate than assuming a shared culture between residents of New Zealand and those of Mississippi. This point has been made strongly by William Beezley and Judith Ewell in their volume *The Human Tradition in Modern Latin America*, in which they note it is patently absurd to use a general term like "Latin American" to indicate a common experience.[10]

While it is folly to imagine that "Hispanic Culture" can be described simply, it might be useful to mention some high points of Latin American literature so the enormity may begin to be comprehended. In his study of the colonization of the Americas, *The Hispanic Labyrinth*, Xavier Rubert deVentós' comments on the breadth of indigenous civilization, noting that "their genius for the monumental was curiously allied with a sensitivity for the minimal and a skill for detail.... The Mayan culture, which, having discovered the vault and the calendar, a numbering system including zero, and a partially phonetic writing system, was already in decline by the time of Charlemagne.... The Nahuatl culture which, upon the literary and architectural base of the Olmecs, Toltecs, and Teotihuacans, had built a political-military empire and elaborated a complex moral theogony."[11]

For the general reader, an attempt to survey the literature of Latin America is so daunting as to discourage. After all, each of these nations has a history of written literature dating to the 1500s and often including the poetry and tales of the indigenous people.[12] In Mexico consider Fray Bernardino de Sahagún (1499–1590), preserver of pre-Hispanic literature such as Nahuatl poetry; Sor Juana Inés de la Cruz (1648–95), legendary in Mexico and Spain and an inspiration to feminists; Fernández de Lizardi (1776–1827), who wrote to transform society; or Octavio Paz, Nobel Prize in 1990, whose visionary mystical work incorporated Mexican cultural tradition, surrealism and social and cultural evolution. In Guatemala, take note of *Popol Vuh* (*Book of Quichés*), the Mayan Bible, translated by Francisco Viménez (1702); Rafael Landívar (1731–1793) with his concern for Indian cultures; José Milla (1822–82), with his typical Guatemalan character; Wyld Ospina (1891–1958), who cultivated *criollism* (creolism); or Miguel Angel Asturias (1899–1974) Nobel Prize in 1967, who used magical realism in his Indianist and political novels to show the opposing worldviews of European and indigenous cultures.

The epic poem *La Araucana* (1569, 1578, 1589), by Spanish nobleman Alonso de Ercilla y Zúñiga, examined the ideological conflict between the values of the Spanish empire and Araucanians in Chile. Much later Juan Egaña, a Peruvian Creole, wrote *El chileño consolado en los presidios* (1826), constituting the reader as public opinion. In this century the Nobel Prizes awarded to Gabriela Mistral in 1945 and Pablo Neruda in 1972 attest to the maturity of the literary tradition.

Gabriel García Márquez, Colombian Nobel Laureate, writer of *Cien años de soledad* (1967), probably the most widely read Latin American novel in the United States, joins others in his nation — from Juan Rodríguez Greyle, author of *El carnero* (1638), to Manuel Zapata Olivella, *Changó, el gran putas* (1983) — in spanning six centuries of African and Afro-American history on three continents.

In Cuba, the *Mirror of Patience* (1608), by Silvestre de Balboa, is rich in classical-tropical elements, a tradition that carries through the literature of that nation to the near mythic work of José Martí. Martí's novel *Amistad funesta* (1885), his poetry, and his essays melded ideology and creation. In Puerto Rico the Spanish-Cuban-American War of 1898 indicated a period of colonialism, with novels such as Juliá Mavín's *Tierra adentro* (1911) or *La gleba* (1912) treating the impact of the United States on the people of that island.

Clearly the possibility of understanding Latin American literature in Argentina, Bolivia, Brazil, Chile, Colombia, Costa Rica, Cuba, the Dominican Republic, Ecuador, Guatemala, Haiti, Honduras, Mexico, Nicaragua, Panama, Paraguay, Peru, Puerto Rico, El Salvador, Uruguay and Venezuela over four centuries is the work of many scholarly lifetimes. This brief and idiosyncratic discussion is meant to provide only an indication of the general lack of knowledge and the need to comprehend.

The Trejo Foster Foundation for Hispanic Library Education

The complexity of the idea of culture and the difficulty in defining Hispanic culture have provided formidable challenges to U.S. librarians. When people and cultures cross borders — or, in the case of many people of Hispanic descent in Texas and California, are invaded or conquered — there is transformation. In their essay "Latino Writings in the United States," Santa Arias and Erlinda Gonzales-Berry note,

> Many worlds overlap in Latino literary discourse articulating new positions. It is the cultural expression of a borderland space where language, class, gender, and racial ethnicity are the interrelated themes in the Latino ethos. As expressed not only in the content of the text, but in the rhetorical and formal construction of expression, language and identity have been major concerns of Chicanos, Boricuas (Puerto Ricans), and Cuban American writers.[13]

It could not be expected that mainstream U.S. librarianship would work to accommodate these concerns. In 1971 REFORMA, the National Association to Promote Library Services to the Spanish Speaking, was founded with Dr. Arnulfo Trejo as its first president.[14] The association, through meetings held concurrent with the American Library Association, publication of the substantive *REFORMA Newsletter*, establishment of scholarships and awards, and promotion of library services and programs which meet the needs of the Hispanic community has worked to maintain concern and support. However, recognizing that long term preservation of concern for Hispanic culture must begin during the education of librarians and by the sensitization of faculty who teach them, Dr. Trejo established the Trejo Foster Foundation for Hispanic Library Education.[15] The Trejo Foster Foundation serves as a "think tank" for issues concerning library and information services for persons of Hispanic heritage in the United States. It also provides support to finance research as well as seminars, workshops and other activities that will promote and enhance library education for Hispanics. Mrs. Ninfa Trejo, who has chaired the REFORMA Scholarship Committee, serves as secretary of the foundation and has provided invaluable service in recording the foundation's achievements.

Under the aegis of the foundation, four institutes have been held:

1. *Status of Hispanic Library and Information Services: A National Institute for Educational Change*, July 29–31, 1993, University of Arizona-Tucson, University of Arizona — School of Information Resources and Library Science, chaired by Director Charlie D. Hurt, and Dr. Arnulfo Trejo
2. *Latino Populations and the Public Library*, November 12–15, 1995, University of Texas–Austin, Graduate School of Library and Information Science, chaired by Dean Brooke Sheldon and Dr. Arnulfo Trejo
3. *Hispanic Leadership in Libraries*, August 8–10, 1997, Rutgers University, School of Communication, Information and Library Studies, chaired by Dr. Betty Turock, Professor of Communication, Information and Library Studies, Mr. Martín Gómez, Executive Director, Brooklyn Public Library and Dr. Arnulfo Trejo
4. *Library Services to Youth of Hispanic Heritage*, March 12–14, 1999, University of South Florida, School of Library and Information Science, Tampa, chaired by Director Kathleen de la Peña McCook, Ms. Catherine Jasper, Tampa-Hillsborough County Public Library System, and Dr. Arnulfo Trejo

As these institutes have moved to different schools of library and information science, they have received support from local libraries and associations.[16] Each institute has consolidated commitment to developing services aimed at the Latino population and has strengthened the network of librarians who share common goals. The Trejo Foster Foundation has been a well-spring bringing together librarians from our hemisphere to analyze, deliberate and plan for the future.

Notes

1. For a history of the contributions of the various ethnic groups to U.S. librarianship,

scc the summer 2000 issue of *Library Trends*, edited by Kathleen de la Peña McCook, with essays on the achievements of the American Indian Library Association, the Asian Pacific American Librarians Association, the Black Caucus, the Chinese-American Library Association, REFORMA, and overall the efforts to achieve diversity.

2. Kate Lippincott, Kathleen de la Peña McCook and Sara M. Taffae, *25 Years of Outreach: A Bibliographic Timeline of the American Library Association, Office for Literacy and Outreach Services* (Tampa: University of South Florida, School of Library and Information Science, Research Group, 1996) ERIC ED 396 755.

3. Thomas McFarland, "The Decline of Cultural Forms," in *Shapes of Culture* (Iowa City: University of Iowa Press, 1987), pp. 1–36.

4. Charles W. Nuckolls, *Culture: A Problem That Cannot Be Solved* (Madison: University of Wisconsin Press, 1998), pp. 37.

5. Jeffrey C. Alexander, "Analytic Debates: Understanding the Relative Autonomy of Culture," pp. 1–27 in *Culture and Society*, eds. Jeffrey C. Alexander and Steven Seidman (Cambridge: Cambridge University Press, 1990).

6 Fred Inglis, *Cultural Studies* (Oxford: Blackwell, 1993).

7. Johan Fornäs, *Cultural Theory and Late Modernity* (London: Sage Publications, 1995), pp. 161–162.

8. Bennett M. Berger, *An Essay on Culture: Symbolic Structure and Social Structure* (Berkeley: University of California Press, 1995), pp. 26–27.

9. Berger, p. 30.

10. William H. Beezley and Judith Ewell, *The Human Tradition in Latin America* (Wilmington, Del.: Scholarly Resources, 1997), p. xix.

11. Xavier Rubert de Ventós, *The Hispanic Labyrinth: Tradition and Modernity in the Colonization of the Americas* (New Brunswick, N.J.: Transaction, 1991), p. 2.

12. David William Foster, *Handbook of Latin American Literature*, 2nd ed. (New York: Garland, 1992); the basis for these literary comments.

13. Santa Arias and Erlinda Gonzales-Berry, "Latino Writing in the United States," in *Handbook of Latin American Literature* (New York: Garland, 1992), p. 651.

14. Norman Oder, "REFORMA Comes of Age," *Library Journal* 121 (October 1, 1996): 38–40.

15. The Trejo Foster Foundation has been named after Annette M. Foster Trejo, the late wife of Arnulfo and co-founder of Hispanic Books Distributors, Inc. (HBD). As business manager of HBD she specialized in the selection and acquisition of Spanish language books for young adults and children. Days before her death she assisted in the establishment of the Trejo Foster Foundation for Hispanic Library Education. The Foundation has become a living memorial to her. See "In Memoriam: Annette M. Trejo," *REFORMA Newsletter* 11 (Fall/Winter, 1993): 11.

16. Institutes have received generous support above all from REFORMA and the American Library Association. The Texas State Library, Brooklyn Public Library, University of Puerto Rico, Florida Library Association, Florida Association for Media in Education, Tampa Bay Library Consortium and Los Amigos de la Biblioteca Pública de Tampa all provided support for institutes held in their respective regions.

From Doña Blanca to Don Quijote

Isabel Schon

I vividly remember the early meetings in Arizona in the 1970s when Dr. Trejo with his characteristic optimism would get us together with ideas and suggestions to promote library services to the Spanish-speaking.

I had just arrived from my native Mexico City, where I had been a librarian. As a single mother, my first concern was, of course, my nine-year-old daughter. How was my daughter going to adapt to such a different culture? Could she learn English soon enough to adjust to a different school? I was still having my own troubles with the English language. Could we survive culture shock? No family? No real Mexican food? Friends?

Fond memories that kept me going were my weekly trips with my father to the only library in Mexico City at the time. As the oldest of eight brothers and sisters, I had the privilege of going with him. But children were not allowed inside the library in Mexico City; I had to wait outside, until my father came out with our weekly surprises. Certainly Dr. Trejo's wonderful dreams reinforced what I had always wanted as a child for my brothers, my sisters, and myself and, now, for my own daughter and the many Spanish-speaking children like her.

And, like every Spanish-speaking parent that I've ever met in the U.S., of course, I wanted my daughter to learn to speak, read, and write in English as well as her Anglo peers. I also knew the research in language acquisition and reading. I knew that reading is a process — an easily transferable skill — and that her improvement in reading in Spanish would increase her reading abilities in English. But, most importantly, I wanted my daughter to grow up to become an independent, self-assured human being. I wanted her to learn to respect herself, her Mexican background and culture. I knew that only then she would have the inner strength and courage to cope with a new society and culture that made so many different demands of us.

Through my father, I grew up admiring the works of the great Spanish-speaking writers. My father pointed out how Octavio

Editor's Note: These remarks, under the full title "From Doña Blanca to Don Quijote: Serving the Reading Needs of Spanish-Speaking Youth," were presented as the Alice G. Smith Lecture, which was the keynote address at the Fourth Institute of the Trejo Foster Foundation for Hispanic Library Education, at the University of South Florida, School of Library and Information Science, Tampa, March 12, 1999.

Paz, the finest contemporary essayist in Spanish and one of the Spanish language's great poets, dared to examine aspects of Mexican life previously considered untouchable. He admired and respected the Argentine Jorge Luis Borges, the master of fantastic literature. He introduced me to Don Quijote's ingenious adventures that transform reality into idealistic dreams and facts into poetic fantasies.

Through my mother, I grew up admiring strong women. She personified the rationalistic attitude and mystical conceptions of nature of the prolific writer of the baroque, Sor Juana Inés de la Cruz. She admired the intensely lyrical Chilean poet Gabriela Mistral and rejoiced when Mistral accepted in 1945 the first Nobel Prize ever awarded to a Latin American writer.

Together, we read the marvelous poetry of the second Latin American to receive the Nobel Prize (1971) for literature, Pablo Neruda. We delighted in Gabriel Garcia Marquez's chronicle of the mythical town of Macondo, *Cien años de soledad,* which provoked, in the words of the Peruvian novelist Mario Vargas Llosa, a "literary earthquake" in Latin America and made its author "almost as famous as a great soccer player or an eminent singer of boleros."

Another event that made a great impact in the thoughts and feelings of many of us in Mexico City was when Octavio Paz, the Mexican poet and 1990 Nobel laureate, resigned his job as Mexico's ambassador to India after the Tlaltelolco massacre of 1968, in which the Mexican army slew hundreds of protesting students in downtown Mexico City, carting their bodies away to secret graves.

My parents definitely influenced my values as a mother, a librarian, and an educator. My greatest wish is to instill in my daughter, and all Spanish-speaking children and young adults, the capacity for critical judgment and the enthusiasm for Spanish-language literature in particular and world literature in general that will enrich their lives as individual human beings, that will develop insights into and understandings of their own lives and their realities, and that will develop an interest in reading as a leisure-time activity.

Very often I get calls or e-mails asking me to list the top 10, 20, or 50 books that all Spanish-speaking children or young adults should read. While I have prepared several lists, I am always reluctant to do so. Because, as we all know, the emotional impact of any book depends on our personal histories. Furthermore, it is always difficult to know which book will impact a given child at a particular time in his or her own emotional development.

Of course, we should always consider the qualities of well-written fiction — honesty, integrity, and imagination. Our favorite books provide us with a sense of wonder and satisfaction that is further enhanced by memorable characters, a true portrayal of life, a fine literary style, emotional impact, and other characteristics of distinguished books for the young.

On my list of favorite books for Spanish-speaking children, I always include books by the wonderfully creative Argentine author María Elena Walsh; popular folktales by Pura Belpré; Violeta Denou's charming illustrations; Manuel Alonso's poignant, honest stories; Joan Manuel Gisbert's imaginative novels; Manuel Afonseca's works, crafted with fresh, natural style; Miguel Fernández-Pacheco's engrossing novels; and delightful stories, novels, and poems by outstanding Latino authors such as Gary Soto, Nicholasa Mohr, Sandra Cisneros, Pat Mora, Julia Alvarez, Cristina García, Alma Flor Ada, and Lucía González. Some of the Latino illustrators that we all admire are Lulu Delacre, Leyla Torres, and Leovigildo Martinez.

On my recommended lists of outstanding works that Spanish-speaking young adults should be exposed to, I include works by several of my longtime favorite authors as well as such classics as Alejo Carpentier's masterpiece, *Los pasos perdidos*; Carlos Fuentes' most important work, *La muerte de Artemio Cruz*; Isabel Allende's first and most popular novel, *La casa de los espíritus; San Manuel Bueno Mártir*; a brief novel by the great Spanish writer and influential thinker of the Generation of 1898, Miguel de Unamuno; a novelette, *Santa Balbina, 37, gas en cada piso*, by Spain's contemporary Nobel laureate, Camilo José Cela; and several wonderful collections of Latin American writers.

A serious concern of all of us who serve Spanish speakers is the current explosion of books for the young translated into Spanish. Fortunately, an increasing number is now wonderfully rendered in Spanish. We now have marvelous Spanish renditions from such masters of the language as Elena Poniatowska, Osvaldo Blanco, and María Puncel. Their translations resonate with the beauty, rhythm, and cadence of the Spanish language. Unfortunately, too, many U.S. publishers continue to get away with linguistic and literary butchery: For a long time now, many of us have been complaining about the great number of literal translations. Hence, I will emphasize again that no degree of literal fidelity can compensate for the betrayal of a good writer by "Spanishing" him or her in a limp, ludicrous style. It is important to note that none of these inferior translations has resulted in a Spanish-language book with an enduring and memorable style. These linguistic aberrations are especially evident in the numerous so-called bilingual books that are now published and sold in the U.S.

In California, a state where nearly 50 percent of the 5.6 million students in kindergarten through high school are Latino, the still unanswered question is, what about the bilingual debate? There is no question that we must find a way to educate the more than half of the Latino students who speak little or no English.

And, considering that these past few years, Mexico and other countries in Latin America have had more than their normal share of sensation and scandal: political murders, the fraternization of drug lords and government officials, the creeping up of mysterious bank accounts — corruption everywhere. The resulting economic catastrophes have brought on, as well, political instability, high unemployment, and increasing poverty. Little wonder, then, that Latin Americans continue to risk their lives to immigrate to the U.S. So far this year, undocumented immigrants are dying in unprecedented numbers as they try to cross the border. They die without water and without hope in sweltering heat or frigid conditions. Despite the horrible plight that new immigrants must endure and the ever-present threat of eventual imprisonment by U.S. immigration officials, many Latin Americans see coming to the U.S. as their only hope. In the words of one immigrant recently quoted in *The San Diego Union-Tribune*, "I would rather die crossing into the U.S. or die trying, than go home with only my hands in my pockets."[1]

It is interesting to note that U.S. farmers want to bring back the *bracero* program. As reported in numerous newspapers in the past few months, when harvest season draws near, U.S. farmers complain of too few farm hands to pick the crops, and they are pushing Washington to take action. Apparently we now have two opposing political movements. On the one hand, there is a growing demand for Spanish-speaking workers in the U.S.; on the other, there is a strong and vociferous group that insists that the only way to educate Spanish-speaking children is to give them one year of English immersion before placing them in mainstream classes.

Despite the controversy about bilingual education in California and elsewhere, we know that home and parental involvement are crucial to the academic success of all children. Consequently, if we want parents to participate in the education of their children, we must provide them with books that they can read and understand and thus enjoy with their own children. Moreover, considering the sad realities of many Latin American countries, we must be prepared for an ever-increasing Spanish-speaking population in the U.S. These children and their parents need our support.

Hispanic-heritage youth who prefer to read in English should be exposed to the cultures of Latino people through noteworthy books. Fortunately, there is an increasing number of wonderful books in English for children and young adults that assist them in their efforts to better know and comprehend the marvelous richness and diversity of Latino people's values and beliefs. Whether we call these youth English-language learners (as we now do in California), or Latinos, or Spanish speakers, our hope is that they will expand their interests into the fascinating cultures of Latino/Hispanic people. It is interesting to note that many school districts in California are more selective in the use of the term "bilingual programs": many now prefer "foreign-language programs" or "biliteracy" for all students. Yet, the children and their needs are still the same. Regardless of language, they need books that thoroughly engage them.

Our task is to ignore longstanding myths and arbitrary doctrines that continue to discourage Hispanic youth from the pleasures of books and reading and to concentrate on our wonderful mission of providing young readers with beautifully written books that appeal to the universal likes, wishes, dreams, and aspirations of children and young adults everywhere.

Note

1. *The San Diego Union-Tribune,* August 31, 1998, p. A–13.

Part II : Programs

Developing Culturally Integrated Children's Programs

Lucía M. González

Libraries can no longer depend on traditional programs that highlight special Hispanic celebrations and holidays to attract and serve Hispanic children. Culture is not a costume that one wears on certain days. These children's cultural heritage is their unique identity, which constantly seeks self-expression.

Developing culturally integrated children's programs at libraries serving Hispanic communities is a manifold process. These programs, which may take many forms, must continuously incorporate into the overall picture of the library the interests and special needs of Hispanic children. They represent a constant and conscientious effort to include the history, art, music, folklore and other cultural manifestations of the Hispanic heritage into mainstream programming. The words *continuous* and *integrated* are used within the context of this article as opposed to special, short-term programs, as well as to those programs resulting from grants and other external sources of funding. The ultimate goal of culturally integrated programs is to make a long-lasting contribution to the library and its patrons by redefining and expanding the scope of the library's core programs.

With the purpose of integration in mind, this article provides practical programming ideas for librarians working with Hispanic children. Two programs from the Miami-Dade Public Library System are discussed: *La hora de cuentos* and *Project Colorín-Colorado*. The ideas and sample programs presented here could easily be adapted and implemented without much need for additional funding.

General Programming Ideas

Library programs aimed at integrating Hispanic children must be well planned before being implemented. General objectives for the overall program, as well as specific objectives for each subprogram, should be formulated, and the ways of accomplishing the objectives should be determined. For example, a Homework and Reading Partners program may be aimed at helping all children in the community improve their school performance and reading skills. If the library recruits bilingual volunteer students from high schools in the area as "partners," then, this program will specifically benefit Hispanic children who may not receive help at home because their guardians struggle with language or have little education.

These programs should be based upon the needs and interests of the children who will be involved. Just as it is wise to determine the size and characteristics of the population and to make an assessment of library needs before initiating library programs for Hispanic children, it is also necessary to ascertain the kinds of programs and subjects which interest the children and meet their needs. This can be best learned by talking to the children, their parents and the teachers in the area schools. The linguistic preferences and abilities of the children must also be considered in light of the fact that Hispanic children may speak only Spanish, only English, or both languages, with a proficiency in either one or the other.

Library Services for Hispanic Children: A Guide for Public and School Librarians, edited by Adela Artula Allen, discusses aspects of programming (criteria, goals, objectives and resources), socio-cultural and linguistic characteristics of Hispanic children, and the implications of these characteristics for library programming.[1] Authors Camila Alire and Orlando Archibeque offer a more recent list of resources in their book *Serving Latino Communities*.[2]

Types of Programs

Toddlers and Preschoolers

Programs for this age are the most fun and easiest to integrate. Many of the children in this age group tend to be monolingual. For many of them, this will be their introduction to a culture and a language other than the home culture. By introducing rhymes, chants, and songs from the Hispanic children's oral traditions alongside those of the mainstream culture, librarians help children build bridges to reconcile both cultures. These culturally integrated programs help children with the socialization process by allowing them to become aware of cultures and ways different from their own and to learn others' perspectives.[3]

Bilingual preschool story hours are always popular and easy to prepare. If the librarian is not bilingual, then help from a bilingual staff member or from a parent in the group is often available. Speaking the language is not enough, though. The person conducting the program needs to be well trained and qualified to present a fun and successful story hour.

There are a variety of materials and programming resources to use with this young audience. Popular folktales such as "Perez and Martina," as retold by Pura Belpré; "*La Hormiguita* / The Little Ant" or "The Billy Goat in the Vegetable Patch," as retold by Judy Sierra in *Multicultural Folktales: Stories to Tell Young Children* (1991); or my very own *The Bossy Gallito* (1994) and "Medio pollito" (Little Half-Chick), retold in *Señor Cat's Romance* (1997), all make great flannel board stories. Furthermore, a great number of bilingual books and Spanish translations target this age group. Many of the most popular titles in English are translated into Spanish. As a matter of fact, in the words of the major publishers of children's books in Spanish, the most popular route for them to follow has been to issue Spanish translations of popular English titles.[4] Characters like Spot, Clifford, the Cat in the Hat, and others, populate the Spanish books shelves.

One of the objectives of a bilingual story hour should be to convey the message of how important it is to read to children at this early age. Parents and grandparents who do not have a command of the English language should be encouraged to read to their children in Spanish. Sometimes Hispanic children miss out on the joys of reading because the adults in their family are not aware of what is available in Spanish at the library. All displays should include Spanish and bilingual titles together with the English ones.

School Age Children

Discussions of two very successful programs from the Miami Dade Public Library System follow: *La hora de cuentos,* at the West Kendall Regional Library, and *Colorín-Colorado.* The first, *La hora de cuentos,* is a branch program, the success of which can be measured by an attained popularity that transcends its immediate community to attract patrons from other parts of the county. The latter, *Colorín-Colorado,* is a system wide project that brings together Spanish-speaking and non–Spanish-speaking librarians and support professionals from all the libraries in the system to develop Hispanic heritage programs. The ready-made programs include puppet shows, oral storytelling, flannel board and creative dramatics stories, games, songs and music.

La Hora de Cuentos

The Spanish story hour started at the West Kendall Regional Library in April of 1994 as an answer to patrons' requests for such a service. At the time, the department's library assistant, Nubya Sanchez, was the only Spanish-speaking person in the staff. Guided by the expertise of other Hispanic professionals in the system, Ms. Sanchez started a Spanish story shelf and developed a basic collection of flannel board stories.

The main objective of *La hora de cuentos* was to promote an enjoyment and appreciation of the Spanish language and traditions through stories, songs, and games. The program attracted a mixed audience of Spanish-speaking and non–Spanish-speaking children of all ages. The Spanish-speakers saw it as a way to preserve their language and traditions, while the non–Spanish-speaking saw it as a means for their children to learn Spanish.

Following is an example of a typical *La hora de cuentos* program:

1. Opening routine "Cancion de los elefantes."

This is a very contagious and easy-to-learn counting song. A short, bilingual version of this song is found in Lulu Delacre's *Arroz con leche* (1989).

2. Book *Los zapaticos de Rosa,* by Jose Martí and illustrated by Lulu Delacre.

This poem is a classic of Hispanic children's literature. The books selected for sharing are generally originally written in Spanish or translations of English books that are relevant to the experience of Hispanic children in the U.S.

3. Rhymes, riddles or never-ending stories

Parents participate by sharing with the group those favorite rhymes and riddles they remember from childhood.

4. Oral story: "The Day Tio Conejo fooled Tio Zorro."

This story belongs to a number of trickster tales about Tio Conejo or Uncle Rabbit. They are very popular in Venezuela, Colombia, and many parts of Central America.

5. Book: *Fabula de la ratoncita presumida,* by Aquiles Nazoa.

6. Closing routine Games and songs.

The program always ends with *A-La-Rueda-Rueda,* the Spanish version of Ring-Around-the-Roses, and the game *Lobo* (Wolf).

The composition of the audience reflects the diversity of the Hispanic community in the West Kendall area of Dade

County. The program is regularly attended by Colombians, Cubans, Venezuelans, Nicaraguans, Peruvians, and Argentinians, just to name a few. It is a joy to see parents discussing the different ways in which they sang the same songs, heard the same stories, or played the same games in their countries of origin. In this way, *La hora de cuentos* brings the community and the generations together.

La hora de cuentos is now in its fifth year. It has become vital to the programming scheme of the West Kendall Regional Library's children's department. It has received a good amount of publicity from local Spanish radio stations and community newspapers, and this coverage has attracted audiences from other communities. According to the library's monthly statistical report, for the year 1997-98 *La hora de cuentos* had an average attendance of 65 to 75 children per program. During the summer, more than 100 children attend regularly. Other libraries in the system are now starting similar programs.

On March 25, 1996, the Spanish edition of the *Miami Herald*, *El nuevo herald*, wrote a full page article titled "Al-animo, al-animo, a la biblioteca."[5] Many of the parents interviewed said that by playing games and listening to stories in Spanish, their children now want to use the language more often, are motivated to take Spanish in school, and want to learn more about their roots.

Project Colorín-Colorado

This program started in 1993 at the Miami Dade Public Library System as an effort to provide special Hispanic programs to small and medium size libraries to celebrate Hispanic Heritage Month. A group of Hispanic librarians, myself included, met with youth services coordinator Sylvia Mavrogenes to develop a plan. It was then that we thought of forming a group composed of Spanish-speaking and non–Spanish-speaking librarians and support professionals to create, rehearse and perform this special Hispanic heritage program at the different libraries. We decided to call the group "*Colorín-Colorado*."

One of the objectives was to generate special programs for Hispanic Heritage month by consolidating the efforts and expertise of librarians in the system, without need for additional funding or outside performers. In addition, non–Hispanic librarians serving Hispanic children would benefit by participating in the group and learning stories, songs, and activities which they could then adapt and perform in their libraries throughout the year. The original group was composed of 14 members, of which only eight members were Hispanic.

The Youth Services Administrator contacted all branch managers in the system to make sure they allowed a member of their children's staff to participate in *Colorín-Colorado*. The encouragement and support of the administrator has been vital for the effectiveness and continuity of the project. Without those memos from the administration it would have been difficult for the children's staff to attend the meetings.

The group decided to concentrate on creating new puppet shows adapted from well-known Hispanic tales. Marta Garcia, children's department manager at the West Dade Regional Library was the leader and soul of the group. She had worked for several years at the New York Public Library where she learned the art of storytelling and puppet-making from Pura Belpré. The first year, the group created four sets of puppet shows of Belpré's *Perez and Martina* to be housed at each one of the four regional libraries. The meetings were puppet-making workshops, where we all learned to make papier-mâché puppets the old-fashioned way. Each set had two copies of the play's script, one in English and one in Spanish. In this way, the show could be performed in one language or the other, according to the preference of the audience or the language ability of the performers.

Besides the puppet show, the four sets of programs also consisted of a bilingual flannel-board story, bilingual finger-plays, a participatory story, and music. The group met twice to complete the puppets and compile all the other materials. The third and fourth meetings were to rehearse and finalize the performance schedule.

Colorín-Colorado is now in its sixth year. During this time the group has created eight puppet shows (in sets of four, housed at each regional library). During the past five years the group has performed (in chronological order) *Martina: The Little Cockroach*, by Pura Belpré; *The Adventures of Don Quixote and Sancho Panza* (humorous adaptation of Cervantes' work); *The Tiger and the Rabbit*, by Pura Belpré; *Juan Bobo and the Bunuelos*, by Lucía M. González; *Ote*, by Pura Belpré; *Menique*, adapted from a story by Jose Martí; and *The Three Feathers*, a story from the Venezuelan folklore.

Needless to say, *Colorín-Colorado* has been overwhelmed by demand. Of the 31 libraries in the system, up to 24 branches sign up for the program each October. Each show includes English and Spanish scripts — all-original adaptations of Hispanic tales —flannel board stories, creative dramatics, and music. The emphasis has been on providing the same materials in the two languages. The group's efforts have brought about a wealth of Hispanic materials to be used year-round in libraries throughout the Miami-Dade County Library System.

Conclusion

Successful programs do not always depend on an influx of new funds or additional staff. Sometimes all it takes is a lot of enthusiasm, initiative, and administrative support. The programs and ideas discussed above require little money, but plenty of commitment and cooperation on the part of the staff involved. Librarians serving Hispanic children need to re-evaluate the scope of each of their existing programs with an eye toward incorporating different aspects of Hispanic culture.

Often, I hear librarians complaining about how hard it is to get Hispanic children to attend library programs. They prepare elaborate programs for *Día de las madres, Cinco de mayo* (even in places where this date has no significance), *Día de la raza*, and so forth. While it is fine to highlight these events, it is not enough. Hispanic children are entitled to know as much as possible about the richness of their culture, about the contributions of others like themselves to the society at large. They need to discover their literatures and their history. All this they must do within the context of society at large. Culturally integrated programs are like the minerals and nutrients in a good soil: The richer the soil, the stronger and healthier its crops.

Notes

1. Adela Artola Allen, ed., *Library Services for Hispanic Children: A Guide for Public and School Librarians* (Phoenix, Ariz.: Oryx, 1987).
2. Camila A. Alire and Orlando Archi-

beque. *Serving Latino Communities: A How-to-Do-It Manual for Librarians* (New York: Neal-Schuman, 1998).

3. Janice N. Harrington, "The Need for Cultural Diversity in Preschool Service," *Journal of Youth Services in Libraries* 6, no. 2 (Winter 1993): 175–180.

4. Sally Lodge, "Speaking Their Language," *Publishers Weekly* 242 (August 28, 1995): 86–89.

5. Teresa Santiago, "Al-animo, al-animo, a la biblioteca," *The Miami Herald / El nuevo herald,* Tuesday, March 25, 1997, sec. C, 3–5.

La hora de cuentos and Colorín-Colorado: A Bibliography of Sources

Belpré, Pura. *Perez and Martina.* New York. Viking Press, 1960

_____. *Ote: A Folktale from Puerto Rico.* New York: Pantheon Books, 1969.

_____. *The Tiger and the Rabbit and the Rabbit and Other Tales.* Illustrated by Kay Peterson Parker. Boston: Houghton Mifflin, 1944.

Carrera, Pilar Almoida, comp. *Habia una vez: 26 cuentos.* Caracas, Venezuela: Ediciones Ekare-Banco del Libro, 1985.

Castellon, Silvia, ed. *Cúcuru mácara: poesia folklorica.* Bogotá, Colombia: Editorial Norma, 1987.

Cuentos de enredos y travesuras. Caracas, Venezuela: Ediciones Ekare-Banco del Libro, 1986.

Delacre, Lulu. *Arroz con leche: Popular Songs and Rhymes from Latin America.* New York: Scholastic, 1989.

Fiesta Musical: A Musical Adventure Through Latin America for Children. Music for Little People (compact disc), 1994.

González, Lucía. *The Bossy Gallito.* Illustrated by Lulu Delacre. New York: Scholastic, 1994.

_____. "Juan Bobo and the Buñuelos" and "The Little Half-Chick." *Señor Cat's Romance and Other Favorite Stories from Latin America.* New York: Scholastic, 1997.

Grupo Cañaveral. *Cantemos con los ninos Hispanos,* vols. 1, 2, 3. Trapiche Publications (compact disc), 1995.

Lizcano, Hugo, and Javier Galue. *Infantiles,* vol. 1. Anes Records compact disc, 95006, 1994.

Marti, Jose. "Meñique." *La edad de oro.* 1889. (*La edad de Oro* was a Spanish language children's magazine published by Jose Martí from New York. He dedicated the magazine to all the children of the Americas. The nine issues that appeared have been compiled and published as a book with the same title.)

_____. *Los zapaticos de Rosa.* Illustrated by Lulu Delacre. New York: Lectorum Publications, 1997.

Nazoa, Aquiles. *Fabula de la Ratoncita Presumida.* Caracas, Venezuela: Ediciones Ekare, 1982.

Orozco, Jose Luis. *De colores and Other Latin-American Folk Songs for Children.* Dutton, 1994.

_____. *Diez deditos: Ten Little Fingers and Other Play Rhymes and Action Songs from Latin America vol. 12.* Arcoiris Records, (compact disc), 1997.

Sierra, Judy, and Robert Kaminski. "The Goat in the Chili Patch." *Multicultural Folktales: Stories to Tell Young Children.* Phoenix, Arizona: Oryx, 1991.

Uribe, Veronica, ed. *Cuentos de espantos y aparecidos (Tales about Ghosts and Spectres).* Caracas, Venezuela: Ediciones Ekare-Banco del Libro, 1984.

BUENOS DÍAS/GOOD MORNING: BILINGUAL PROGRAMS FOR CHILDREN

Rose V. Treviño

Reading and interacting with children in a storytime environment can be most rewarding for the child and the presenter. In our culturally rich society, the introduction of nursery rhymes, songs, and stories in a language other than English will provide the child with the beginnings of an appreciation for the similarities and differences between people.

The following are program plans to be used by children's librarians who are committed to fostering the desire in others to learn more about the Hispanic culture.

Program Plan No. 1: Toddlers, Ages 24–36 Months (10–15 Minute Program)

The attention span for toddlers is very short. Share a story and then recite a nursery rhyme or sing a song. Keep a circulating display of board books to be checked out by your storytime group immediately following your storytime.

Books to Share

Alexander, Martha. *La bota de lalo/Willy's Boot.*

Brown, Margaret W. *Buenas noches luna/Goodnight Moon.*

Walsh, Ellen S. *Pinta ratone/Mouse Paint.*

Song

Diez deditos/Ten Little Fingers (sung to the tune of "Ten Little Indians"): *Uno, dos, tres deditos* (one, two, three little fingers), *cuatro, cinco, seis deditos* (four, five, six little fingers), *siete, ocho, nueve deditos* (seven, eight, nine little fingers), *y uno mas son diez* (and one more makes ten).

Rhyme

El día en que tú naciste/"On the Day You Were Born": *El día en que tú naciste* (on the day you were born), *nacieron las cosas bellas* (beautiful things were born). *Nació el sol* (the sun was born), *nació la luna* (the moon was born), *y nacieron las estrellas* (and the stars were born).

Finger play

La luna/"The Moon": *Ahí viene la luna* (here comes the moon), *[ponga los dedos juntos en forma de la luna* (form a moon by putting your arms above your head)], *comiendo una tuna,* (eating prickly-pear fruit), *[pretenda comer con los dedos,* (pretend to eat with your fingers)], *echó las cáscaras en esta laguna,* (throwing the peel into the pond), [*haga cosquillas en el estómago del niño,* (tickle child's tummy)].

Program Plan No. 2: Preschool Children, Ages 4–5 (15–20 Minute Program)

As an introduction, be sure to inform your storytime children that the songs and nursery rhymes are those sung and recited in Mexico and other Latin American countries. Again, use variety in your storytime, alternating stories with rhymes and songs.

Books to share:

Brusca, María C. *Tres amigos: Un cuento para contar/Three Friends: A Counting Book.*

Carle, Eric. *The Very Hungry Caterpillar/La oruga muy hambrienta.*

Mora, Pat *Oye al desierto/Listen to the Desert.*

Songs:

Buenos días/"Good Morning": *Buenos días, buenos días* (Good morning, good morning), *¿Cómo estás? ¿cómo estás?* (How are you? how are you?), *Muy bién gracias* (Very well, thank you), *muy bién gracias* (very well, thank you). *¿Y usted? ¿y usted?* (And you? and you?).

Buenas tardes, buenas tardes (Good afternoon, good afternoon) *¿Cómo estás? ¿cómo estás?* (How are you? how are you?), *Muy bién gracias* (Very well, thank you), *muy bién gracias* (very well, thank you), *¿Y usted? ¿y usted?* (And you? and you?).

Los pollitos/"The Baby Chicks": *Los pollitos dicen* (Baby chicks are singing), *"Pío, pío, pío"* ("Pío, pío, pío"), *"Cuando tienen hambre"* ("Mama we are hungry"), *"Cuando tienen frio"* ("Mama we are cold").

La gallina busca (Mama looks for wheat), *El maíz y el trigo* (Mama looks for corn), *Les da la comida* (Mama feeds them dinner), *Y les presta abrigo* (Mama keeps them warm).

Bajo sus dos alas (Under mama's wings), *Acurrucaditos* (Sleeping in the hay), *Hasta el otro día* (Baby chicks all huddle), *Duermen los pollitos* (Until the next day).

Rhyme:

This little rhyme has traditionally been recited when a child injures himself. Have the child pretend he has just hurt his hand. The child should begin rubbing the hurt hand in a circular motion while reciting "*Sana, Sana.*"

Sana, sana/"Heal, Heal": *Sana, sana* (Heal, heal), *colita de rana* (Little frog tail), *si no sanas hoy* (If you don't heal today), *sanarás mañana* (you'll be healed tomorrow).

Finger play:

This fingerplay is well known all over Latin America. Children can point to their own fingers, starting with the thumb and ending with the pinkie, or an adult can help.

Mi familia/"My Family": *Este chiquito es mi hermanito.* (This tiny one is my little brother). *Esta es mi mamá.* (This one is my mother). *Este altito es mi papá.* (This tall one is my father). *Esta es mi hermana.* (This one is my sister). *Y este chiquito y bonito soy YO!* (And this little pretty one is ME!)

Program plan No. 3: School-Age Children, Ages 6–8 (30–40 Minute Program)

Books to share:

Aardema, Verna. *Borreguita y el coyote/Borreguita and the Coyote.*
Ada, Alma Flor. *Mediopollito/Half-Chicken.*
Belpré, Pura. *Perez y Martina/Perez and Martina.*
Ehlert, Lois. *Cucú: Un Cuento Folclórico Mexicano/Cuckoo: A Mexican Folktale.*
González, Lucía. *El gallo de bodas/The Bossy Gallito.*
Soto, Gary. *Qué montón de tamales/Too Many Tamales.*

Song:

Children in Spanish-speaking countries know *Pimpón* very well. In a circle, sing the words and act them out. Hold up your hands to show *Pimpón's* hands. Pretend you are washing your face and hands, combing your hair, wiping away tears, and holding hands. Open and close your fingers to show the twinkling stars in the last stanza. Make your hands into a pillow and close your eyes for the last two lines.

Pimpón/"Pimpón": *Pimpón es un muñeco* (Pimpón is a nice doll), *con manos de cartón* (with hands made out of cardboard). *Se lava la carita* (He likes to wash his face), *con agua y con jabón* (with soap and lots of water).

Pimpón es un muñeco (Pimpón is a nice doll), *con manos de cartón* (with hands made out of cardboard). *Se lava las manitas* (He likes to wash his hands), *con agua y con jabón* (with soap and lots of water).

Se desenreda el pelo (He disentangles his hair), *con peine de marfil* (with an ivory comb). *Y aunque no le gusta* (Although he doesn't like it), *no llora, ni hace así* (he doesn't cry or fuss).

Pimpón dame la mano (Pimpón give me your hand), *con un fuerte apretón* (with a big and strong grip). *Que quiero ser tú amigo* (I want to be your friend), *Pimpón, Pimpón, Pimpón* (Pimpón, Pimpón, Pimpón).

Y cuando las estrellas (And when the stars are blinking) *comienzan a salir* (up in the pretty sky), *Pimón se va a la cama* (Pimpón closes his eyes), *Pimpón se va a dormir* (Pimpón lays down to sleep).

Poetry:

Read poems from one of the following collections.

Ada, Alma Flor. *Gathering the Sun: An Alphabet in Spanish and English.* New York: Lothrop, Lee & Shepard, 1997.
Mora, Pat. *Confetti: Poems for Children.* New York: Lee & Low Books, 1996.

Game:

Doña Blanca

This is a circle game and there is no limit to the number of players. The words can be sung or chanted.

To play choose a *Doña Blanca* and a *Jicotillo* (hornet). *Doña Blanca* stands inside the circle, while *Jicotillo* remains on the outside. Children join hands and circle around *Doña Blanca* as they sing or chant. After the second verse, *Jocotillo* tries to break through clasped hands to catch *Doña Blanca.* When *Jicotillo* succeeds in entering the circle, she chases *Doña Blanca. Doña Blanca* cannot run outside of the circle. When she has been caught, *Doña Blanca* chooses a new *Jicotillo* before she becomes part of the circle. The old *Jicotillo* is now the new *Doña Blanca.*

Doña Blanca está cubierta (Doña Blanca is surrounded), *con pilares de oro y plata* (by pillars of silver and gold). *Romperemos un pilar* (Break a column now), *para ver a Doña Blanca* (if Doña Blanca you will hold).

Quién es ese Jocotillo (Who is this hornet), *que anda en pos de Doña Blanca?* (who chases Doña Blanca?) *Yo soy ése, yo soy ése* (I am [s]he, I am [s]he) *que anda en pos de Doña Blanca!* (who's trying to catch her!)

Group Participatory Activities:

La Tía Monica

Children form a circle and will do all the movements to the song. Have them say, "Ooh la la!"

Tenemos una tía (We have an aunt), *la Tía Monica* (our Aunt Monica). *Que cuando va al mercado* (And when she goes to town), *le dicen, "Ooh la la!"* (people say, "Ooh la la!") *Ooh la la!* (Ooh la la!)

Así mueve cadera (Here's how she moves her hip), *así, así, así* (like this, like this, like this). *Así mueve cadera* (Here's how she moves her hip), *la Tía Monica* (our Aunt Monica).

Tenemos una tía (We have an aunt), *la Tía Monica* (Our Aunt Monica). *Que cuando va al mercado* (And when she goes to town) *le dicen, "Ooh la la!"* (people say, "Ooh la la!") *Ooh la la!* (Ooh la la!)

Así mueve los hombros (Here's how she moves her shoulders), *así, así, así* (Like this, like this, like this). *Así mueve los hombros* (Here's how she moves her shoulders), *la Tía Monica* (our Aunt Monica).

Tenemos una tía (We have an aunt), *la Tía Monica* (our Aunt Monica). *Que cuando va al mercado* (And when she goes to town) *le dicen, "Ooh la la!"* (people say, "Ooh la la!") *Ooh la la!* (Ooh la la!)

Así mueve cabeza... (Here's how she moves her head...) Repeat first stanza.

Así mueve los pies... (Here's how she moves her feet...) Repeat first stanza.

Así mueve las manos... (Here's how she moves her hands...) Repeat first stanza.

Así se mueve toda... (Here's how she moves all over...).

La canción Doodley-Do/"The Doodley-Do Song"

Sitting down, participants will sing this using hand motions.

Haridiasha (Please play for me), *Haridiasha* (That sweet melody) *Doodley-do, doodley-do* (That goes doodley-do, doodley-do).

Haridiasha (I like the rest), *Haridiasha* (but what I like the best), *Doodley-do, doodley-do* (goes doodley-do, doodley-do).

Es muy fácil puedes hacerlo (Simplest thing there isn't much to it), *solo tienes que aprenderlo* (all you've got to do is doodley-do it), *me gusta mucho pero ninguno* (I like it so wherever I go), *como el doodley, doodley, Quak, Quak* (I just doodley, doodley Quak Quak).

Juanito/"Little Johnny"

In this delightful song, you get to shake, jiggle, and twist different parts of your body as you sing. Clap your hands, too! Get your whole body in motion, from head to toe, as the song progresses.

Juanito cuando baila (When little Johnny dances), *baila, baila, baila* (he dances, dances, dances). *Juanito cuando baila* (When little Johnny dances), *baila con el dedito* (he dances with his pinkie), *con el dedito, ito, ito (*with his pinkie, pinkie, pinkie). *Así baila Juanito* (That's how little Johnny dances).

Juanito cuando baila (When little Johnny dances), *baila, baila, baila* (he dances, dances, dances). *Juanito cuando baila,* (When little Johnny dances), *baila con el pie* (he dances with his foot), *con el pie, pie, pie* (with his foot, foot, foot), *con el dedito, ito, ito* (with his pinkie, pinkie, pinkie). *Así baila Juanito* (That's how little Johnny dances).

Juanito cuando baila... (When little Johnny dances...) *la rodilla, dilla, dilla...* (knee...) *la cadera, dera, dera...* (hip...) *la mano, mano, mano...* (hand...) *el codo, codo, codo...* (elbow...) *el hombro, hombro, hombro...* (shoulder...) *la cabeza, eza, eza...* (head...)

References

Aardema, Verna. *Borreguita and the Coyote.* New York: Alfred A. Knopf Books for Young Readers, 1991. A clever lamb outwits a scheming coyote.

_____. *Borreguita y el coyote.* New York: Scholastic, 1993.

Ada, Alma Flor. *Mediopollito/"Half-Chicken."* New York: Doubleday Books for Young Readers, 1995. Little half chick goes out to explore the world and finds adventure along the way.

Alexander, Martha. *La Bota de Lalo.* Glendale: Continental Book, 1993.

_____. *Willy's Boot.* Cambridge: Candlewick Press, 1993. Willy loses his boot when he helps Lily put the toys away.

Belpré, Pura. *Perez y Martina.* New York: Viking Children's Books, 1960.

_____. *Perez and Martina.* New York: Frederick Warne, 1966. A sad and funny tale about a too-particular cockroach and her string of suitors.

Brown, Margaret W. *Goodnight Moon.* New York: HarperCollins Children's Books, 1947.

_____. *Buenas Noches Luna.* New York: HarperCollins Children's Books, 1995. A bunny says goodnight to everything, including the moon.

Brusca, María C. *Three Friends: A Counting Book/Tres amigos: Un cuento para contar.* New York: Holt, 1995. Learn to count from one to ten and see some animals along the way.

Carle, Eric. *The Very Hungry Caterpillar.* New York: Putnam, 1969.

_____. *La oruga muy hambrienta.* New York: Putnam, 1989. A small and hungry caterpillar eats his way through different foods on different days of the week, then builds himself a cocoon until it's time to emerge as a butterfly.

Ehlert, Lois. *Cuckoo: A Mexican Folktale/Cucu: Un cuento folklórico Mexicano.* San Diego: Harcourt Brace, 1997. A traditional Mayan tale which reveals how the cuckoo lost her beautiful feathers.

González, Lucía. *The Bossy Gallito/El gallo de bodas.* New York: Scholastic, 1994. A bilingual version of a traditional cumulative tale about a rooster, who, while on the way to the wedding of his Uncle Perico, is tempted by a small kernel of corn.

Mora, Pat. *Listen to the Desert/Oye al desierto.* New York: Houghton Mifflin, 1994. Listen to the gentle sounds of the desert in this book about the beauty found in an unlikely place.

Soto, Gary. *Qué montón de Tamales.* New York: Putnam, 1996.

_____. *Too Many Tamales.* New York: Putnam, 1996. While helping make tamales, Maria tries on her mother's wedding ring. To her dismay, the ring is lost and panic ensues.

Walsh, Ellen S. *Mouse Paint.* San Diego: Harcourt Brace, 1989.

_____. *Pinta ratones.* Glendale: Continental Book Company, 1994. Three mice have fun dipping themselves in paint and then painting on a piece of paper.

Connecting Readers' Advisors and Youth

Dana Watson

"Every reader his book."
— Ranganathan

"It is not enough that Melvil Dewey put the books in order on the shelves. We must take them down, read them, and give them to the people" Margaret Edwards.[1]

Readers' advisory, an essential library service for all children and young adults, connects readers with appropriate books and resources. This service involves knowledge and skills beyond those typically applied within the reference arena. Readers' advisory service today provides guided access to fiction collections of school and public libraries. The goal is to help young people connect with materials they want or need, making the right match, for the right child, at the right time.[2] The scope of this process is daunting, given the amount of fiction available for young people, but can be even more challenging when the needs and interests of youth demand specialized resources. To meet this challenge, librarians need knowledge of available resources, expertise in working with youth, and a commitment to readers' advisory.

This article reviews readers' advisory strategies for librarians working with children and young adults in public and school libraries. Secondarily, this discussion will focus on avenues for implementing, improving, and expanding service to youth of Hispanic heritage.

Basic to any readers' advisory service are the bone-deep beliefs that reading is intrinsically important and eminently enjoyable. Many studies document the relationship between pleasure reading and reading achievement and identify the impact of pleasure reading on such skills as decoding, literacy development, vocabulary growth, understanding of grammar, and writing. Beyond these skills, however, reading has the potential for pure enjoyment and provides opportunity to identify with others.[3] Oralia Garza de Cortés, in her discussion of children's literature for Hispanic Americans, reaffirms Walter Dean Myers' view that minority youth, reading literature reflective of their own cultural experiences and history, and seeing themselves in that literature, are empowered to visualize their own future within the society in which they live.[4]

Librarians need to develop the skills and expertise necessary to deliver readers' advisory services to children. Margaret

Edwards, who wrote *The Fair Garden and the Swarm of Beasts* and served young people for more than 30 years at Enoch Pratt Free Library, put readers' advisory at the center of library service to young adults, insisting that new librarians receive extensive training in youth literature. Her approach is still valid: "In my preliminary thinking I realized that work with young adults is as simple as ABC. All there is to it is: (A) a sympathetic understanding of all adolescents; (B) firsthand knowledge of all the books that would interest them; and (C) mastery of the technique of getting these books into the hands of the adolescents. Simple."[5] While Edwards provides a succinct and incontrovertible summary, readers' advisory is a complex process. Certainly, a knowledge of the literature is critical; yet, getting books — the right books — into the hands of young people demands creativity and involves both active and passive approaches.

Active Readers' Advisory

Readers' advisors actively seek to match book and reader by discovering the patron's preference(s) and subsequently recommending appropriate titles according to that stated preference. The appeal is determined through an interview process which solicits information on what it is about a book that interests the patron. Elements of appeal can include such aspects as geographical or chronological setting, character type, writing style, theme, and genre. No one book, of course, will appeal to all readers.

Victor Nell, in *Lost in a Book: The Psychology of Reading for Pleasure*, states that pleasurable reading is determined by three factors: a high degree of reading competency, positive expectations about reading and correct book selection.[6] Readers' advisors, therefore, need to consider reading levels of children when recommending titles and strive to interest and motivate young people with the judicious choices of books they suggest. Readers make subjective judgments about whether a book is "good" or not. In Nell's study of "ludic," or pleasure reading, the literary merit and difficulty of a book (as evidenced in its vocabulary and sentence structure) had a definite influence on readers' perceptions. Perhaps even more important, however, was the "trance potential," defined as the capacity of the book to enthrall the reader. "Quite often," he says, "readers' judgments of trance potential will override judgments of merit and difficulty."[7] Many young people, for example, choose to read Tolkien's *Hobbit* or *Lord of the Rings* despite unfamiliar vocabulary and complex structure because they become caught up in the story.

Because personal choice is so integral to the process, librarians often provide a selection of titles from which to choose. They also strive to develop good, low-key working relationships so young people feel suggestions can be accepted or rejected. Again, the selection of titles a patron is offered may be determined by the readers' advisory interview. While maintaining a working list of key questions to determine a reader's preference is standard practice (What was the last book/author read that you especially enjoyed? Have you heard of one you think you would like? Is there a particular genre you favor? Do you like short/long books? Short stories? Poetry?) sometimes young people can be unsure or noncommittal. Keeping them talking about their other interests, what they enjoy and what they like to see and do can often open other avenues for book suggestions. Readers' advisors try to explore all options to ensure pleasurable reading experiences of suggested titles.

Passive Readers' Advisory

Young people are often too shy to ask for help or may not realize librarians are available to assist them in their book selection needs. A passive readers' advisory service, one which provides reading guidance through a variety of materials, can address this audience. Young adult librarian Patrick Jones believes many young adults today can be reached through the use of documents and self-service strategies. He suggests card files, lists, newsletters, catalogs, reviews and displays.[8] A user-friendly approach can do much to connect young people with books. Signage, in more than one language when applicable, can direct them to appropriate sections of the library. Young adult and children's areas that are comfortable and appealing can encourage young people to investigate what is available and recommended.

Many promotional techniques used in passive readers' advisory are familiar to librarians: new book collections, genre collections, bulletin boards, displays, bookmarks, annotated booklists and pocket size lists. Especially helpful in readers' advisory services are booklists that link authors, books, or types of books. For example, "If You Like (this author), Then Try (another author)." Jones, in *Connecting Young Adults and Libraries*,[9] provides examples of many of these strategies. Another passive readers' advisory technique is compiling a collection of recommended booklists created in-house or acquired through other sources and placing that collection in an easily visible location. Lists of books in series or award winners are also helpful. Library newsletters, general or specifically focused on youth services, can include recreational reading suggestions for young people. This can be especially effective to invite young people into the library and to assist adults who select books for their children.

Since young adults spend time on the web, readers' advisors may also wish to take advantage of this medium and suggest materials through the library web site or provide a more active online readers' advisory service. A web-based readers' advisory interview may take the form of a template and include some of the same questions asked in the face-to-face readers' advisory encounter. However young people identify titles of interest, the momentum is lost unless libraries make resources easily accessible and have sufficient copies of popular titles and books placed on display, booktalked, and otherwise promoted.

Dynamic Readers' Advisors

Readers' advisors need skills and expertise to help young people find the books and materials they want and to encourage reading interests. Unlike most adults, children are often unable to articulate what they would like to read and cannot categorize their likes into typical genres (mystery, science fiction, fantasy). This underscores the need for expertise in interacting with youngsters and a thorough knowledge of available literature. There is no substitute for advisors' having read the books they recommend. Enthusiasm for the book is easier and more genuine and understanding of the story's nuances is greater. Consequently, providing that "right" match between reader and book becomes more assured. It is impossible, of course, to read all the books that are available; however, readers' advisors can depend on a combination of their own knowledge, their colleagues, and local and commercial resources. Library staff often develop areas of expertise and become local "experts." Individual efforts can combine to develop readers' advisory expertise among all involved personnel through formal review sessions, ongoing training, development of annotated lists, compilation of genre lists, and other activities. Developing this expertise can take time and effort, but it ultimately enhances the ability of readers' advisors to match a young person's reading interest with an appropriate title.

Readers' advisors also need a knowledge of reading interests of different age groups. For example, librarians come to know young adults are often interested in the genre reading categories of romance and adventure/mystery and science fiction genres. One way to relate more directly to young people and learn about their reading preferences is to be aware of and respect their interests and opinions and to keep current with what is happening in popular culture. Time spent by librarians in the youth section can assist in discovering these interests, provide opportunity to know individual patrons, and develop that invaluable reputation of approachability (or "coolness"). Holding youth book discussion groups is another avenue to promote books and encourage young people's reading; also effective is promoting video titles and books-on-tape—alone or in combination with their print counterparts.

Readers' Advisors and Community

Librarians throughout the country need to know the recreational reading needs of youth of Hispanic heritage and what Hispanic literature is available for young people. This is not a concern only for libraries within a specific geographic area. Today's Hispanic community in the United States, while predominantly an urban population, is not restricted only to those states along the southern border or the East or West Coast. According to 1990 census statistics, the Hispanic population is a rapidly growing segment of the U.S. and is a younger group than the general population. Nearly 40 percent are under 20 years of age, compared with 28 percent of the general population. Clearly, public and school librarians need to plan and provide services for this substantial and growing community.[10]

Librarians also need to recognize that this diverse population chooses to describe itself in a number of ways. In their thoughtful discussion of the history and rationale for such diversity in terminology, Alire and Archibeque write, "No universally accepted term describes the incredibly diverse population.... For the overall population the most popular terms currently in use are *Latinos*, *Hispanics*, *Hispanic-Americans* and *Spanish-speaking*."[11] Indeed, Oralia Garza de Cortés writes, "The term 'Hispanic Americans' is a relatively new one within the library profession, one that offers the most precise classification of the literature about a group whose ethnic roots stem from the cultural heritages of Mexico, Puerto Rico, Cuba and the Caribbean, and Central and South America but whose home and dual cultural context is the United States of America."[12] Hazel Rochman, in *Against Borders*, uses the term *Latino* but acknowledges some prefer *Hispanic*.[13] Within these broad categories, of course, are many smaller groups "united by a common Spanish language and cultural heritage... divided by geography, country of origin, class, and the time and circumstance of their arrival. Each subgroup is distinct and best understood individually."[14] The choice for which term is appropriate is, of course, decided by each community and by individuals. For this discussion the term *Hispanic* has been used in an encompassing manner. Sensitive librarians will seek out appropriate information about terminology from local residents as they engage in community assessments.

A community assessment is an established information-gathering procedure in libraries and one which is critically important to support constituents and their needs. This information is especially significant when planning programs and services for the Hispanic community. Information about length of residence in the U.S., language facility in both English and Spanish, reading preferences and abilities, needs and interests, types of reading material preferred and usual sources of reading material can assist in delivering effective and relevant service. Previous library experiences (or lack thereof) can also provide useful information. An assessment would, of course, reflect the needs and interests of youth of Hispanic heritage.

Understanding the diversity of backgrounds in a community can help shape services libraries provide. We know children obtain significant amounts of recreational reading books from their school and public library and with knowledge of the community, libraries can address the specific fiction needs and interests of Hispanic youth.[15]

Readers' Advisors and Hispanic Youth Literature

Whether a child requests fiction, popular culture, or book topics that reflect a young person's own life or heritage, librarians need to provide these materials. Librarians conscientiously prepare for these requests by identifying and evaluating titles, purchasing the resources, and becoming familiar with them. Acquiring Hispanic fiction for young people is a component of this process. Unfortunately, building an Hispanic fiction collection for young people is a difficult endeavor. Available materials, especially for young adult fiction, are scarce. A look at the number of books being produced can explain some of the problem: "Of the 4500 children's books published in 1995, 100 titles were created by black authors and illustrators, and 70 titles from Hispanic authors...."[16] Although there are some adult fiction titles by Hispanic authors to supplement young adult reading, the dearth of material means librarians have to seek out the literature using every possible approach. Selection aids, such as those provided in the "Selected Resources" section at the end of this chapter, are invaluable resources for identifying Hispanic books and other appropriate materials for youth of Hispanic heritage.

Communication with young people and others in the community may indicate that nontraditional materials such as novels in picture form (fotonovelas) and comic book formats are popular and appreciated in libraries. Sales of comic books in Mexico have been traditionally very high and the format is used for romance novels and other genres.[17] Hispanic youth may also enjoy more poetry, songs, short stories, and cartoons than Anglo youth.[18] Ongoing communication between library and community can help determine local needs and preferences. This communication with the community, and indeed many readers' advisory functions, can be enhanced with the presence of bilingual librarians.[19]

Not only do libraries need to have Hispanic literature within the collection, but the available materials should reflect a variety of interests, reading levels, and complexity to ensure appeal to all age levels. It is important to have materials available for young people in both Spanish language editions and English and often in a bilingual (parallel texts in Spanish and English) format, as well. Young people may be more comfortable reading in their preferred language, and this may have a positive affect on reading attitudes.[20] Bilingual texts can give monolingual parents opportunity to read to and with their children. Interlingual texts (with selected Spanish words and phrases inserted into the text as appropriate) are also welcomed. A 1994 overview of Spanish language selection tools, published in the *Journal of Youth Services in Libraries,* can assist librarians in accessing these materials.[21]

Nonfiction materials aimed at Hispanic youth are more readily available than fiction. Oralia Garza de Cortés explains: "The reality is that nonfiction subjects are much easier to write about and yet less likely to be the target of criticism by librarians and scholars eager to attack the work on the basis of stereotyped images or lack of diacritics. Too, authors from outside the culture have generally been more successful in writing nonfiction, which relies upon factual research and the quality of its presentation, than in depicting the subtle aspects of language, experience, and emotion necessary for a compelling work of fiction."[22] To ensure that right book for the right child at the right time, whether fiction or non-fiction, librarians need to be knowledgeable of Hispanic authors, titles, and sources, and make sure these materials are in their collections.

Readers' Advisors and Best Practice

How can libraries and librarians best prepare for optimal readers' advisory service to youth of Hispanic heritage? How can libraries build relevant and authentic collections for youth of Hispanic heritage? What is the role of the library? These are questions responsive library professionals are striving to answer.

A basic step for each librarian is to read young people's literature, in particular that of Hispanic authors and subjects. This involves fiction, including genre fiction, and a range of formats: picture books, folktales, hardcover fiction, paperbacks, magazines, comics, and so forth. Reading what young people are reading will expand background knowledge of titles and authors to include an understanding of young people's interests. Librarians with limited knowledge of Hispanic culture will want to read the history of Spanish-speaking communities both abroad and in the U.S. Reading adult fiction such as Mexican-American writers Rudolfo Anaya, Sandra Cisneros, Juan Felipe Herrera, and Gloria Anzaldua can also contribute to cultural understandings.

Individual librarians can learn more about Hispanic culture and how to better serve Hispanic communities by seeking out such resources as *Serving Latino Communities,*[23] *Library Services for Hispanic Children,*[24] and Dyer's "Hispanics in the U.S.: Implications for Library Service."[25] Knowledge of the culture will support readers' advisory activities and will also enhance the librarian's ability to assess materials for accuracy and authenticity. Many children's books published earlier this century and still available in libraries present inauthentic and patronizing images of Hispanic people. Librarians will want to recognize these materials when they find them. Assessment criteria are provided in thoughtful introductory essays in *Latina and Latino Voices in Literature,*[26] *Our Family, Our Friends, Our World,*[27] and *The New Press Guide to Multicultural Resources for Young Readers.*[28] *Teaching Multicultural Literature in Grades K–8* includes a chapter particularly useful for the Mexican-American perspective.[29]

Many librarians are unfamiliar with youth literature in general as well as Hispanic children's literature. A useful strategy to internalize knowledge of children and young adult literature is to maintain a reading log and develop annotations and records for future booktalks and advisory sessions. Short annotations with major themes, suggested appeal topics, and subject headings can provide valuable reference in future readers' advisory interviews. These records can later be used to identify titles to incorporate into book lists and displays, whether organized by theme, genre, or designed for an ethnic celebration. Familiarity with the literature also facilitates integration of Hispanic and Spanish titles into all youth book displays and booktalks. This, in turn, provides outreach to all young constituents of the library.

Librarians new to the readers' advisory interview can work together with colleagues and mentors to hone skills. Study groups, book review sessions, and role playing can help develop expertise. Published descriptions of actual readers' advisory proceedings such as "The Nature of the Readers' Advisory Transaction in Children's and Young Adult Reading," for instance, can be instructive for group discussions.[30] While no one librarian can have total mastery of the young adult literature universe, working collaboratively is a practical approach. Librarians often need to refer questions outside their expertise to more knowledgeable colleagues, whether in their own building or beyond, and they can consult an increasing number of useful published and online resources. Readers' advisory electronic sources such as *NoveList* and *What Do I Read Next?* can be useful in searching out that perfect title. Also relevant are the print counterparts to *What Do I Read Next? What Do Children Read Next? What Do Young Adults Read Next?* and *What Do I Read Next? Multicultural Literature.*[31]

As readers' advisors to young people, in particular those of Hispanic heritage, librarians want to provide books patrons request. To enable this process, they call on their knowledge of sources and titles to make purchase recommendations. This helps enrich their fiction collection and allows them to respond positively to requests. A number of resources can assist them in this process. While most librarians are aware of the Newbery and Caldecott awards, many do not realize there are special awards for Hispanic children's literature. These children's book awards, the Arroz con Leche Award, Pura Belpré Award and the Américas Award for Children's and Young Adult Literature highlight literary contributions to youth of Hispanic heritage. These titles would be noteworthy additions to a library's collection. Library review journals like *Booklist* and *School Library Journal* include reviews and bibliographies of Hispanic titles for children and alert librarians to new publications. Isabel Schon evaluates recently published titles for children in a *Multicultural Review* column. She also maintains a web site, the Center for the Study of Books in Spanish for Children and Adolescents, which provides information about recommended books in Spanish.[32] Knowledge of small press publishers like Arte Público Press and Children's Book Press is also useful to seek out quality materials produced by non-mainstream publishers.

Libraries ensure effective readers' advisory services by making it an integral part of the mission of the library. This means it is incorporated into policy statements, job descriptions, allocated a portion of the budget, and publicized. Ongoing training, in-service and continuing education opportunities, critical to develop expertise, are essential. All library staff should be involved in planning and evaluation activities and contribute to developing the collection.

Libraries need to involve the community, in formal or informal ways, both to gather input and direction for the library and to foster communication. Local communities should be informed about services the library can provide. This may need to be communicated in both Spanish and English and in a variety of venues. Librarians may need to promote their readers' advisory services through community centers, churches, schools, malls, and the media. A user-focused library will ensure the community is well served and that all youth of Hispanic heritage know what they can expect at their library.

Celebrating the Connection

To connect with youth of Hispanic heritage, readers' advisors can adapt Margaret Edwards' approach and embrace the opportunity to engage young people in conversation, increase their personal awareness of Hispanic literature, and perfect and utilize a variety of techniques to get the "right" book into the hands of the reader. This ongoing process demands an understanding of the intrinsic complexity of the readers' advisory transaction and a firm knowledge of available resources for youth. It also requires a thorough knowledge of the community and a firm commitment on the part of the library. And while this may seem overwhelming at times, what readers' advisor can resist a young reader's call to find another "good book just like this one"?

Notes

1. Margaret A. Edwards, *The Fair Garden and the Swarm of Beasts: The Library and the Young Adult*, reprinted (Chicago: ALA, 1994): p. 107.
2. Sarah Barchas, "Strategies for Involving Children in Reading Literature," in *Library Services for Hispanic Children: A Guide for Public and School Librarians*, ed. Adela Artola Allen (Phoenix: Oryx, 1987): p. 76.
3. Sandra L. Pucci, "Supporting Spanish Language Literacy: Latino Children and School and Community Libraries," in *Literacy, Access and Libraries Among the Language Minority Population*, ed. Rebecca Constantino (Lanham, Md.: Scarecrow, 1998): pp. 18–19.
4. Oralia Garza de Cortés, "United States: Hispanic Americans," in *Our Family Our Friends Our World: An Annotated Guide to Significant Multicultural Books for Children and Teenagers*, ed. Lyn Miller-Lachmann (New Providence, N.J.: Bowker, 1992): p. 123.
5. Edwards, 12.
6. Victor Nell, *Lost in a Book: The Psychology of Reading for Pleasure* (New Haven, Conn.: Yale University Press, 1988): pp. 256–261.
7. *Ibid.*, 146.
8. Patrick Jones, *Connecting Young Adults and Libraries: A How-to-Do-It Manual* (New York: Neal-Schuman, 1992): pp. 81, 88.
9. *Ibid.*, 88–94.
10. U.S. Bureau of the Census, *Current Population Reports: Population Projections of the United States by Age, Sex, Race, and Hispanic Origin: 1995 to 2050*, prepared by the Economics and Statistics Administration, Department of Commerce (Washington, D.C.: U.S. Government Printing Office, 1996.)
11. Camila Alire and Orlando Archibeque, *Serving Latino Communities: A How-to-Do-It Manual for Librarians* (New York: Neal-Schuman, 1998): p. 2.
12. Cortés, 121.
13. Hazel Rochman, *Against Borders: Promoting Books for a Multicultural World* (Chicago: ALA, 1993): p. 207.
14. Yolanda Cuesta, "From Survival to Sophistication: Hispanic Needs = Library Needs," *Library Journal* 115 (May 15, 1990): 26.
15. Pucci, 23–24.
16. Daphne Muse, ed. *The New Press Guide to Multicultural Resources for Young Readers* (New York: The New Press, 1997): p. 15.

17. Cuesta, 27.
18. Pucci, 26
19. *Ibid.*
20. *Ibid.*, 32.
21. Alan Bern, "Selection Tools for Materials in Spanish for Children and Young Adults," *Journal of Youth Services in Libraries* 8 (Fall 1994): 55–67.
22. Cortés, 123.
23. Camila Alire and Orlando Archibeque, *Serving Latino Communities: A How-to-Do-It Manual for Librarians* (New York: Neal-Schuman, 1998).
24. Adela Artola Allen, ed., *Library Services for Hispanic Children: A Guide for Public and School Librarians* (Phoenix: Oryx, 1987).
25. Esther Dyer and Concha Robertson-Kozan, "Hispanics in the U.S.: Implications for Library Service," *School Library Journal* 29 (April 1983).
26. Frances Ann Day, *Latina and Latino Voices in Literature for Children and Teenagers* (Portsmouth, N.H.: Heinemann, 1997): pp. 5–8.
27. Lyn Miller-Lachmann, *Our Family Our Friends Our World: An Annotated Guide to Significant Multicultural Books for Children and Teenagers* (New Providence, N.J.: Bowker, 1992): pp. 15–21.
28. Daphne Muse, ed., *The New Press Guide to Multicultural Resources for Young Readers* (New York: The New Press, 1997): pp. 17–19.
29. Rosalinda B. Barrera, Olga Liguori, and Loretta Salas, "Ideas a Literature Can Grow On: Key Insights for Enriching and Expanding Children's Literature About the Mexican-American Experience," *Teaching Multicultural Literature in Grades K–8*, ed. Violet J. Harris. (Norwood, Mass: Christopher-Gordon, 1992): pp. 203–241.
30. Pauletta Brown Bracy, "The Nature of the Readers' Advisory Transaction in Children's and Young Adult Reading," in *Guiding the Reader to the Next Book*, Kenneth D. Shearer, ed. (New York: Neal-Schuman, 1996): pp. 21–43.
31. This series is available from Gale Publishers.
32. The web site URL is: *http://coyote.csusm.edu/cwis/campus_centers/csbs/intro_eng.html*

Parents' Workshops

Judith Rodriguez

The most exciting outreach program I have done with the Connecting Libraries and Schools Project (CLASP) of the New York Public Library is the parent workshops for Latino families. Initially funded by DeWitt Wallace Reader's Digest to develop the necessary activities to bring new readers to the library, CLASP is directed at those who think the library has nothing to offer them. For example, people who do not want to read, or do not know how, or who cannot read English. To do the outreach job, the library has liberated a team of librarians from their desks who go into the community to make people aware of library services. These CLASP staffers visit community organizations, class rooms and offer teacher and parents workshops.

I have been with CLASP in School District no. 6, which covers the Hamilton Grange, Washington Heights, Fort Washington and Inwood neighborhoods, since 1991. Out of a population of 198,192 in Northern Manhattan, 132,722 — roughly 67 percent — are Latinos. The actual percentage, however, may be significantly higher, because illegal aliens abound in the neighborhoods. These Latinos speak only Spanish and have to wait a long time to be admitted to an English as a Second Language (ESL) class. Several community agencies, including the library, offer free classes, but the capacity per class is from 20 to 30 people. How do these numbers compare with thousands on the waiting list? Further complicating matters is the lack of a basic education among the aliens; many do not even read in their own language.

Why Parents' Workshops?

Reading at home and visiting the public library is something very natural for people in the United States. However, in Latin America, most of the cities have only a central library, and for people in the poor neighborhoods it is out of reach. Absorbed by the economical and social difficulties, an education is out of the question.

Once in the U.S., Latinos are again at a disadvantage. As the children begin to fit into the culture of the United States and learn the language, the parents have little chance to keep pace with their children's education. As parents struggle to put some food on the table, the gap between them and their children grows, because some kids stop talking in Spanish, and the parents are very limited in English.

In 1990 I was a young adult librarian at the Hamilton Fish Library, in another very Hispanic neighborhood, the Lower East Side of Manhattan. While there I realized that even though I was presenting booktalks to the kids every day and they seemed delighted with the stories, they failed to check out the books I discussed. Instead, the children begged me to tell them how the story ended, as they would never read as many pages as there are in a chapter book. I think that this would not happen if their parents had started reading to them at an early age.

Parent workshops are intended to make parents aware that even with language limitations they still have a culture to transmit to their children. They can accomplish this by talking to their children about their own childhood, by telling them folkloric tales from their countries and by reading to them in Spanish. Reading to children every day (or night) starting from an early age, is a very pleasant activity that both parents and children equally enjoy, establishing a very close relationship between them.

How to Get Parents' Attention

To get parents' attention is a challenge. If the parents are not highly motivated, they will not go to the library to hear a librarian talk about reading. The same is true if the workshop is about acquiring library skills. If they assume you are going to ask them to read or to fill out an application for a library card they will not come; for those not yet proficient in English, such simple tasks represent daunting challenges fraught with potential embarrassment. Of course, they realize how wonderful it is that their children can read, but they are ashamed that they themselves cannot read, spell or write.

A good place to find parents is at the schools in the mornings or nights when the principal calls them for a mandatory meeting. The job-training sessions in different neighborhood agencies, the English as a Second Language classes, or any adult education courses (like the GED or Even Start Program) are also good places to find parents because they are already assembled and bound to the program. Once they are gathered, it may be easier to command their full attention, so long as the workshops are entertaining, alive, and the information is appealing to them.

First CLASP staff contacts the agency or school, calling on, for instance, the principal or assistant principal, the family worker, the school librarian, the English as a Second Language coordinator, or the Parent Teacher Association to coordinate the program. Then the schools send home a flyer announcing the workshop and requesting that the parents attend.

It is an excellent idea to follow the first parent workshop at the school or agency with a second at the library. The workshop at the library allows parents to take books home right away. Even though workshops have conducted for as many as 70 to 100 parents, it is more effective to have small groups of 15 to 20 parents so you can exchange some ideas with them, and keep their attention.

It is important to start on time; delays give the audience an excuse to leave. The parents' attention span is often as short as the kids (between 20 to 40 minutes), and if they do not find what is said important or enjoyable they might leave or, worse, fall asleep.

I remember when we first started the workshops. They were pretty much speeches telling the parents how important reading was and how easy it was to get a library card. I remember translating for the CLASP director while the parents dozed. Guessing that the group might better relate to me, a Spanish speaker, Latina and mother, I asked my supervisor to allow me to take over the meeting. With some apprehension, he accepted. After that, the meeting went smoothly, and when I told them anecdotes about my own children and my frustrations as a working parent, they responded with enthusiasm and participated.

Now we do reading aloud, storytelling, flannel board stories, or origami stories and booktalks, no more than four minutes each. Many times we get the parents to volunteer a story or song. We talk about the library services and rules in between activities and book presentations. The conversation is in simple language — their own language.

It is interesting to see that at the beginning of the session some parents refuse to take off their coats and sit down. They all stay near the door as if planning to escape. Little by little as they find themselves captivated by the stories, and find their own concerns answered, they start sitting down and participating in the event, even sharing their own views and doubts. At the end they are pleased that they stayed, and they are anxious to have the books in their hands. Many times when we come back from the school workshop, we find the parents already at the branch, looking for the book we have booktalked.

We promote picture books with beautiful artwork and stories, ranging from those with no words to those with a few English sentences. We have had marvelous results using bilingual picture books and short tales that can be shared in a few minutes by the entire family. Preparation of the materials for the workshops is basic. Participation in the selection of the books is very important because the presenter has to enjoy the stories too. Also we have noticed very often that any story CLASP staff members read aloud or booktalk in a workshop is probably the one the parents will want to try at home first, simply because this material is familiar to them.

We also introduce the parents to adult books they can enjoy. We let them know about useful collections like the "Adult Spanish" collection, "Learning English" material, and "Life-Long Learning" collections. We finish the presentation by giving them library cards and allowing them to examine the books we brought to the presentation. They then have the chance ask questions about library services.

The program cannot take place without some kind of refreshments; otherwise, parents might be anxious to go home to eat. The refreshments can be donated by any school grant, or even by the library.

Some Ideas We Give the Parents

We use the "10 Tips for Parents" bookmark produced by the American Library Association. The CLASP staff translated this bookmark to Spanish and put the neighborhood libraries' schedules on the back.

We try to make these parents feel proud of their language, encouraging them to talk to their children in Spanish, if for no other reason than the ease with which they can use it. I remember when my daughter was in elementary school and she had never passed a math test. I decided that with all my degrees, I could teach her math. I start teaching her in the language I feel more confident talking: Spanish. She stopped me and said, "Mama, I do not understand Spanish." So I tried my luck with the English and soon she stopped me and said, "Mama, your accent is so difficult that I cannot understand your English." From that day on I taught her Spanish so we could understand each other; she cannot correct my Spanish, but my English she always will! If parents speak Spanish to their children at home, they will become bilingual, a valuable asset in a demanding society. It is also a way for parents to transmit their culture to a generation that needs an identity. We let parents know that despite their lack of education, they possess a treasure that will enrich their children's spirits: their language and their culture.

Many parents have expressed their frustration at not being able to help their children with math or English. We let them know that, if they cannot be their children's tutors, they *can* be pals, sharing books and stories.

Reading a book at bedtime, or at any time a child might be more receptive, will likely whet the appetite for more stories, more special moments. Their attention will improve as they become good listeners. They will nurture the stories with their own imagination. As a consequence, they will become more at ease with writing. Parents can do such beautiful work, helping to expand the creativity of their children without spending a dime, just by going to the public library to check out as many books as they want to share with their children. Even when the parent does not know how to read, a quick trip to the library will turn up beautiful wordless books like Tana Hoban's.

There are no special skills in reading aloud or telling a story. We suggest that the parents use those moments when they and their children face each other every day. This quality time is not the time for complaints or demands. But the joy of reading or telling a story has to be authentic: the story has to entertain, not simply bear a message the parent wants to deliver.

The parents' workshop is even more necessary with new immigrant parents. It is easy to tell somebody to go to the library and find books to take home. But think about it: a regular-size children's collection at the local library has 10,000 books. These parents will find themselves overwhelmed by the choices. What decisions can they make in selecting books if they do not even speak English? How will they know what is good for their child's age? After a parents' workshop they will be more aware of the library services, the type of material they can find, and they will be familiar with at least a few titles, any of which might prove their child's favorite and the impetus to a lifetime of reading.

Services to Migrant and Seasonal Farmworkers

Catherine Jasper

Migrant and seasonal farmworkers are often referred to as an "invisible" population. They live in their own communities, away from the rest of the population. If their employers supply buildings to live in and stores to buy food from, the adults have little reason to interact with society at large. Because they are new to the country, they often do not know how government agencies function and do not utilize social services. In other words, they keep to themselves, don't ask for much, and don't get much. My experience supports these ideas. How else could I live in a county with an estimated 20,000 migrant workers and never come in contact with a single one? They don't go to my grocery store or my mall or my movie theater. Until I went to the Institute on Library Services to Migrant and Seasonal Farmworkers in Florida, they truly were an invisible population for me.

Still a library school student, in June 1998 I attended the six-day institute, sponsored by the University of South Florida School of Library and Information Science and funded through the Department of Education by monies provided under the Higher Education Act, Title II-B. I didn't know what I was going to learn, only that I had a lot to learn. We crammed about as much learning into those six days as is humanly possible. The experience added an invaluable dimension to my library education that will stay with me throughout my career.

Sunday June 14, 1998

The institute started Sunday afternoon. As we went around with initial introductions, I was surprised. Because I was so unaware of the migrant and seasonal farmworker population, I was surprised at the specificity of people's purposes in attending the institute. Repeatedly I heard, "I am here because there are many migrant children in my school and I need to know how to better serve them," or, "Sometimes migrant workers come into my library and I'm at a loss for how to help them." I realized that if I am to be a librarian in Florida, this is an issue that probably will affect me.

We were then introduced to the major aspects of the issue with the classic 1961 documentary *Harvest of Shame*. Done by Edward R. Murrow, this film documented the conditions of migrant workers in the 1960s. Not since *The Grapes of Wrath* had a work so raised the consciousness of the U.S. public. Murrow talked to migrant workers, a crew leader, growers, the local police chief, a local minister, the president of the Farm Bureau, and the secretary of Labor. Boldly aired on Thanksgiving day, *Harvest of Shame* revealed the horrible living and working conditions of migrant workers and their families. Most powerful for me was the revelation of the cyclical nature of the system. Children started working in the fields as soon as they were big enough to be useful and continued throughout their lives until they were too old and weak to keep going. Despite the film's power, after the video we were told that conditions for the migrant and seasonal workers had not greatly improved in the 27 years since this film was made.

Monday June 15, 1998

Monday we received background information on who migrant workers are and where they can be found. Donna Parrino, the director of University of South Florida's Latin Community Advancement, spoke to us on the status of Latinos in America. We learned from her more surprising information. Hispanics have three times the poverty rate of white non–Hispanics; Hispanics' poverty rate is higher than African-Americans'. Hispanics' dropout rate is three times that of white non–Hispanics and two times the rate of African-Americans. Although Hispanics account for only 10 percent of the workforce, they represent over 40 percent of the farmworker population and more than 30 percent of the cleaning staff and servants of this country. On the other side, they represent only 3 percent of all the university and college professors and only 1.7 percent of the journalists. These are just a few examples that illustrate that as a job's salary increases, Hispanic representation goes down. I was so surprised by these figures because having spent a lot of time in central and south Florida, I know many Hispanics, and they are all solidly middle class or upper middle class, well-educated, and employed in well-paying professions. Once again, I realized the invisible nature of the migrant population. I don't know their situation because I don't come in contact with them.

Linda Grisham, from the Florida Department of Education, Adult Migrant Program and Services, gave us background on farmworkers' situations and imparted strategies for contacting them. To make contact with farmworkers, she recommended going first to agencies and organizations that serve them — churches, Head Start programs, day cares, migrant health clinics, anyplace that serves the migrant population. After contacting people who work with migrant workers, you are ready to make contact with community members. Suggestions included the stores where they buy food, flea markets, laundromats, Mexican restaurants, anywhere that migrant workers congregate. She warned to be sensitive to the time of day and the time of year. Know what crops your target population is working and work around their schedule. Take advantage of rainy days. In short, know and understand the population before you try to implement programming.

After Linda Grisham spoke, we heard from Kathleen de la Peña McCook, professor and director of the University of South Florida School of Library and Information Science. She pointed out ALA and FLA both have need-assessment guidelines that can be interpreted to require services to migrant populations. She recommended being familiar with these guidelines so that you can use "their" (the administration's) vocabulary to fight for what you want. And she reminded us to ask ourselves, "When visions are being formed, when long-range plans are being created, who is sitting at the table? And who will be the voice for those who cannot come?" The migrant population is a passive group. Serving them well requires advocacy on our part.

We later heard from Gloria Vales of the Area Health Education Center, Joan Turner of the Agriculture and Labor Program Inc., Ann Cranston-Gingras from the USF College of Education, two lawyers from Florida Rural Legal Services and Lucas Benito from the Coalition of Immokalee Workers. Their topic was "Information Needs of Migrant and Seasonal Farmworkers and their Families." Opinions on what farmworkers need included information on health care, child/infant care, labor rights, community services, and agencies and organizations that can help. One of the lawyers pointed out that many farmworkers do not understand that the Department of Labor can help them, that its purpose is not soley to investigate illegal workers and send them home. Also needed at libraries are materials about farmworkers — stories of labor struggles, books on their native cultures. Lucas Benito pointed out that there are many resources, including computers and the Internet, at the library, and librarians may need to teach farmworkers how to use them. Farmworkers need more access to libraries through bookmobiles and extended hours, and they need greater awareness of libraries' services and resources.

By this point, we had been inundated with information on how horrible migrant workers' situations are, we had been told how complicated and established the political and economic systems that rely on their labor really is, and we had been told that libraries are currently doing little to reach this population. It was, frankly, disheartening. Luckily, Tuesday offered hope.

Tuesday June 16, 1998

Tuesday the theme shifted to what has been done and what we can do. We heard from Patrick Donne from the High School Equivalency Program offered through the USF College of Education. This is a summer program that enables the children of migrant workers to either advance to the next grade when they re-enter school in the fall or, in some cases, graduate. Three graduates of the program told us about the needs of migrant workers. They told us to remember that the children of migrant workers are intimidated by teachers, by the workload the U.S. education system and by computers. These children often miss the library orientation at the beginning of the year because they start back later than other students. And while many may be capable of earning scholarships for college, few know these scholarships exist or how to go about applying for them. They often live in cramped quarters and have no place to study. They have usually been uprooted from their homeland and are living in a strange culture. These three successful adults had very specific suggestions about what migrant children need from libraries: they need a warm, welcoming face; their own library orientation; after-school tutoring and extra help with the computers; information on scholarships and financial aid programs; a quiet place to study after school; and materials on their own countries and culture to boost their sense of identity and self-worth. All of these needs can be easily addressed by school media centers and public libraries.

Next we heard about the needs of adult learners from Linda Grisham. She recommended that adult education programs employ real-life applications and be group-oriented, supportive and non-competitive.

Because of the low self-esteem of many adult students, positive feedback must be frequent. Migrant workerss lack of transportation must be accommodated. It doesn't matter how many people want to come to your program; it matters how many want to *and are able* to come.

Afterward, we heard some examples of programs that have been tried in libraries. They have not all been successful, but those librarians have started to figure out what works and what doesn't work. In the evening we heard from Patrice Koerper from the Tampa-Hillsborough County Public Library System on how to publicize the services and programs you provide. She suggested that librarians be specific about their goals, know their target market, and be prepared to present their message a number of ways in a variety of formats.

Wednesday June 17, 1998

Wednesday we had our field trip. We left our notebooks at the hotel and got on a bus to see a few examples of migrant workers' living and working conditions. Dr. Stauffer reminded us that, of course, what we were going to see were examples of close to ideal situations because these are the employers who are proud and want to show off what they do. The employers at the places that do not provide such good conditions wouldn't let us visit. In Dover we visited the Adult Migrant and Seasonal Farmworker Program. Here adults actually receive a small wage to attend classes and get an education. The program works with the Redlands Christian Migrant Association to provide daycare. They have many new facilities and a great computer lab. Next we went to Sanwa Growers in Wimauma. Here we witnessed the benefits of conscientious business practices. Sanwa Growers does not employ seasonal or migrant workers, only year-round farm workers. This dependable income and stability allows these workers to establish roots, buy homes, let their children go through school.

Next we visited Wimauma's Beth El Mission, where the goal is to promote self-sufficiency through education and prayer. Its director was a powerfully inspirational man. He believed that as long as the system requires migrant and seasonal workers, those who are helped on to a better situation will only be replaced by others. He wondered why millions of dollars can be spent to research agricultural products, methods and techniques, but nobody is looking for a system of manual labor that would ensure year-round work and give these people a better life.

Last we visited the Deseret Farms housing facilities. These are the best of the housing, and they are in fact quite livable. The sad thing is that all employers and landlords don't feel a moral responsibility to provide such housing for their workers and tenants. The lesson of the day seemed to be that through caring business owners, landlords and service agencies, a better life is possible for migrant workers.

Thursday June 18, 1998

Thursday was devoted to collection development, which is essential because almost all services and programs are supported by the collection, and a good collection is the base that will keep people coming back to the library. Nelida Miranda from the Tampa-Hillsborough County Public Library system talked to us about her experiences.

She pointed out that librarians must either work within the established collection-development policy or change the policy to reflect what their goals really are. She reminded us that a good collection meets the recreational, educational, and informational needs of all ages. Libraries must not only provide the materials, but they must also make them accessible through appropriate signs, displays and bibliographies. All of the principles of usual collection development apply, but the librarian must also check for cultural relevancy (which required that the librarian know the targeted cultures) and information accuracy. She strongly recommended using a vendor because they are in touch with what is popular and can help you determine quality.

Casey McPhee from the Pasco County Library system talked to us about her experiences building a Spanish language collection at her library. She warned us of mistakes that she made. First, she tried to do it alone. She soon realized how helpful a vendor is in this situation. Second, she started off creating a Spanish version of the existing collection. Now she understands that different communities have different needs and tastes, and this must be reflected in the collection a librarian builds. The importance of knowing the population was once again emphasized. Linda Goodman of Bilingual Publications spoke to us about what she can offer as a vendor who specializes in Spanish language materials. She recommended that librarians build a relationship with at least two specialists to help them in collection development.

Friday June 19, 1998

On our last day, we had time to talk about what we had learned and what we planned to do. Dr. Perez led us through a structured activity that forced us to think in concrete terms about what we would actually do when we returned to work. Though I was a student, this activity gave me an opportunity to think about how I would be able to translate the experience and knowledge gained at the institute into real-life programs, services and resources at a library. The underlying message of all of our activities and presenters was clear: Know the people in the community you serve. Know where they live, where they're from, where they work, what they harvest, when they come, when they go, how they live, how they play, what they want, what they eat, what they like, what they fear, what they dream, who they are. Until you know who they are, you cannot serve them.

Bridging Cultures Through Literature

Tim Wadham

Introduction

My journey began thirteen years ago when I started working as the children's librarian in a neighborhood with a large Latino population. I spoke fluent Spanish but quickly discovered that there were few resources to help me find materials that would utilize my language skills. In my programming, I wanted to include materials that were indigenous to Latin American countries instead of just using translations of material originally presented in English. I began to gather rhymes, finger plays, and stories from disparate sources, focusing particularly on books by Latino authors, whether in English or Spanish or both, and books originally published in Spanish from Latin American countries. These last are not given very much attention in this country, and many of them deserve more. It is from these materials that I began to develop a feeling for the richness of the Latino cultural heritage.

After surmounting the challenge of finding books, I worked to connect children and young adults with the material I had discovered. This required bridging cultural barriers that sometimes make traditional library programming inadequate. In this article, I will discuss briefly the cultural issues relevant to library programming in Latino communities, then discuss experiences I've had doing programming and outreach in the Latino community.

Cultural Issues

With a heritage rich in culture from many countries, Latinos are the fastest-growing ethnic group in the United States. Many Latino children are bilingual, but they score consistently lower on language-skills tests than their English-speaking counterparts. I have seen firsthand the difference that librarians, teachers, and caregivers can make by modeling the Spanish language and reinforcing cultural heritage. It is also advantageous for all children, regardless of their background, to have a sense of the beauty and richness of the Spanish language and Latino culture. For the professional to begin forming bridges through literature, it is important to understand Latino cultures, and the differences and similarities between those cultures. I have found that these differences are manifested primarily through language variations and issues relating to national origin.

Recognizing the diversity represented in national origin is extremely important when working with Latino children. There are some major differences in Latino cultures. A common thread to the history of Mexico and Central and Latin America is the story of native peoples conquered and assimilated by the Spanish. This has led to populations of mixed origin living alongside those native peoples who have managed to maintain their identity. Countries such as Argentina and Uruguay exhibit a great deal of European influence, whereas countries such as Guatemala, Bolivia and Peru are shaped more by Indian influences. The native cultures continue to thrive in these countries. Mexican culture is a mixture of Spanish and Indian influences.

Beyond these cultural differences there are also differences in language. As you look over a group of children in a bilingual storytime you might see children who have recently arrived from any number of countries and who have little or no knowledge of the English language. One child may come from a family who speak English better than Spanish — perhaps the grandparents immigrated here, but the parents grew up in an English-language environment, and the child may speak no Spanish at all. Behind this child may be another from a family who immigrated a few years ago, one in which the parents may speak no English, but the children have learned English in the public schools and are fully bilingual. Each child in the audience, then, may have a different socio-economic status and bring with him a particular set of cultural values from his native land, or, in the case of the children born here, the Latino-American culture.

Latinos are linked and separated by the Spanish language. Spanish is spoken by over 400 million people and is one of the world's major languages, yet there is constant disagreement over what constitutes "bona fide" Spanish. The differences in spoken and written Spanish from country to country and within regions can be compared to the disparity between the English spoken in England and that spoken in North America and the accents and slang of regional speech found across the United States. Latinos have generally learned to celebrate these differences and have little trouble understanding one another. Many cultural differences are reflected in the use of language, and maintaining the language in a new country helps preserve a sense of identity.

To understand how language differences translate into cultural differences, we need to understand how language reflects culture. For an example of how cultural attitudes toward public libraries are manifested through language, you need only look at the words *Libería* and *Biblioteca.* Since there is no strong tradition of free public library service in many Latin American countries, a Latino patron will likely refer to a public library as a *Libería,* which suggests a bookstore, rather than *Biblioteca,* which suggests a library. This is often an obstacle to be overcome in serving these patrons.

Another concept that is extremely important in understanding Latino culture is that of the extended family. In working within Latino communities, programs that include the entire family will likely be the most successful. Single caregiver or single child programs rarely succeed because they are not an option for Latino parents with larger families. An overriding concern for most Latino parents is for their children and their children's education. This attitude stems from a cultural association of books and reading primarily with school and education, rather than with recreational reading. It is this same emphasis on education that is a primary reason that, at least until recently, there has been relatively little creative literature for children emerging from Latin America. Cultural issues must be treated in a positive light, as something to build on, rather than as something negative that needs to be changed. For example, library services can be marketed to emphasize the educational priorities of Latino parents. Ultimately, cultural barriers can be overcome with outreach into the Latino community by dedicated and enthusiastic librarians who can articulate how the library is a relevant institution.

Programs

The following are examples of specific types of programs that I have found work well in the Latino community. I will illustrate these by citing actual programs that I have implemented. The primary focus of these programs has always been to share books, and the ones I discuss are among the best.

Family Programs

Since the family unit is integral in Latino culture, many schools and libraries have met with success bringing parents or grandparents and children together for programs. This programming goes beyond traditional storytimes (where a child is brought by one parent, or a day-care provider), bringing entire families together. There are many examples of successful programs, but the one thread they have in common is parent-child involvement. It is possible to build from this foundation and to offer instructional programs just for parents, teaching them how to read to their children and how to model a reading habit. Librarians or teachers can demonstrate how to read a book with a child and suggest activities to be used with particular books. One format that has worked for me is to have a meeting with parents in one area of the library while a storytime (which can include craft activities, so that the entire time does not have to be filled with stories) is being held for the children in another. At the end of the program, parents and children are brought back together. Obviously, this requires more than one staff person, so staff or volunteer cooperation is essential. You can also seek out guest speakers, such as Latino artists or storytellers from the community. This sort of programming can be organized as a once-only program or as a series of workshops.

In my library we had a particularly successful program of this type using Eduardo Robles Boza's book *Cuatro letras se escaparon* (*The Four Letters That Escaped*). This book relates the tale of four letters, *p*, *e*, *o* and *r*, which escape from a large book. They play around and decide to form words together. But the only words they can form have slightly negative connotations: *pero* (meaning "but") and *peor* (meaning "worse"). They even form English words! (*rope*). They return to their book and tell *a* and *z* their problem. Together with those two letters, they are able to form the word *proeza*, defined as an exploit, feat or heroic deed. Robles Boza tells us at the end that it is through the exploits of the four letters that the word *proeza* was, in fact, invented.

The adult portion of the program began with a welcome speech from the library manager, followed by an introduction to library services. Then a discussion of the types of children's literature available in Spanish was held, using examples from the library collection. This was followed by a discussion of the importance of reading to children, focusing on the educational aspect.

While the parent program was going on in one part of the library, the children were enjoying a storytime in the library auditorium. The staff and children rehearsed the "Four Letters" story and prepared to present it. As the discussion with the parents ended, they were brought into the auditorium and treated to a program by their children. The children acted out the story, holding up signs representing each letter and rearranged themselves when the letters spelled out different words.

Other elements that would work well in a program of this type include book displays and printed booklists highlighting library collections that participants can take home. Refreshments can be served, and parents should be offered a tour of the library. The primary key to making a program like this work is parental involvement, and the key to that is reaching the parents in a way that will make them want to participate.

Other variations on this theme include the American Library Association's "Born to Read" format which reaches out to expectant mothers, giving them instruction and materials. As the women apply for library cards they are provided incentives such as "Born to Read" t-shirts or rompers for their children. Library programs are held in which the ideal for parent-child interaction with books can be modeled by librarians. In other libraries, grant-funded programs have sent librarians to Latino homes to work with individual families. Targeted families receive a bag containing books, a puppet or finger play, and library publicity materials. Staff talk to the parents about the importance of reading themselves and of reading to their children, with the goal of bringing these families to programs into the library. Another excellent model for an intergenerational program is *Gente y cuentos,* or "People and Stories" developed by Sarah Hirschman, which is a program where young adults and senior citizens meet to read and discuss short stories and poetry that have significant cultural content. The simple idea of reading stories and then discussing them can be adapted to work in many different group situations.

After-School Programs

Before obtaining my professional position, I worked for a time as an aide in a school library. There I realized that school librarians have one significant advantage over public librarians: they have a captive audience and are able to have a special impact on students who visit their library for programs on a weekly basis. To duplicate that experience, I began to develop after-school programs in my library that would allow me to work with the same group of students over an extended period of time. These programs were often developed to serve specific schools. When a teacher asked me to develop a program for her charges who were teenage children, all new immigrants, and spoke no English, I jumped at the chance. We had a weekly program that always began with choral poetry reading. We read and discussed Latino folklore and literature. I had long realized that one of the most effective ways of sharing folktales is through creative dramatization because so many tales lend themselves well to dramatic treatment. During the course of our after-school program I asked the students to choose their favorite folktale to dramatize. They picked "Pedro de Ordimalas." Pedro is a character found in stories throughout Latin America. In some of them Pedro is a hero trying to correct injustices, but in most he is more of a trickster, trying to get rich or to get out of having to do work. He loves to trick the mostly foolish and greedy people with whom he comes in contact. He can make bandits believe that money grows on trees. He even wins a battle of wits with the devil. In another tale Pedro gets Saint Peter to let him into heaven. Together, we wrote a script based on the story in which Pedro tricks his way into heaven, and we put on the production, complete with costumes, for an appreciative audience of parents and friends. There was not enough time to memorize lines, so the children carried their scripts. We did our production twice, once in Spanish, and then again in English. Since these children knew little English, it was a challenge, but one that they enjoyed.

There are two excellent books of Pedro stories by María Cristina Brusca and Tona Wilson. *The Blacksmith and the Devils* tells the basic story that we used, but transforms Pedro into a character named Juan Pobreza who lives in the Argentine pampas. A Spanish translation of this book is available entitled *El herrero y el diablo. Pedro Fools the Gringo, and Other Tales of a Latin American Trickster* is a hysterical collection of Pedro stories, including "Pedro Goes to Heaven." All of these stories cry out to be dramatized.

STORYTIMES

The basic principles for creating an effective bilingual or Spanish storytime are not much different from those any children's librarian would follow when preparing any other type of storytime. They simply must be adapted to the culture and specific needs of the audience. You must know your audience and prepare books that are age-appropriate. The librarian must also face the issue of deciding when is the best time for a bilingual storytime. Bilingual or Spanish storytime should be done when children and parents can attend together. Beyond the standard topics adapted for a bilingual audience, I like to do special storytimes with books based on Latino cultural themes such as holidays. One particularly successful storytime was based on *El Día de los Muertos* (*Day of the Dead*). The Mexican Day of the Dead is marked with unique artistic and culinary creations. The major motif is the skeleton. I used the book *Pablo Remembers: The Fiesta of the Day of the Dead*, by George Ancona, combining it with a craft project. The gorgeous photographs in this Pura Belpré honor book for illustration show all the color of these skulls, or *calaveras*, as well as the altars created to honor the spirits of the departed. These things are not viewed as morbid — a little girl preparing to do the craft project asked if she could draw her grandfather's skeleton. Programs such as this can touch a chord with the audience. After my program, a mother expressed her lament that the day was no longer celebrated as it had once been in Mexico. It is true that Mexicans in the United States who no longer have access to their family cemeteries in Mexico often express dissatisfaction and disappointment in the holiday and its less spiritual U.S. transformation. The good news is that this holiday seems to be growing in popularity in the United States as the influence of Latino culture grows. Ancona's book is also available in Spanish translation as *Pablo recuerda: La fiesta de el día de los muertos*.

The ideal book to use when introducing students to the library and the joys of books is Pat Mora's *Tomás and the Library Lady*, which is truly a gift to librarians working with Latino children. This is the moving true story of the influence of an Iowa librarian on the life of an author and University administrator, Tomás Rivera. I've seen this story bring tears to the eyes of jaded school principals.

A book I discovered early on and which has become my all-time favorite is *El caballito que queria volar* (*The Horse Who Wanted to Fly*), by Marta Osorio. This is a beautiful story about a wooden carousel horse who wants to become a bird so that he can fly. Made from the carpenter's last piece of tree trunk, which had a large open gash, he is different from the carousel horses. Two church bells overhear his wish and dispatch an owl to work some magic. The book is filled with glorious language. It is a long story which demands to be read in one sitting. I have seen audiences sit mesmerized for the entire length of the tale. If you can find the right audience and the right setting, you will create an experience through this book that those present will never forget.

There are many opportunities for outreach, both in and out of the library, using this same format. I've had success in working with teachers to have bilingual classes, particularly the younger grades, arrange field trips to the library. This lets the children know where the library is, and an enthusiastic storytime can be followed up with eager children picking out their own books to read. Obviously the storytimes I've described can also be taken "on the road" to schools, and other agencies like Head Start. I've done parent education classes off-site for PTAs and at meetings of parents whose children go to a particular day care agency. I am always looking for tales that can be told without a book which are memorable enough to use in school settings when talking to a large group makes the use of a book somewhat ineffective. In these settings you want to create an impression, and give children something that they will remember and connect with the library. The story I most often use for this purpose is *The Terrible Tragadabas*, retold by Joe Hayes. This is a great monster story in the form of a cumulative tale. Three sisters, one by one, get scared up in into a tree by the Tragadabas, who has taken up residence in the store to which each of the girls go, in turn, to get tortillas and honey. The Tragadabas gets stung by a bee and the girls return home safely to their grandmother.

Beyond Literature: Computer Literacy Programs

When I was transferred to a branch library which had been constructed in the early sixties, it was immediately apparent that the library collection had not kept pace with the ethnic shift in the surrounding community. Much of the collection seemed irrelevant for a neighborhood which had become predominantly Latino, and in which Spanish was spoken more than English. As I traveled to various schools in the neighborhood, I learned of the dual struggle that bilingual education presented the teachers: the need to keep students on track with the grade-level curriculum while at the same time dealing with basic language issues that had to be resolved before any subjects could even be taught. As I investigated further, I found that the reading test scores of Latino children in these schools lagged behind those of their English-speaking counterparts. Then I realized a great fundamental truth. Before my collection of fiction and picture books in both Spanish and English could be truly relevant, before any of these stories could make a difference in these children's lives, we were going to have to teach them how to read. In conjunction with the school district, I developed a grant proposal to create a computer lab in the library where children could use software that would help develop their literacy skills. The program became very popular. It was gratifying to see parents sitting with their children, learning together at the computer. I remember one child in particular, a first grader whose reading was so poor that she was to be held back and not allowed to advance with her classmates to the second grade. She came to the computer lab workshops diligently throughout the entire summer. Her parents reported to me later that when this young girl went to school in the fall she was retested and allowed to move on to the second grade. The parents wrote a touching letter indicating that they attributed her increased reading skills to her work in the computer lab. When I talked to this little girl later, she told me that she had found the computer games to be a challenge, and this challenge motivated her to return to the lab regularly to master them. Her mother is now a valued library employee.

Obviously, a computer-aided literacy project such as the one I'm describing requires money and staff time. We found that the very tangible rewards, such as a child's learning to read, justify the time and effort spent in obtaining funds and implementing the program.

Conclusion

Each of these programs is linked by the idea of books becoming literal bridges between children and their culture. For the after-school teens, folklore bridged the gap between their new home and the homes they had left behind. In schools and Head Start centers, children make cultural connections through books such as *Tomás and the Library Lady*, which, with the photo and brief biography of Tomás Rivera included at the end, teaches them that regardless of their circumstances, they can become anything they wish to be. Parents make these connections as well through stories such as *Pablo Remembers*, which serves as a reminder of a lost heritage waiting to be recovered. These experiences have made me a passionate advocate of the importance of library service to Latino children, and most especially, of the rich heritage of Latino materials available. The challenge is to find the books, share the books, and build the bridges.

References

Ancona, George. *Pablo Remembers: The Fiesta of the Day of the Dead.* New York: Lothrop, Lee & Shepherd, 1993.

Brusca, María Cristina, and Tona Wilson. *The Blacksmith and the Devils.* Illus. María Cristina Brusca. New York: Holt, 1992.

_____. *Pedro Fools the Gringo, and Other Tales of a Latin American Trickster.* Illus. María Cristina Brusca. New York: Redfeather (Holt), 1995.

Hayes, Joe. *The Terrible Tragadabas/El terrible tragadabas.* Illus. Lucy Jelinek. Santa Fe, New Mexico: Trails West, 1987.

Johnston, Tony. *Day of the Dead.* Illus. Jeanette Winter. New York: Harcourt, 1997.

Mora, Pat. *Tomás and the Library Lady.* Illus. Raul Colón. New York: Knopf, 1997.

Osorio, Marta. *El caballito que queria volar* (*The Horse Who Wanted to Fly*). Illus. Maite Miralles. Valladolid: Editorial Miñon, 1982.

Robles Boza, Eduardo. *Cuatro letras se escaparon* (*The Four Letters That Escaped*). Illus. Rebeca Cerda. Mexico: Editorial Trillas, 1986.

Wells, Rosemary. *Léale a su conejito.* Trans. Susana Pasternac. New York: Scholastic, 1997.

The Support Role of Community Colleges Library/ Learning Resources Programs in Academic Success

Derrie Perez

The Hispanic population of the United States is defined as Mexican-American, Puerto Rican, Cuban-American, and those from the Caribbean and Central and South America. Hispanics are found primarily in the states of Arizona, California, Colorado, Florida, Illinois, New Mexico, New York, Puerto Rico, and Texas. At the time of the report *Our Nation on the Fault Line*, "sixty-four percent of Latino Americans [were] U.S. born citizens residing in the United States" and "the vast majority" of Latino immigrants were legal. It is predicted that by the year 2050, Hispanics will be the largest population in the United States and will make up nearly 25 percent of the population of the county. Moreover, the report suggests that by 2030 "Latino students age 5 to 18 will number almost 16 million — 25 percent of the total school population."[1] As of July 1998, the U.S. Census Bureau estimated that percentage already at 15 percent, and newer predictions are that the numbers will reach 20 percent by the year 2020. These increases are related to continued Hispanic immigration and high birth rates among Latina women. [2]

According to a report of the National Council of La Raza (NCLR) based on recently released census data, Hispanics are making economic progress, but they remain the poorest of the minority groups for three reasons: 1) low educational attainment levels, 2) decline in the value of wages, and 3) concentration in lesser paying industries. The NCLR believes that "sustained and significant economic improvement for Latinos can only be achieved by addressing ... low levels of educational attainment."[3]

Highest Dropout Rate

Hispanics have the highest high school drop out rate, a cumulative 30 percent,[4] compared to 12.6 percent for African-Americans,[5] and 7.7 percent for whites.[6] While the percentage of African-Americans and whites enrolled in higher education has doubled over the past 20 years (to 25 and 33 percent, respectively), the percentage of Hispanics enrolled has risen only from 13 to 20 percent.[7]

To complicate the situation, only a small percentage of Hispanic youth take a pre-college or college prepatory curriculum in high school; rather, they are tracked into courses that satisfy only their high school requirements. Of those who do attend college, approximately half attend a community college, and few transfer to a four-year institution.[8]

Studies of the Intent to Persist

In his 1990 research, Halpin provided a review of studies from the discipline of student development that analyze the intent of students to persist to complete a college education, to get a degree, or to transfer from a community college to a 4-year institution.[9] Unlike university students who reside on-campus, community college students live and usually socialize outside the institution. Therefore, their feelings of community with the institution are practically nonexistent. Halpin's study indicates that the factors that account for the greatest contributions of the institution to the academic success of students in the community college are academic and intellectual development faculty concern for teaching and student development, and faculty-student interaction.[10] Halpin concluded that

> the creation of institutional mechanisms to maximize student/faculty contact is likely to result in greater levels of integration and hence persistence. Small, interactive classes, numerous office hours, active, developmental academic advising systems, mentoring and small group learning projects, and a generally accessible, involved faculty may be a significant portion of the prescription for retention in nonresidential, open-door community colleges.[11]

Research done by Solis indicated that the factors that play the most significant roles related to an Hispanic student's persistence are motivation to persist and commitment to attend.[12] A few of the factors that Solis analyzed were motivational indicators, including peer and family support systems, use of tutorial services, participation in specialized remediation course work, and quality of academic services.[13] Nora also found that, along with high school grades, "encouragement by others before entering a community college" was a significant factor in the retention process.[14] These factors were also identified by Cabrere et al., who found that the largest "effect on Persistence was accounted by Intent to Persist, followed by GPA, Institutional Commitment, [and] Encouragement from Friends and Family," of which, institutional commitment had the greatest impact.[15]

Rendon and Valadez identified factors related to those of Solis. Their research on the influences of Hispanic student transfer identified five major factors influencing the transfer of community college students to four-year institutions: (a) importance of the family, (b) economic considerations, (c) knowledge of the system, (d) cultural understanding, and (e) relationships with feeder schools and senior institutions.[16] Family has a strong effect on decisions affecting both female and male Hispanic students; that familial influence includes education. As indicated, U.S. Hispanics continue to be the poorest among the U.S. populations, so naturally, they tend toward majors that would prepare them for immediate employment. Many Hispanic students come from immigrant families with limited or no knowledge of the U.S. educational system. The understanding of the Hispanic culture by a predominantly white faculty puts the Hispanic student in an environment of limited sensitivity. The relationship between universities and feeder schools is not always cooperative.[17] This combination of factors surely has contributed both to the serious high school dropout rate and to the lack of college persistence of Latino students.

Following in this research direction,

the University of La Verne (Calif.) began the First Generation Student Success Program during the academic year of 1996-97. The program is a three-year study of the obstacles faced by first-generation students and includes workshops and classes for both students and parents on such topics as financial aid, admissions, costs, calendars, career opportunities, motivation, and the culture of college life and requirements. As Reisberg reports, parents often underestimate the importance of their child's immersion in the college lifestyle: "Their son or daughter may need to go to campus simply to study in the library...."[18] The workshops help the students learn ways to explain college life in discussions with their parents. Although the study's findings are not yet conclusive, University of La Verne officials are already impressed with retention rates of participants in this specialized program of workshops, classes, parental involvement, scholarships, small class size, security, and mentors.

Library Services

The development of library services for Hispanics did not begin until the late sixties.[19] It was during that time that special libraries and collections were developed in universities such as UCLA. During this period, Dr. Arnulfo Trejo and a few other interested Hispanic librarians gave birth to the organization REFORMA, the National Association to Promote Library Services to the Spanish Speaking.

In both public and academic library settings, there are a number of services and programs currently offered that have been specifically developed for the Hispanic or Spanish-speaking population, or for minority populations in general. The most complete source of such services for public libraries, and a must-have resource for all libraries, is the recent monograph by Alire and Archibeque, *Serving Latino Communities*.[20] Academic librarians with an in-depth interest in this topic might also consult the classic *Developing Library and Information Services for Americans of Hispanic Origin*.[21] Some of the outreach services noted throughout the library literature include[22, 23]:

- Special institutional, pre-college programs, like specialized library instruction for a summer high school program on campus
- Library instruction directed to students of a foreign language institute or an English as a Second Language program
- Library orientation programs and tours offered each academic term, both in the library and in classrooms, and perhaps in other languages
- Cultural and foreign language materials collections
- Cultural exhibits, colloquia, displays, author series, book displays
- Identification efforts, such as procuring campus mailing lists of minority students to determine their perceived needs
- Outreach programs to other areas of the institution or community
- Targeted special populations, such as migrant families[24]
- Peer information counseling[25]

Libraries might also consider the possible need for specialized signage, the use of group study rooms, and the role of special collections departments in providing materials for cultural services. Libraries must consider the diversity of staffing patterns, the need for bilingual staff, and staff sensitivity training. Especially in the academic setting, the library can certainly be seen as an open classroom.[26]

Library Contributions to Academic Success

As noted above, studies have indicated that an institution can contribute to the academic success of students in a variety of ways. The institution can make a commitment to provide students with faculty who are passionate about teaching and about their students' learning. The institution can help assure that faculty members are sincerely concerned about the academic and intellectual development of students, and that they are accessible to students and involved in student activities. Furthermore, the institution can provide for the student at least a few of the situations proven to enhance their learning and academic success: small classes, numerous office hours, mentoring, and small group projects.

To the extent that studies also indicate that motivation by family, friends, and peers contributes to the success of Hispanic students, institutions can provide on-campus or college-related activities that would bring these constituents together and help them understand the impact of the college learning experience on students and their families. Since immigrant families and their children often have no experience with the U.S. system of higher education, and since many Hispanic students would be first-generation students, institutions must consider the depth of information needed by the students and their families. Institutions should provide activities that would specifically help the Hispanic student work through the mazes of first-time college admission. If the institution makes a commitment to contribute to the academic success of students, particularly Hispanic students, then each unit within the institution must make the same commitment. Therefore, the community college library/learning resources (CL/LR) program should have a contribution to make as well. This contribution would then link the CL/LR program squarely to the "overall educational enterprise" and would provide "a culture of evidence that documents progress and contributions toward the realization of desired [institutional] outcomes."[27]

Hispanic Serving Institutions (HSI)

In the United States, there is no designation of historically Hispanic colleges parallel to the historically black colleges. There are, however, about 3,000 two-year and four-year institutions in the United States and Puerto Rico designated as "Hispanic Serving Institutions." The current criteria for the these colleges is as follows: (1) student enrollment is 25 percent Hispanic; (2) no less than 50 percent of the Hispanic students are low-income and first-generation college attendees; and (3) an additional 25 percent of the Hispanic students are either low-income or first-generation college attendees.[28]

In February 1998, the U. S. Department of Housing and Urban Development announced that twelve community colleges received special grants under the Hispanic Serving Institutions Work-Study program.[29] Those awards included two community colleges in New York, one in Illinois, seven in California, one in Texas, and one in New Jersey. In an article on academic success, a program at Triton College in suburban Chicago was cited for its extraordinary effort to provide specialized services for the immigrant population. The program is known as *Nuevos Horizontes* (New Horizons) and is located at a center in a community near the main campus. [30]

Community College Library/Learning Resources Involvement

While it was considered that the college-wide work-study grants and the innovative *Nuevos Horizontes* program might impact the attitude, concern, and programs of the libraries/learning resources programs of the individual community colleges noted above, the depth of such a research project prohibited that study at this time. However, as a sample for this paper, contact was made with library/learning resources program (L/LRP) representatives at four community colleges to ask about the library services offered to the Hispanic population.

The representatives were asked to complete a chart to indicate activities of their L/LRP that might contribute to the increased chances of academic success of Hispanic students at their institutions. The activities those four libraries provide to students in each of the ten categories do appear to provide what development researchers say students need to increase their chances of academic success. While not all of the responding libraries single out Hispanic students, the activities they provide for students in general are extended to all the population groups. Column 3 of the chart below provides a composite summary of the above libraries' activities.[31]

What Students Need to Increase Their Chances of Academic Success	Contributions of the Library to Students' Academic Success	Library Activities Associated with Students' Academic Success
Faculty concerned about teaching	Librarians concerned about library-use instruction and student learning	Library-use instruction (LUI) for classes, including ESL and development; reference librarians at all campuses; hands on; exercise sheets; study guides in Spanish and Asian languages; one-on-one instruction; LUI included in special minority study skills project; librarians are faculty and involved in college-wide governance
Faculty concerned about student intellectual development	Librarians concerned about student development in information literacy	Computer literacy course; course in information literacy of Internet and electronic databases; classes on search engines and networked CDROM technology

What Students Need to Increase Their Chances of Academic Success	Contributions of the Library to Students' Academic Success	Library Activities Associated with Students' Academic Success
Faculty involved and accessible	Librarians involved and accessible	Offices in reference area; library in charge of student email and newsgroups for college; librarians introduced during orientations; reference librarians available all hours; multiple librarians available during peak times; librarians serve on college-wide committees on academic and student issues
Small classes	Library as open classroom	Instruction classroom with computers; one-on-one, over the shoulder instruction; LUI courses offered in library; tours and orientations for classes, small groups, and individuals
Numerous office hours	Extended hours of operation, including nights and weekends	Seven-day operations from as early as 7 AM to late as 10 PM
Mentoring programs	Library staff involvement in college-wide or library mentoring program	No student mentoring programs mentioned; faculty mentoring on information skills; teach faculty how to integrate skills into classroom
Small group projects	Support of small group library projects	Small group study rooms; web links to help students working on group projects; librarians available for small groups and individual consultation
Motivation by peers, friends, family	Inviting atmosphere with culturally diverse library staff	Culturally diverse staff and materials; Spanish speaking librarian or staff member available in each public service area; international student assistants; includes Hispanic, Asian, Hawaiian, African-American, etc.

What Students Need to Increase Their Chances of Academic Success	Contributions of the Library to Students' Academic Success	Library Activities Associated with Students' Academic Success
An understanding of the college system	Provision of information or access to information about college operations and library as part of college system	Link from library web page to college web page; library houses placement materials; circulating textbook collection for indigent students; official disseminator of college information to students and public
An understanding of the college culture	Provision of information about college culture	Displays on academic events, monthly cultural displays; permanent and temporary Hispanic art displays; library classes; brochures; study guides

Since the community college libraries/learning resources contacted offer these services, it might be construed that the library can certainly take an active role in the academic success of Hispanic young adults. An in-depth study of a large portion of the over 1200 community colleges in the United States would certainly give insight into what exactly the community college libraries/learning resources are doing to contribute to academic success. It would also provide a formidable checklist of activities and programs that might support the commitment to attend and the motivation to persist of Hispanic young adults in U.S. community colleges.

Notes

1. President's Advisory Commission on Educational Excellence for Hispanic Americans, *Our Nation on the Fault Line: Hispanic American Education* (Washington, D.C.: White House Initiative in Educational Excellence for Hispanic Americans, 1996): pp. 23, 26–27.
2. Linda Jacobson, "Hispanic Children Outnumber Young Blacks for the 1st Time," *Education Week*, 5 (August 1998): 6.
3. Kaydee Kirk and Eric Rodriguez, "Hispanics Reap Benefits of Hard Work, as Incomes Rise and Poverty Drops," *Agenda* 14, 3 (1998): 9.
4. Charles Dervarics, "Can a Rift Be Avoided? Blacks, Hispanics Vie for Same Funds," *Community College* Week 10, 8 (1997): 3.
5. National Center for Education Statistics, *Dropout Rates in the United States* (Washington DC: U.S. Department of Education, Office of Educational Research and Improvement, 1993): 102.
6. Lynn Schnaiberg, "U.S. Report Tracks High Dropout Rate Among Hispanics," *Education Week* 11 (February 1998): 7.
7. National Center for Education Statistics, *The Condition of Education* (Washington, D.C.: U.S. Department of Education Office of Educational Research and Improvement, Center for Education Statistics, 1996): 203.
8. President's Advisory Commission, 36–37, 39, 47–48.
9. Richard L. Halpin, "An Application of the Tinto Model to the Analysis of Freshman Persistence in a Community College," *Community College Review* 17, 4 (1990): 22–24.
10. *Ibid.*, 30.
11. *Ibid.*, 31.
12. Enrique Solis, Jr., "Regression and Path Analysis Models of Hispanic Community College Students' Intent to Persist," *Community College Review* 23, 3 (1995): 12.

13. *Ibid.*, 11.

14. Amaury Nora, "Determinants of Retention Among Chicano College Students: A Structural Model," *Research in Higher Education* 20, 1 (1987): 54.

15. Alberto F. Cabrera, Amaury Nora, and Maria B. Casteneda, "College Persistence: Structural Equations Modeling Test of an Integrated Model of Student Retention," *Journal of Higher Education* 64, 2 (1993): 134.

16. Laura I. Rendon and James R. Valadez, "Qualitative Indicators of Hispanic Student Transfer," *Community College Review* 20, 4 (1993): 30.

17. *Ibid.*, 32–34.

18. Leo Reisberg, "To Help Latino Students, a College Looks to Parents." *Chronicle of Higher Education* (15 January 1999): A43.

19. Roberto P. Haro, "The Development of Library Programs for Hispanics in America: 1962–1973," in *Activism in American Librarianship, 1962–1973*, eds. Mary Lee Bundy and Frederick J. Stielow (New York: Greenwood, 1987): pp. 141–151.

20. Camila Alire and Orlando Archbeque, *Serving Latino Communities* (New York: Neal-Schuman, 1998).

21. Robert P. Haro, *Developing Library and Information Services for Americans of Hispanic Origin* (Metuchen, N.J.: Scarecrow, 1981): pp. 152–189.

22. Lois Buttlar, "Facilitating Cultural Diversity in College and University Libraries," *Journal of Academic Librarianship*, 20, 2 (1994): 12.

23. Camila A. Alire and Frederick J. Stielow, "Minorities and the Symbolic Potential of the Academic Library: Reinventing Tradition," *College and Research Libraries* 56 (1995): 513–16.

24. Kathleen de la Peña McCook and Kate Lippincott, "Library Services to Farm Workers in West Central Florida," in *Poor People and Library Services*, ed. Karen M. Venturella (Jefferson, N.C.: McFarland, 1997): 154–65.

25. Barbara MacAdam and Darlene P. Nichols, "Peer Information Counseling: An Academic Library Program for Minority Students," *Journal of Academic Librarianship* 15, 4 (1989): 205.

26. Dario J. Villa and Jane Jurgens, "Minority Students in Higher Education: A Challenge for the '90s," *Illinois Libraries* 72 (1990): 626.

27. Bonnie Gratch Lindauer, "Defining and Measuring the Library's Impact on Campuswide Outcomes," *College and Research Libraries* 59 (1998) 560–561.

28. "Bill Alters Classification of Hispanic Schools," *Community College Week* 10, 7 (1997): 3.

29. "Housing Agency Awards Work-Study Grants," *Community College Week* 10, 14 (1998): 3.

30. Robert A. Rhoads and Sylvia Solorzano, "Multiculturalism and the Community College: A Case Study of an Immigrant Education Program," *Community College Review* 23, 2 (1995): 31–45.

31. Responses from El Centro College (Dallas, Tex.), El Paso Community College (Tex.), Austin Community College (Tex.), and Seminole Community College (Sanford, Fla.); February 1999.

Part III : Collections

OUTSTANDING LITERATURE: PURA BELPRÉ AND AMÉRICAS SELECTIONS WITH SPECIAL APPEAL IN THE DIGITAL AGE

Eliza T. Dresang

Introduction

All young people deserve the opportunity to read the outstanding contemporary literature recognized by the Pura Belpré and Américas awards. With its overview of these recently established awards designed to celebrate books with elements of Latino culture, this chapter brings to the attention of all librarians one of the ways in which they can locate a number of the best books published in any given year. These titles provide a welcome richness to a library collection.[1]

Librarians who select and use books with youth from Hispanic backgrounds will be among those who especially value these distinguished books—first and foremost because Latino and Latina children will find their own cultures and traditions reflected authentically in them. Each book on these best books lists offers multiple treasures to be mined. I suggest, however, one unique approach for singling out those titles that may especially attract and challenge young readers of the "net-generation." Hispanic youth in the United States are growing up in a high tech, digital society. In the quest to help these children and young adults gain the necessary experiences for 21st-century literacy, strategies to cement connections between the print and digital world are essential.

Awards and Distinctions

Awards and distinctions for outstanding writing and illustration for children have enjoyed a long history in the United States. In 1919 Macmillan was the first American publisher to set up a separate children's book department. Soon after, Frederic G. Melcher, an American editor and publisher, proposed the Newbery Award to the American Library Association (ALA). Since 1922 this award has been given annually to the author of the year's "most distinguished contribution to American literature for children." It is named for John Newbery, one of the first British publishers of children's books and a bookseller. Its purpose is "to encourage original creative work in the field of books for children." This recognition of distinguished writing has served as both an inspiration for authors as well as a standard against which librarians, teachers, and parents measure other books for youth. Throughout the century several other national awards and distinctions to encourage outstanding writing and illustration in books for children and young adults have been established.[2] The companion to the Newbery, also suggested by Frederick Melcher, is the Caldecott Award (1938) for best illustrated book of the year published in the United States. The most recent award established is the Best Young Adult Book of the Year (working title) approved by ALA in January 1999 and first presented in the year 2000. Notable Children's Books and Best Books for Young Adults present lists of the award winners annually.[3] In 1970 the Coretta Scott King Awards, which recognize an outstanding African American author and illustrator each year, were initiated to bring visibility and recognition to literature with cultural substance from African and African American heritage.[4] In the last decade of the 20th century two new awards focused specifically on books reflecting Latino culture joined this group of recognitions that contribute to setting standards of excellence for children's and young adult literature.[5]

Established in 1996, the Pura Belpré Award is presented biennially to a Latino or Latina writer and illustrator whose work best portrays, affirms, and celebrates the Latino cultural experience in an outstanding work of literature for children and youth. Awards are given for narrative and for illustration, with honor books in each category. The award is named after Pura Belpré, the first Latina librarian at the New York Public Library. As a children's librarian, storyteller, and author, she enriched the lives of Puerto Rican children in the United States through her pioneering work of preserving and disseminating Puerto Rican folklore.

Pura Belpré (1897–1985) grew up in Puerto Rico. Following her sister to New York in 1926, Belpré put her first tale in writing as a student at the Library School of the New York Public Library, in her storytelling class. Subsequently for more than two decades she delighted children who attended her participative, bilingual storyhours and puppet shows in the New York Public Library. Belpré's efforts were not limited to storyhours, but included widespread advocacy on behalf of and opportunities for the Puerto Rican community. Belpré's published tales are in many libraries, and some have recently been reissued.[6]

The Belpré Award is co-sponsored by REFORMA, the National Association to Promote Library Services to the Spanish Speaking, an American Library Association (ALA) affiliate, and by the Association for Library Service to Children (ALSC), a division of the ALA. It was first awarded in 1996, from books published in the U.S. between 1990 and 1995. Subsequent awards are based on the previous two years of publishing. For a complete list of Belpré winners, see the Association for Library Service to Children's webpage (*http://www.ala.org/ alsc/Belpré.html*).

In 1993, the national Consortium of Latin American Studies Programs (CLASP) bestowed the first Américas awards, annual children's and young adults book awards (until 1995 called the CLASP Award). These awards are given in recognition of a U.S. picture book and a work of fiction published in the previous year, in English or Spanish, that authentically and engagingly presents the experience of individuals in Latin America or the Caribbean, or of Latinos in the United States. Authors or illustrators do not have to be of Latino or Latina heritage — as they must be for the Belpré— to have their books considered for the Américas Award. (Note that the Belpré cites the author or illustrator and the Américas the books). Another criterion for the Américas Award selection that differs from the Belpré is consideration of the potential for classroom use: the Américas Award incorporates the concept of both awards (the winner and honorable mention books) and distinctions (a list of commended books). (For a complete list of Américas winners, see *http://www.uwm.edu/Dept/CLA/outreach_americas.html*).

Hispanic Youth Growing Up in a Digital World

All youth, including Hispanic youth, are profoundly affected by the way the computer chip has permeated virtually all parts of daily life in the United States. By asserting that they live in a "digital world," it is not implied that all or even a majority of these youth have access to computers and online resources.[7] It does imply that all youth of Hispanic heritage, whatever their socio-economic background, are immersed in a culture that is dramatically different from that in which young people matured prior to the widespread use of the microchip.

Young readers are fascinated by properties of the Internet, video and computer games, and other digital media that have saturated society. The prime properties of the digital world can be characterized as *interactivity, connectivity,* and *access.* The daily lives of youth are affected by this interactivity, connectivity, and access *even* if they do not have direct access to digital media.

What are the implications of this brave new world?

The hypertextual quality of all kinds of information gathering and reading encounters, from DVDs to the daily newspaper, reinforces the notion that young people can pick and choose the information they want to acquire in the order in which they want to acquire it. In the best digital era media experiences, they are challenged to think harder and to weave together what they know rather than to have it presented to them predigested.

Likewise, young people have been encouraged by the openness and access of the digital society to speak out for themselves in a way they have not previously had the opportunity to do. They are listening, therefore, and responding to multiple points of view on virtually every topic.

A final impact of this digital age has been on the subject matter and subtleties to which youth are exposed. Many more topics are available and in much more depth and more graphic form than previously—from the private life of the president of the United States to the inside story of slaves experiencing the Middle Passage to contemporary war and conflict playing out before their eyes. Real world happenings cannot be shielded from youth.

In short, youth of all ages and backgrounds are more sophisticated in their modes of giving and receiving information. Their expectations for participating in this process without restrictive barriers are becoming more and more apparent. These youth are less likely to respond positively to passive or patronizing experiences. (Although filtered computers may temporarily stop some of this flow of information, young people easily bypass barriers created for them on and off line.)

A century ago John Dewey advocated active learning with periods for reflection. Russian psychologist Lev Vygotsky's research contributed validity to this philosophy. Contemporary youth are embracing this mode of learning which can finally, with the support of sensitive adults, be brought to fruition in the early 21st century. Hispanic youth are among those "growing up digital,"[8] and this must not be overlooked in any aspect of adult–young person interaction.

Distinguished Literature with Special Digital Age Appeal

In careful reading, observation, and interaction with many colleagues for almost a decade, I have developed what I refer to as a "literary lens," a way of identifying books that may be particularly relevant to digital age youth. This literary construct is described in depth in *Radical Change: Books for Youth in a Digital Age.*[9] Radical change as a literary lens emerged from a codification of the characteristics of the digital society (interactivity, connectivity, and access).[10]

Radical Change describes changing forms and formats, changing perspectives, and changing boundaries that have become apparent in the digital world. It can also be applied to identify relevant books from previous eras. Books with these characteristics have always existed. The "radical change" in the digital society is that these characteristics are nurtured and flourish — and books reflecting them have increased in both quantity and kind. Radical Change does not identify "trends" but rather can be used to single out specific books that provide the type of reading experience that, because of their interactivity, connectivity, and access, may appeal particularly to net-generation youth. What these books are like will change as the society around us changes, but these qualities are likely to be valued for many years to come.

Three types of changes in books for youth in the digital age are observed in *Radical Change.* Examples from the Belpré and Américas awards are incorporated, as the properties of each of these three types of Radical Change are explained.

Changing Forms and Formats

Paralleling the advances in computer hypertext, books for all ages of young readers often exhibit the following changes:

- graphics appear in exciting new forms and formats
- words and pictures reach new levels of synergy
- the organization is often nonlinear (not moving forward in a straight line) and nonsequential (events do not always follow one another in a predictable manner)
- they have multiple layers of meanings

Two books that reflect this first type of Radical Change are *Laughing Tomatoes and Other Spring Poems/Jitomates Risueños y otros poemas de primavera* (a 1998 Belpré Narrative Honoree and 1997 Américas Commended Book)[11] and *An Island Like You: Stories of the Barrio*[12] (1996 Belpré Narrative Award recipient 1995 Américas Honorable Mention).[12] The symbolic nature of the titles of each of these books forewarns that they may, indeed, be radical.

The poem "Other Voices/otras voces" in *Laughing Tomatoes/Jitomates Ruisueños* summarizes one of the interactive aspects of these books. "Can you hear the voices between these lines?/ Escuchas las voces entre estas lineas?" Threads and ribbons moving among the open mouths of children in the accompanying illustration symbolize the tying together of the voices between the lines — a clue to the astute reader about the challenge of this radical-change book. The "other voices" in *Laughing Tomatoes/Jitomates Ruisueños* also come from the interactivity and synergy between word and picture. In a metaphoric poem, "Words are birds," a wing-like banner sports the words *peace* and *paz*, concepts not mentioned in the poetry. The words become pictures, sometimes fanciful, sometimes factual; for example, "Orchata es una sabrosa bebida de arroz" is printed as an aside on a tablecloth while "Orchata is a tasty rice drink" becomes a banner on a broom handle. A sidebar at the end of another poem explains (in English and Spanish) that César Chávez was a Mexican-American leader, head of the United Farm Workers. The nonlinear, digital-age reader can weave together the many images and designs to achieve full meaning.

The pictures likewise become words: no text tells us that four Latino children and a vivacious grandmother are the "main characters" of this book — nor that they differ in skin-color, hair-color, gender, likes and dislikes. Magical realism, a literary/life concept familiar to many Latino and Latina children, permeates the pictures without intruding on the design. Is Grandmother's disembodied head really atop the César Chávez tree? Can the children really turn somersaults, hang from clouds or fly amid chile peppers afloat in the sun? Nonsequential surprises abound. Dropped in among concrete poetry celebrating the sun, the dew, roots, and strawberries are symbolic poems about dreams and words and voices — and then there is the combination of the two, the "laughing tomatoes." The note from poet, Franciso X. Alarcón interrupts the text before the final poem, "Universal Spiral/Espiral universal," which portrays a joyous synergy of words and pictures. Lively as the latest video game? Indeed.

An Island Like You: Stories of the Barrio provokes reader interaction solely through the skilled composition of its text. Loosely translated, root words suggest that the basic meaning of *hypertext* is "weaving text together into pattern." *An Island Like You*, multilayered with words upon the background of words and words woven with other words, presents short stories that might well stand alone for a reader dipping into the book here and there, but together cumulatively build and paint a powerful picture of personality and culture. The backdrop is the community, the barrio, where each teenaged protagonist lives. The solidarity of the community becomes more and more evident as the stories are told. Characters at the forefront in one story move to the background in another and vice versa. Causal clues are dropped along the way to later happenings, making mystery that does not need to be solved. The lightness of tone juxtaposed with the seriousness of theme is set down in the first story by a teen who reluctantly goes to visit her grandparents in Puerto Rico; the clear clash of generations provides a backdrop against which much of remaining narrative of the entire book is painted. The last story, in which a theater troupe goes on even after one of their members dies of AIDS, leaves the reader with a reminder of the depth of issues that we all face. Cultural specificity is interwoven with universality, providing yet another level of meaning of the thoughtful reader. The form and format of the stories, with their often nonlinear and nonsequential elements, challenge all readers to read seriously and enjoy.

Changing Perspectives

This second type of Radical Change reflects

- multiple perspectives, visual and verbal (as opposed to a more uniform message in the past)
- previously unheard voices
- youth who speak for themselves

It is at the core of the digital age.

Voices From the Field: Children of Migrant Farmworkers Tell Their Stories (1995 Américas Commended Book)[13] exemplifies the other two principles of this type of Radical Change: multiple perspectives and youth speaking for themselves.[14] Atkin was one of the first authors to employ interviews with youth to portray their perspective, rather than attempting to interpret it for them. In a digital age author-youth partnership, Atkin located and interviewed youth of various ages with differing points of view, provides a brief commentary before their interviews to provide context, then allows them to speak their own piece. Photographs add another dimension to the authenticity of the accounts. Through these young migrant workers from Mexico, laboring in the Salinas Valley in California, we are informed of hopes and dreams as well as hardships and barriers.

Both fictional and non-fictional means can be successfully used to bring the child's perspective to literature. *Snapshots from the Wedding* (1998 Belpré Illustration Award)[15] creates the words of a young Mexican-American flower girl to describe the highlights of a wedding from her perspective, adding artistically created "snapshots" to illustrate the story from her perspective. Photodocumentaries have become a respected way to represent cultural authenticity. An outstanding example of how photography allows young people to speak for themselves is *Pablo Recuerda: La fiesta de día de los muertos* and the English Language version: *Pablo Remembers: The Fiesta of the Day of the Dead* [1996 Belpré Illustration Honor].[16] Ancona's skilled writing and photography document the Day of the Dead celebration (bread, candy, flowers, cardboard skeleton's) from the point of view of Pablo, a participant.

A final type of unheard voice is that of "famous" figures from Hispanic background. *Tomás y la señora de la biblioteca* and the English language version, *Tomás and the Library Lady* (1997 Américas Commended)[17] belong to radical-change literature for numerous reasons. They present, for instance, the perspective of a child migrant worker and a picture book story based on a real incident in the childhood of Dr. Tomás Rivera, who later became chancellor at the University of California at Riverside.[18]

Folktales with cultural substance often bring unheard voices to the forefront. These award-winning tales are not immediately defined as radical-change literature because they are often familiar to the children reading them. Most of the Latin American folktales now appearing in contemporary U.S. literature represent "previously unheard voices" to the majority of youth in the United States and, for them are radical-change literature. However, when we address library service to youth of Hispanic background, we realize that these tales are potentially familiar to many Latino youth.

Even a tale that is generally familiar to its audience qualifies as radical-change literature when it presents a substantially new perspective. Folktales which are selected from the award lists to represent Radical Change (for example, *The Golden Flower: A Taino Myth from Puerto Rico*[19]) either employ a decidedly "digital-age" twist in the telling or present a cultural perspective or place that is not commonly known by youth from Hispanic background.[20]

Changing Boundaries

Books identified by this third and last type of Radical Change are those that push the envelope, that bring topics to previously unreached children. This access has been denied possibly because adults thought children were incapable of understanding complex matters or possibly because young people were considered too vulnerable to encounter harsh realities, or possibly because what was appropriate for children was very narrowly defined. This is changing in the digital age. Children are more and more regarded as "capable and seeking connections," and rather than shunting them aside into their "other," protected world, adults are working with them in mutually beneficial partnerships.

It is important to note that not all such previously forbidden topics are controversial; some have simply been absent from literature for youth. This third type of digital-age book contains

- previously omitted and overlooked subjects and settings
- characters portrayed in new, complex ways
- new types of communities
- unresolved endings leaving interactive readers making more decisions for themselves

Heart of a Jaguar (1995 Américas Honorable Mention)[21] reflects meticulous research into the rituals of the late period of ancient Mayan society. The detailed explorations of Mayan rituals and relationships makes the ultimate human sacrifice (Balam, the 14-year-old protagonist) realistic. Reviewer reaction to this novel ranged from praise for the literary and historical merit to harsh dismissal, calling the book unsuitable for youth. Talbert's novel pushes the boundaries of what has been acceptable for youth in their literature. The point of placing violence in the context of well-researched and well-written literature is to give youth the opportunity to reflect on the why behind the violent happenings (or to observe various means to cope with it) rather than merely to observe its presence.

Parrot in the Oven: Mi Vida (1998 Belpré Narrative Award and 1996 Américas Fiction Award winner)[22] and *Chato's Kitchen* (1996 Belpré Illustration Award and 1995 Américas Award winner),[23] both with contemporary stories in realistic settings, disturb some readers for an entirely different reason. Both books, the first a young adult novel about growing up economically deprived family that is emotionally unstable but supportive in its own way, the second a modern day parable about the cat and the mice (the mice win) set in the barrio of East Los Angeles. In the latter, it is not the fable that is disturbing but rather the implied street culture of the cats, Chato and Novio Boy. That these two books have been selected for awards marks the maturing of Latino literature for youth. A common pattern that has occurred with various ethnic and cultural groups whose representation has been either stereotypic or virtually absent has been portrayal of only what might be considered "the positive" aspects of the culture. Certainly positive portrayals are desirable, but the absence of culturally authentic situations — even those that are undesirable — leave young people in less-than-ideal situations without the opportunity to explore their lives through literature. As the literature matures, and those who write it gain more confidence in young people and their abilities to absorb information in context, the topics proliferate. Literature must not be limited by the notion that the child reader needs protection. To the contrary, in the digital age, children must be regarded as capable and seeking connection.

Settings as well as subjects are identified in the broadening presentation of radical-change literature for youth. Lucia González's *El gallo de bodas / The Bossy Gallito: A Traditional Cuban Folktale* (1996 Belpré Narrative Honoree and 1994 Américas Commended Book)[24] is an example of a radical-change folktale because of the setting in which it is presented. It is widely popular, according to Gonzáles, in various forms throughout Latin America and is known by most youth in Cuba, her country of origin," but illustrator Lulu Delacre has chosen a fresh perspective for the presentation of the story. In her illustrations, the arrogant gallito prances down a street, la Calle Ocho, in a part of Miami known as "Little Havana"—the heart of the Cuban community in Miami. The artist explains the words that appear on signs in the illustrations as Spanish used in the Miami area. In a glossary, she translates this "new" Spanish into "traditional" Spanish terms. The church in the pictures was built in 1917 but is a copy of a Mexican and a European church. Gonzáles' and Dulacre's detailed cultural notes regarding both text and pictures provide added value and interest for the librarian as well as for the young readers.

How Radical Is Outstanding Latino Literature for Youth?

One way to respond to this question is to compare the Belpré and the Américas lists with other lists of outstanding literature for youth during a given year. Following is a chart that compares the percentage of books receiving various selected national awards and distinctions in 1998 and reflecting characteristics identified by Radical Change.

Award or Distinction (Presented in 1998)	Percentage of Books Reflecting Characteristics Identified by Radical Change
Américas	49
Pura Belpré[25]	100
Best Books for Young Adults	59
Bulletin of the Center for Children's Books: Blue Ribbons	39
Booklist: Editor's Choice	41
Book Links: Lasting Connections	71
Randolph Caldecott	75
CCBC Choices	29
The Horn Book: Fanfare	52
Coretta Scott King Author and Illustrator	86
John Newbery	75
Notable Children's Books	50
School Library Journal: Best Books for Young Adults	30

Of these twelve awards or distinctions presented for young people's literature presented in 1998, only four (or one-third) have a higher percentage of Radical Change books than those on the Américas list, and none are higher than the Belpré. In this most recent year for which statistics were available at the writing of this chapter, the books with Latino content appear to be as "radical" as those prounounced most outstanding from the general population of books for youth.[26]

Probing further, and focusing solely on the awards that honor outstanding books reflecting Latino culture, a year by year analysis reveals the following percentage of books that reflect Radical Change characteristics.[27]

Award or Distinction	Percentage of Books Reflecting Characteristics Identified by Radical Change
1998 Belpré	100
1996 Belpré	100
1997 Américas	55
1996 Américas	58
1995 Américas	33
1994 Américas	26
1993 Américas	71[28]

From the beginning, the Latino awards and distinctions have included a sizeable percentage of "radical" books. Taken all together, 45 percent or 69 of the 155 Américas Awards (1993–1997) are radical-change books, and 100 percent of the Belpré books have digital connections.[29]

A librarian, then, can be assured that a substantial percentage of these outstanding Latino books have special appeal for children and young adults accustomed to the lure of the interactivity, connectivity and access of the computer age. A closer analysis of the titles, however, gives more useful information about highlights and gaps in this most outstanding literature with Latino cultural content.[30]

Type One: Changing Forms and Formats

The tradition of magical realism in Latino literature for youth, as reflected in *Laughing Tomatoes,* provides one culturally specific venue for experimentation and radical directions. This specific Latino cultural element, which amazes and delights readers, is found in several books in both illustrations and text. However, beyond this, only a handful of the books on these lists represent multilayered fiction for young adults or even for intermediate readers. In fact, only a few books contain the complex cognitive and visual challenges that characterize the most radical forms and formats of the titles. While the literature brings youth from Hispanic background into touch with uncommon traditions from present and past, it is not moving as rapidly into what I call "handheld hypertext and digital design." These are the visual and intellectual representations of the nonlinear, nonsequential properties of digital media. The implication of this is that the most outstanding literature with Latino content lacks some of the visual and verbal complexity that hypertextual design has to offer.

Type Two: Changing Perspectives

The strength of the radical-change books lies in changing perspectives. Forty-seven percent of the radical-change titles (32 of 69) offer some kind of new perspective to the literature. Of these, 59 percent (19 of 32) are traditional folktales (or 29 percent of all the radical-change books) that add a unique or unusual dimension to the folk literature. Photoessays give emphasis to children telling their own story. The high point of these books is the richness of Latino culture — much needed in the body of literature. They are radical in that they are bringing many previously unheard voices and perspectives into the literature for youth. Very few books, however, have multiple perspectives in one volume.[31] Multiple points of view exist in various books but are not often juxtaposed in a way that forces intellectual interactivity in one book. Rarely do we hear the voices of young people themselves.

Type Three: Changing Boundaries

Many enticing and thought-provoking settings are represented in these award books. Venturing out of the bland into the violent is found in some fiction. However, the inclusion of either controversial topics or those that are new to all books for youth because of their unusual nature is not prevalent. Depth and variety of characters beyond approximately age eight are rare. Few books venture beyond the happy or resolved ending or experiment with unchartered territory.

In Sum

This outstanding literature is rich in cultural elements, but not as daring or risk-taking in subject matter as it might be. Radical-change literature provides many types of connections for young people. The *connectivity* with various elements of the digital world exists in this literature far more than does the *interactivity* brought by hypertextual design or the *access* of barrier-breaking subject matter.

The Implication of This Analysis

Approaching the 155 books that have achieved the distinction of these awards, librarians can be assured of authentic representation of Latino elements. Librarians might, however, be especially sensitive to choosing those books that reflect the less common "radical" characteristics, purposefully featuring them in displays and programs and helping young people to see the interactivity and connectivity and to appreciate the access that is so appealing to them in the digital environment.

This paper does not explain why the particular highlights and gaps exist among these outstanding books, whether they exist in the body of Latino literature for youth or the general youth literature. It does seem, however, that publishers, authors, illustrators, editors, and designers might make note of the opportunity to stretch this excellent literature in directions it has not already moved, the opportunities to experiment with 21st-century formats and subject matter, while continuing to incorporate the distinctiveness that now prevails and offers rich reading experiences for all.

In the last section of this paper, all of the award and honor books on the Belpré and Américas lists that reflect one or more of the types of Radical Change have been annotated, with a note on the types reflected following each annotation. Annotations for all of the commended books on the 1997 Américas list are also included. This annotated list is to provide for librarians working with youth from Hispanic background a concrete guide for observing these characteristics and for selecting and using the most challenging and "connecting" books possible for this growing community of young readers.

Selections from Latino Awards and Distinctions: Reflections of Radical Change[32]

Key to Types of Radical Change:

RC 1 nonlinear, nonsequential, multilayered, interactive, graphic words and pictures

RC 2 multiple perspectives, previously unheard voices, speaking for oneself

RC 3 new subjects, new settings, new characterization, new communities, new endings

1998 Pura Belpré Award Winners[33]

MEDALS

Parrot in the Oven: Mi Vida by Victor Martinez. New York: HarperCollins, 1996. 216 pgs. ISBN 0-06-026704-6 (Ages 9–12) Martinez dares to deal candidly with the difficulties of Manny's struggle with the emotional roller coaster of his family life — including a father who drinks too much — and the racism and poverty which he and his family together face. Simultaneously Martinez skillfully shows Manny developing the inner resistance to survive and finding shelter in family strengths. (Narrative Award; Also National Book Award Winner) **RC 3**

Snapshots from the Wedding by Gary Soto. Illustrated by Stephanie Garcia. New York: Putnam, 1997. 32 pgs. ISBN 0-39-92280-8X (Preschool–3) The unusual three-dimensional tableaux created with clay and objects such as olives and potato chips visually represent snapshots from the point of view of Maya, the flower girl, of the events and mishaps during a Mexican American wedding. (Illustration Award) **RC 1, 2**

HONORBOOKS

Laughing Tomatoes and Other Spring Poems/Jitomates Risueños y otros poemas de primavera by Francisco X. Alarcón. Illustrated by Maya Christina

González. San Francisco: Children's Book Press, 1997. 32 pgs. ISBN 0-89239-139-1 (Ages 3–5) Magical realism permeates the illustrations, and these joyous poems, penned by a much celebrated, award-winning poet and linked by the consistent appearance of four children and a grandmother whose antics reflect the action, real and symbolic. Hypertext-like side bars and picture words add challenge to the reading experience that incorporates visual multiple perspectives. (Narrative) **RC 1, 2**

Spirits of the High Mesa by Floyd Martinez. Houston: Arte Público, 1997. 192 pgs. ISBN 1-55885-198-4 (Ages 6–8) The tug between the intrusive "new-fangled" device of electricity and time-honored customs emerges in a small town in New Mexico as young Flavio's grandfather fights what he believes will destroy traditional culture, a struggle similar to that of newer technologies at the cusp of the 21st century. (Narrative) **RC 3**

In My Family/En mi familia by Carmen Lomas Garza. San Francisco: Children's Book Press, 1996. 32 pgs. ISBN 0-89239-138-3 (K–older) Detailed folk-art style paintings of family and related community life provide fascinating glimpses into the artist's life in Mexico, featuring unique and universal cultural details through personal storytelling. (Illustration) **RC 2**

The Golden Flower: A Taino Myth from Puerto Rico by Nina Jaffe. Illustrated by Enrique O. Sánchez. New York: Simon & Schuster, 1996. 32 pgs. ISBN 0-689-80469-5 (Ages K–3) A creation myth from the Taino Indian culture that was decimated by the arrival of Columbus and his contemporaries with captivating, multilayered illustrations effectively incorporating symbols from the little known Taino culture. (Illustration) **RC 1, 2**

Gathering the Sun: An Alphabet in Spanish and English by Alma Flor Ada. Illustrated by Simon Silva. New York: Lothrop, 1997. 40 pgs. ISBN 0-688-13903-5 (Ages K–3) Unlike many bilingual books published in the United States, the Spanish language provides the structure for this alphabet book portraying in bold red and yellow tones the daily life of Latino farm workers. (Illustration) **RC 2**

1996 Pura Belpré Award Winners

Medals

An Island Like You: Stories of the Barrio by Judith Cofer. New York: Orchard Books, 1995. 165 pgs. ISBN 0-531-06897-8 (young adult) Multiple perspectives emerge from these short stories telling of events experienced by various youth of a Puerto Rican community in New York City. Cofer skillfully weaves together incidents in the life of the various teens into a distinctive portrait of community life. (Narrative) **RC 1**

Chato's Kitchen by Gary Soto. Illustrated by Susan Guevara. New York: G.P. Putnam's Sons, 1995. 32 pgs. ISBN 0-399-22658-3 Cats they may be (in this modern cat and mouse fable), but Chato and his sidekick, Novio, are clearly members of the Latino street culture of East Los Angeles. Soto and Guevara break away from "innocent" portrayal of the Hispanic experience to a reflect more of "real life" in a fun-filled, culturally rich tale. (Illustration) **RC 3**

Honorbooks

The Bossy Gallito: A Traditional Cuban Folktale retold by Lucía M. González.

Illustrated by Lulu Delacre. New York: Scholastic, 1994. 32 pgs. ISBN 0-59046843-X This traditional tale has anything but a traditional setting: Little Havana in Miami brings a unique dimension to a lively, repetitive story. (Narrative and Illustration) **RC 3**

Baseball in April, and Other Stories by Gary Soto. New York: Harcourt, Brace, 1994. Who knows the hurt of being unable to break the barrier of racism (and classicism) to get onto the local little league team? Or the devastation of having one's "almost-Barbie" destroyed? Or the struggle between altruism and a new guitar? Or the pathos of having no dress to wear to the prom? Each of these short stories adds insight into the life of Mexican American youth in a unqiue and provocative telling. (Narrative) **RC 3**

Pablo Remembers: The Fiesta of the Day of the Dead by George Anaconda. New York: Lothrop, Lee, Shepard. 1993. 48 pgs. (Spanish Language edition also.) Photos allow Pablo, his family, and their community to "speak for themselves" as they go about preparing for this November 1 festival day. (Illustration) **RC 2**

Family Pictures/Cuadreso de familia by Carmen Lomas Garza. San Francisco: Children's Book Press, 1990. 32 pgs. ISBN 0-89230-138-3 A Chicana artist shares through her oil, acylic, and gouache paintings and precise words (original in Spanish) such family experiences as Easter egg decoration, a family birthday and wedding, Grandmother telling the traditional story of La Llorona, and other little glimpsed views of Mexican traditional family celebrations. (Illustrations) **RC 2**

1997 Americas Book Award

Winners

The Circuit: Stories from the Life of a Migrant Child by Francisco Jimenez. Albuquerque: University of New Mexico Press, 1997. 134 pgs. ISBN 0-8263-1797-9 (Ages 6–8) This rich cultural mosaic of the daily life a family from rural Jalisco, Mexico, enmeshed in the circuit of migrant laborers who endlessly follow crops, exemplifies hypertext in its original meaning of "beyond weaving." Jimenez intertwines stories from a child's perspective with harsh reality in a multilayered reading experience. **RC 1, RC 3**

The Face at the Window by Regina Hanson. Illustrated by Linda Saport. New York: Clarion, 1997. 32 pgs. ISBN 0-395-78625-8 (Ages K–3) The face at the window is that of Miss Nella, who frightens Dora until her parents help her deal with her own fears and her friends' misconceptions about mental illness. **RC 3**

Honorable Mentions

Mayeros: A Yucatec Maya Family by George Ancona. New York: William Morrow, 1997. 40 pgs. ISBN 0-688-13465-3 (Ages 3–5) Visiting his home land, author and photographer Ancona discovers his own family story as he tells that of a contemporary Mayan family—blending traditions that date back to the great Mayan city-states (A.D. 300–900) with everyday life in the late twentieth century. **RC 2 RC 2**

Commended List

Angela Weaves a Dream: The Story of a Young Maya Artist by Michele Sold. Photographs by Jeffrey Jay Foxx. New York: Hyperion, 1997. 48 pgs. ISBN 0-

78680073-9 (Ages 3–5) A multilayered story, unusual for such a short text, depicts a rite of passage for a young Maya artist in Chiapas, Mexico, who must demonstrate both the skill of weaving and the understanding of seven sacred designs that incorporate elements of Mayan spiritual beliefs into the weaving. **RC 1, RC 2**

Baseball in the Barrios by Henry Horenstein. New York: Gulliver/Harcourt Brace, 1997. 36 pgs. ISBN 0-15-200499-8 (Ages K–3) A nine-year-old Venezuelan boy, Hubaldo, tells about his passionate love for baseball, as popular in his country as in the United States. Spanish words and photographs of Hubaldo and his friends, reproductions of team logos, and baseball cards add to the authenticity of Hubaldo's story. **RC 2**

Buried Onions by Gary Soto. New York: Harcourt Brace, 1997. 149 pgs. ISBN 0-15-201333-4 (Ages 9–12) Nineteen-year-old Eddie must deal with inner city poverty and racism as he drops out of college and unsuccessfully struggles for a way to end the cycle in which he finds himself entrapped—lacking the optimism of "typical" young adult novels. **RC 3**

Butterfly Boy by Virginia Kroll. Illustrated by Gerardo Suzán. Honesdale, PA: Boyds Mills, 1997. 32 pgs. ISBN 1-56397-3) 71-5 (Ages K–3) Communicating with a grandpa who can neither speak nor smile nor walk requires great ingenuity on the part of a determined young boy. Magical realism seems to permeate the illustrations and add celebration to the relationship. **RC 3**

Cocoa Ice by Diana Appelbaum. Illustrated by Holly Meade. New York Orchard, 1997. 52 pgs. ISBN 0-531-30040-4 (Ages K–3) Parallel stories told by two young girls, one in Santo Dominigo, Dominican Republic, one in Maine, USA, give very different perspectives on the "cocoa for ice trade" of 19th century schooners. Cut paper illustrations and text provide a wealth of little-known information. **RC 2, RC 3**

La Cucaracha Martina: A Caribbean Folktale/La Cucaracha Martina: Un cuento folklorico del Caribe by Daniel Moreten. Illustrated by Daniel Moreten. New York: Turtle, 1997. 32 pgs. ISBN 1-890515-03-5 (English edition) 1-890515-04-3 (Spanish edition) (Ages K–3) A traditional Caribbean tale with striking digitally designed illustrations sporting onomatopoeic text. **RC 1**

Cuckoo/Cucu by Lois Ehlert. Translated by Gloria de Aragón Andújar. New York: Harcourt Brace, 1997. 36 pgs. ISBN 0-15-200274-X (Ages K–3) Ehlert retold this Mayan folktale after extensive background research to assure authenticity of text and illustrations inspired by traditional Mexican folkart. **RC 1, RC 2**

Dear Abuelita/Querida Abuelita by Sofia Meza Keane. Illustrated by Enrique 0. Sánchez. Crystal Lake, IL: Rigby, 1997. 24 pgs. ISBN 0-7635-3156-1 (English edition) 07635-3155-3 (Spanish edition) (Ages K–3) Keane uses letter writing, one way in which children "speak for themselves" in contemporary fiction, for Marco to tell his Abuelita about his new house, school and city after he moves from the Yucatán to California. The two worlds are juxtaposed in text and illustration. **RC 2**

Gathering the Sun: An Alphabet in Spanish and English by Alma Flor Ada. Illustrated by Simon Silva. New York: Lothrop, 1997. 40 pgs. ISBN 0-688-13903-5 (Ages K–3) (See 1998 Belpré Honorbooks)

Grannie Jus' Come by Ana Sisnett. Illustrated by Karen Lusebrink. San Francisco: Children's Book Press, 1997. 32

pgs. ISBN 0-89239-150-2 (Ages K–3) Several animals found on all pages promote interactive reading in this joyous Panamanian family story told in dialect by a granddaughter waiting for her Grannie. **RC 1, RC 2**

I Am of Two Places/Soy de dos lugares edited by Mary Carden and Mary Cappellini. Illustrated by Christina González. Crystal Lake, IL: Rigby, 1997. 16 pgs. ISBN 07635-3161-8 (English edition) 0-7635-3160-X (Spanish edition) (Ages K–3) A collection of poetry composed by five Latino children, ages eight to eleven, who speak candidly with compelling images and ideas of living in two cultures. **RC 2**

Laughing Tomatoes and Other Spring Poems/Jitomates Risueños y otros poemas de primavera by Francisco X. Learn. Illustrated by Maya Christina González. San Francisco: Children's Book Press, 1997. 32 pgs. ISBN 0-89239-139-1 (Ages 3–5) (See 1998 Belpré Honorbooks)

The Lizard and the Sun/La largartija y el sol by Alma Flor Ada. Illustrated by Felipe Dávalos. New York: Doubleday Dell, 1997. 40 pgs. ISBN 0-385-32121-X (Ages K–3) This pourquoi tale, set in the Aztec culture of long ago central Mexico, uses repetition and carefully crafted illustrations to engage the reader. **RC 2**

Novio Boy, a play by Gary Soto. New York: Harcourt Brace, 1997. 78 pgs. ISBN 0-15201531-0 (Ages 6–8) Plays written specifically for young actors are unusual — and more so culturally specific dramas. This one addresses serious adolescent issues with humor, placing, for instance, the anxieties of a first date against the cultural context of extended Lationo families. **RC 3**

Señor Cat's Romance and Other Favorite Stories from Latin America by Lucía M. González. Illustrated by Lulu Delacre. New York: Scholastic, 1997. 48 pgs. ISBN 0-590-48537-7 (Ages 3–5) These well-told tales, including a Cuban version of Pura Belpré's "Perez and Martina," are familiar to many youth from Hispanic background. The "radical" feature of these tales is the variety of background setting chosen by Delacre, including Velasquez's Spain for the concluding tale. Unusually distinguished source notes from both author and illustrator explain the origin and cultural contexts. **RC 3**

Spirits of the High Mesa by Floyd Martinez. Houston: Arte Publico, 1997. 192 pgs. ISBN 1-55885-198-4 (Ages 6–8) (See 1998 Belpré Honorbooks)

The Story of Doña Chila/El cuento de Doña Chila by Mary Capeliinni. Illustrated by Gershom Griffith. Crystal Lake, IL: Rigby, 1997. 24 pgs.ISBN 0-7635-3267-3 (English edition) 0-7635-3266-5 (Spanish edition) (Ages K–3) An unusually serious subject for a picture book, this story relates the dilemma that Oscar's mother experiences as she tries to decide whether he should be treated by a medical doctor or the local curandera after a scorpion bites him. **RC 3**

Tomás and the Library Lady by Pat Mora. Illustrated by Raul Colón. New York: Knopf, 1997. 32 pgs. ISBN 0-679-80401-3 (Ages K–3) Based on an incident in the childhood of a chancellor of the University of California at Riverside, the importance of the library lady to a young boy whose family is in town as part of a migrant worker family in the 1930s — and his hope and dreams — is sensitively told and illustrated. **RC 2**

White Bread Competition by Jo Ann Yolanda Hernández. Houston: Pihata Books, 1997. 208 pgs. ISBN 1-55885-210-7 (Ages 8–10) Hernández tells the story of Luz, a ninth-grade Mexican

American girl who wins a spelling contest, setting up ambivalent reactions in her family, through multiple narratives that can be read either as a single story or a series of short stories. **RC 1**

1996 Americas Book Award

Winners

In My Family/En mi familia by Carmen Lomas Garza. San Francisco: Children's Book Press, 1996. 32 pgs. ISBN 0-89239-138-3 (Ages K–older) (See 1998 Belpré Honor)

Parrot in the Oven: Mi Vida by Victor Martinez. New York: HarperCollins, 1996. 216 pgs. ISBN 0-06-026704-6 (Ages 9–12) (See 1998 Belpré Medal Books)

Honorable Mention

So Loud a Silence by Lyll Becerra de Jenkins. New York: Lodestar, 1996. 154 pgs. ISBN 0-525-67538-8 (Ages 9–12) Seventeen-year-old Juan Guillermo gets caught up in an ideological struggle between guerrillas and the government. Such intense political conflicts are unusual in books for youth. (Narrative) **RC 3**

1995 Américas Book Award[34]

Winner

Tonight by Sea by Frances Temple. New York: Orchard Books, 1995. 152 pgs. ISBN 0-531-06899-4 (young adult) A novel of political intensity and sensitivity tells of Paulie's decision to join others in her Haitain village and escape government brutality by sea. A character who gains inner resilience through her connections. (Narrative) **RC 3**

Honorable Mentions

An Island Like You: Stories of the Barrio by Judith Ortiz Cofer. New York: Orchard Books, 1995. 165 pgs. ISBN 0-531-06897-8 (young adult) (See 1996 Belpré Medal)

Chato's Kitchen by Gary Soto. Illustrated by Susan Guevara. New York: G.P. Putnam's Sons, 1995. 32 pgs. ISBN 0-399-22658-3 (picture book) (See 1996 Belpré Medal)

Heart of a Jaguar by Marc Talbert. New York: Simon & Schuster, 1995. 197 pgs. ISBN 0-689-80282-X (young adult) Balam, a boy living in the Yucatan peninsula during the era of the great Mayan kingdoms, struggles to achieve manhood and to help end the severe drought in his community. Neither Balam nor the reader knows that the story will end with his sacrifice, an authentic ritual of his people. The graphic violence and well-done dispassionate telling are both extraordinary. **RC 3**

1994 Américas Book Award Winner[35]

The Mermaid's Twin Sister: More Stories from Trinidad by Lynn Joseph. Illustrated by Donna Perrone. New York: Clarion Books, 1994. 63 pgs. ISBN 0-395-64365-1 (young reader) Decidedly a previously unheard voice in literature for young readers, Tantie, a *griot* (storyteller) on the Island of Trinidad, speaking in the Caribbean vernacular, passes her bamboo "storyteller" beads on to her niece,

Amber, explaining to her how she can find stories anywhere. **RC 2**

1993 CLASP Book Award Winner[36]

Vejigante Masquerader by Lulu Delacre. New York: Scholastic, 1993. 40 pgs. ISBN 0-590-45776-4 (picture book) Since 1858, Carnival has been celebrated in Puerto Rico by men and boys wearing papier mâché masks. Delacre, who grew up in Ponce, Puerto Rico, invites reader participation in this bilingual story of young Ramon, who works hard to be allowed to participate. The book includes 28 hidden lizards in the illustrations (one for each day of February, the month of Carnival). **RC 1, 3**

Notes

1. The number of books by Latinos and about Latino themes and topics has increased since 1993, but is still only a small fraction (approximately 2 percent) of the overall 4,500 children's books published annually during these years. According to the librarians of the Cooperative Children's Book Center, School of Education, UW-Madison (Wisc.) who keep annual statistics, in 1994 there were 90 Latino titles; in 1995, 70; in 1996, 103; and in 1997, 88. See Kathleen T. Horning, Ginny Moore Kruse, and Megan Schliesman. CCBC *Choices 1997* (Madison, Wisc.: University Publications, 1997). Latina author Pat Mora explores the reasons why so few Latino/Latina books are published in the U.S. and suggests ways to improve the situation. These recently established awards and distinctions are one way to increase visibility of Latino excellence and to encourage, as Mora suggests, publishers to seek out the talent among this cultural group as well as to tap into the $200 billion in purchasing power among the Latino population. Pat Mora, "Confessions of a Latina Author," *The New Advocate* 11, 4 (Fall 1998): 279–290.

2. In this chapter the following definitions are used: an *award* singles out "one best book" while a *distinction* goes to a book that is one of several books receiving honor and recognition.

3. For a list of major annual national and international awards and distinctions see *http://www.soemadison.wisc.edu/ccbc/awards.htm.* Those under the auspices of the American Library Association are also listed at *http://www.ala.org/alsc/awards.html*

4. Henrietta M. Smith's *The Coretta Scott King Awards Book: From Vision to Reality* (1994) contains a history of the founding and development of these awards as well as a complete description of each book. A revised edition will soon be issued. Henrietta M. Smith, ed. *The Coretta Scott King Awards Book: From Vision to Reality* (Chicago: ALA Editions, 1994).

5. A more comprehensive review of recommended books about Latino people and cultures can be found in Isabel Schon's *The Best of the Latino Heritage: A Guide to the Best Juvenile Books About Latina People and Cultures* (1997), with a selective recent supplement in "Delightful Recent Books about Latinos" (1999). As Director of the Center for the Study of Books in Spanish for Children and Adolescents (*http://www.csusm.edu/campus centers/csb/*), Schon updates the center's website weekly. Isabel Schon, *The Best of the Latino Heritage: A Guide to the Best Juvenile Books About Latino People and Cultures* (Metuchen, N.J.: Scarecrow, 1996) and "Delightful Recent Books About Latinos/as," *Book Links* (January 1999).

6. Pura Belpré's collected papers (18.75 feet of shelf space), which document the rich contribution she made as a librarian and an author are available at the Centro Library and Archives of Hunter College, City University of New York, divided into Personal and Biographical Information, Correspondence, Writings, Subject File, and Photographs. For more information about this archive, see *http://myst.hunter.cuny.edu/centro/archives/aids/Belpré.html.* A 30-minute videotaped interview is available from Temple University. See Belpré's career as touched upon in an interview of Lillian Lopez conducted by Lilia Vazquez in *Women of Color in Librarianship,* ed. Kathleen de la Peña McCook (Chicago: ALA, 1998): pp. 81–103.

7. Both the U.S. government legislation and private donors such as the Bill and Melissa Gates Foundation and AT&T may make at least limited access through schools and public libraries a reality in the near future.

8. Don Tapscott, *Growing Up Digital:*

The Rise of the Net Generation (New York: McGraw-Hill, 1997).

9. Eliza T. Dresang, *Radical Change: Books for Youth in a Digital Age* (New York: H.W. Wilson, 1999).

10. This literary construct, which grew out of a collaboration with Kate McClelland, assistant director and head of children's services at the Perrott Memorial Library in Old Greenwich, Connecticut, has been explicated in other places as well. See Eliza Dresang and Kate McClelland, "Radical Books," *Book Links* (July 1996); Eliza Dresang, "Radical Change: The Influence of Digital Media on the Handheld Book," *Library Trends* (Spring 1997); or Eliza Dresang and Kate McClelland, "Reading in the 21st Century," in *Theory Into Practice.* Forthcoming.

11. Francisco Alarcón, *Laughing Tomatoes' and Other Spring Poems/Jitomates Risueños y otros poemas de primavera,* illus. Maya Christina (San Francisco: Children's Book Press, 1997).

12. Judith Ortiz Cofer, *An Island Like You: Stories of the Barrio* (New York: Orchard/Melanie Kroupa, 1995).

13. Beth S. Atkin, *Voices from the Field: Children of Migrant Farmworkers Tell Their Stories* (New York: Little Brown, 1993).

14. Books are not limited to one type of Radical Change, of course. *An Island Like You,* for example, is also a Type Two book in that it tells the story from multiple perspectives. It was used here to illustrate Type One.

15. Gary Soto, *Snapshots from the Wedding,* illus. Stepanie Garcia (New York: Putnam, 1997).

16. George Ancona, *Pablo Remembers: The Fiesta of the Day of the Dead* (Lothrop Lee & Shepard, 1993).

17. Pat Mora, *Tomas and the Library Lady,* illus. Raul Colon (New York: Knopf, 1997).

18. For more about *Tomás and the Library Lady,* see Julie Cosaro. "Talking with Pat Mora," *Book Links* 7, 1 (September 1977): 25–30.

19. Nina Jaffe, *The Golden Flower: A Taino Myth From Puerto Rico,* ill. Enrique O. Sánchez. (New York: Simon & Schuster, 1996).

20. *The Stinky Cheeseman and Other Fairly Stupid Tales* (Scieszka/Smith 1992) provides an example of a new telling of Western European tales that are identified as radical-change literature because of the form and format in which they are told. (Jon Scieszka, *The Stinky Cheese Man and Other Fairly Stupid Tales,* illus. Lane Smith. New York: Viking, 1993.) *Puss in Boots* qualifies as Radical Change because of the new perspective portrayed in the illustrations, that of the cat (Charles Perrault, *Puss in Boots,* illus. by Fred Marcellino. New York: Farrar, Straus & Giroux, 1990). *Señor Cat's Romance and Other Favorite Stories from Latin America* (1998 Américas Commended Book) were selected as those stories "most widely known" through Spain and Latin America (Lucía González, *Señor Cat's Romance and Other Favorite Stories from Latin America,* illus. by Lulu Delacre. New York: Scholastic, 1997). González now lives in the U.S. (Hialeah, Florida), where she works as a children's librarian and a storyteller. The illustrator's notes describe her choice for various settings for the tales.

21. Marc Talbert, *The Heart of a Jaguar* (New York: Atheneum, 1995).

22. Martinez, Victor, *Parrot in the Oven: Mi Vida* (New York: HarperCollins, 1996).

23. Soto, Gary, *Chato's Kitchen,* illus. by Susan Guevera (New York: Putnam, 1995).

24. Lucía M. González, *The Bossy Gallito: A Traditional Cuban Folktale,* illus. Lulu Delacre. (New York: Scholastic, 1994).

25. The Belpré, Américas, and Coretta Scott King awards, although given for both artists and illustrators (or picture books and text), are selected by a single jury or committee while the Caldecott and Newbery Awards are selected by separate committees. For this reasons the former awards are listed as one for this analysis while the latter are not.

26. At the end of this chapter is a complete list of the Belpré and Américas books I have identified by applying Radical Change. Each title is annotated to indicate the radical-change characteristics reflected.

27. Only seven 1993 books were chosen for the Américas award, Honorable Mention, and Commended lists, compared to 39 1994 books, 36 1995 books, 39 1996 books, and 33 1997 books.

28. In this one year, Belpré, Newbery, and Caldecott, given to only a few books each time they are awarded, showed a higher percentage of radical-change books than do the larger categories.

29. This analysis does not include recommended reader age levels, but a quick glance reveals a heavy emphasis on picture books for an elementary or preschool audience and little to interest or challenge preteen or teenage youth.

30. These lists include *only* those books identified as incorporating characteristics of Radical Change.

31. The form and information of the citations in this annotated list follows that of the

official Américas Award lists, but I have inserted the type(s) of Radical Change identified in each title and have written original annotations directed specifically at radical-change elements.

32. Through 1995, only one Américas Award was given each year.

33. Through 1994 no honorable mention books were selected.

34. In the first year, the Américas Award was called the CLASP Award.

Give Them What They Need

Oralia Garza de Cortés

Invisible Barriers: A Story

Pepe walked through the doors of the Eastside Branch of the Oakview Public Library one afternoon shortly after school had let out.[1] He was a big fellow with an equally large smile that conveyed a sense of friendliness and humor. Trailing him was his sister, who seemed slightly younger and much more reserved. Pepe was a student from the neighboring middle school, looking for information on Zachary Taylor. He approached the front desk and asked the library clerk on duty for some information on the Confederate general. "Sorry," she said after checking, "We don't have any books about him in the library." I had overheard part of the request. When I saw the disappointed look on Pepe's face, I immediately sensed there was something wrong and set out to help this middle school student find the answer to his probing question. But I, too, quickly came up short. In the meantime, I asked the library assistant to look in the *World Book Encyclopedia* to see if we could at least get this young man started. After Pepe glanced through the article, he came back up to the service desk, a sad disappointed look on his face. "Nope," he said, " It's not there." His seventh grade history teacher had offered a large bonus to students who could correctly answer the question If Zachary Taylor was from the South, why was he for the Union?

Frustrated by the limited resources at our disposal, I sat down with Pepe and began to read the encyclopedia article. There was plenty of biographical information about the life of this famous general and the role he played in the Mexican War. But Pepe was right, there was not much else. The library aide, meanwhile, had checked the holdings of the central library and found that a biography of Zachary Taylor was available for checkout. Could we get this book for him? she asked. "No," said Pepe, he needed this for tomorrow.

Apologizing for our branch's shortcomings, I explained to Pepe that he could go to the central library to complete his research. I asked him if he had ever been there. His negative reply confirmed what we knew all too well of Hispanic youth from Oakview's East Side who live not far from the central library, but who seldom cross the invisible border that divides East and West Oakview. Our border was a freeway, a visible yet invisible barrier that separated race and classes of peoples from each other. In all of Pepe's fourteen-some-odd years, neither he nor his sister had ever stepped foot inside the central library. I gave Pepe and his sister directions along with a strong nod of encouragement as they walked out the door, as hopeful and full of life as when they walked in. It was not until I went back to my office that I allowed my anger to steam. The incident was a classic example of how bureaucratic rules and regulations militate against low income communities and poor children in particular when it comes to book budgets. The Oakview Public Library, as most public libraries during this time, was in the practice of systematically allocating book budgets to each branch library based on a formula that was heavily weighted on the circulation rate of each branch. So for example, if a literate, well-read community branch circulated more books, then that community received a larger share of the allocation. On the face of it, the formula was a logical one. But when you began to compare the book budget allocations of the cluster of low income, minority communities, then it became clear from the allocated funds that the formulas were stacked against these communities. Put bluntly, on the face of it, the formulas smacked of inequality.

Upon cooling down, I proceeded to go about my normal business. I was scheduled to go to the central library for book exam to view and select new acquisitions. I left the branch and headed for Central. Who should I encounter at the door if not Pepe, his sister, Pepe's mother, and an older brother, the family driver, all in tow, trekking in, single file through the front doors. I was elated that Pepe had heeded my advice. But knowing full well that there would be no one at the central children's desk on a weekday afternoon to help him with his reference search, I seized the opportunity to be able to guide him once again. Like the Pied Piper, I led Pepe and his family through the rows and rows of books. Pepe was in awe. Like Lily and her teacher, his most frequently uttered expression became " Wow! So many books, ma'am."[2] Like Crocodile Dundee walking through the concrete jungle of Manhattan, so too Pepe was awash in amazement of his new-found discovery, the central library. Once in the children's section, we found the book he needed, and once more I sat down with Pepe and his family. After skimming through the book I found some relevant information and handed it to Pepe for his review. After reading through it he declared, "Nope, it's not there." I scanned through the book again, this time pointing to the pages that he needed to pay close attention to. Pepe read through them and still could not find it. After closer reading, I proceeded to explain to Pepe the significance of the information. I began by reading aloud key paragraphs from the book. Sadly for Pepe, though, he could neither grasp the concepts nor the implication of what I was reading. It was only then that I realized that Pepe's critical thinking skills may not have been sufficiently developed for him to understand the question properly. It seemed so unfair for his teacher to raise up so much expectation only to have the students fall short, once more. I was sad for Pepe, but proud of him for having tried his best and going the extra mile. I advised him to tell his teacher that Mrs. Cortés, the librarian, said that this was a trick question and that he should get credit for his investigative work. I told him to be sure to point out to his teacher that he had searched in two libraries. I shook his hand and wished him and his family well.

In the course of my work at the Eastside branch in the Hispanic neighborhoods of Oakview, I met and befriended a sharp, creative journalist, herself Latina. In the course of our conversation, the "Pepe story" surfaced. The incident was fresh, and it became my rallying cry for the need for changes in how we attempt to serve low-income inner city youths. I did not want to embarrass Pepe in any way; I was trying to point out children's efforts and frustrations in doing homework when the tools they need for their homework are not readily available to them. The reporter, armed with her probing, investigative and research skills, began to ask questions.

When her article appeared in the local press there was a stunned silence from our colleagues, the branch managers from the neighboring "at-risk" libraries. We took their silence as a signal that we may well have "gone too far," jeopardizing our positions in our effort to be library advocates on behalf of our constituents while at the same time being required to play the role of dutiful city library employee. Late that afternoon the long awaited call I anticipated came through from a top administrator. She had read the article, and had one question, and one question only. After prefacing the question at least five times with "I know you know this, but I have to ask," she proceeded: "Did you tell this young man that you could route the information he needed to the Eastside branch?" "Of course we did," I answered, emphatically, "but he needed it right away." "Well, I knew you knew," she responded, "I just had to ask it," she said, and she hung up the phone.

Lucky for us, there were no major repercussions. We did receive a few calls from concerned citizens from the other side of town. One offered to donate some old, outdated college books to our branch. Another offered time and talent in helping us find funding sources. Other citizens, mostly educators and professionals offered to give us their children's books both old and new. We accepted them kindly, but nonetheless, we were bewildered. No citizens cried foul, wrote letters to the editor, or raised their fist at the injustice and indignation of it all.

Four years later I discovered that the book budget formulas had indeed been reconfigured for all the branches in question after the library conducted in-house use surveys. The Eastside branch book budget has doubled since this incident. That was in the early nineties, and the Oakview Public Library had just received a national award that recognized the library system for its creativity and innovation in "managing in the face of dwindling resources," a concept that continues to diminish the library's chances of restoring staffing and funding and continues to demoralize library staff since the days of the collapse of the real estate market in Oakview over ten years ago. Yet in spite of an upward turn and a booming economy, the library system and the city of Oakview continue to chip away at children's services. One lost staff position left the central library with no professional children's librarian. But for services for children in the Latino community, the cuts are the worst kind of travesty. Where the Eastside branch had a full time children's librarian six years ago, today the branch has no regularly scheduled children's storytime for toddlers or preschoolers in English, much less in Spanish. Rather, the branch has adopted a storyhour-by-demand approach that requires the presence of ten or more children in order that a storyhour take place, and the children's librarian is shared with a neighboring branch, a handsome new facility that took over six years to build, ranking fourth in construction priority among 1992 voter approved projects. Meanwhile, for an upper-middle class branch that was built to meet the demands of the growing suburban areas incorporated by the city, the construction of the library ranked first in priority of all the 1992 Library Bond projects. Staffing at that branch includes a full-time children's librarian who conducts approximately six children's programs per week.

The Robinson Model: How It Fails At-Risk Communities

While one could say some libraries appear to be discriminating in the manner in which they provide services to Latino and Spanish-speaking children, the fact is that these facilities operate as "Charlie Robinson Libraries," a model that defines the public library as a "middle-class institution" that caters to the needs and demands of the middle class.

The motto "Give them what they want," made famous by Mr. Robinson, has been the guiding principle for Baltimore County for the last 25 years. The model described in a *Library Journal* interview adapts a corporate management style that treats people as customers and consumers rather than citizens.[3] These concepts drive the organization, and the institutions devote their energies to insure they are meeting the demands of their "customers." But their customers consist of persons who walk through the library doors and avail themselves of services and programs. The model, when refined for efficiency, adapts a self-serve supermarket store approach. It assumes that you know what you want and know where you can find it. This model is the guiding principle for many urban libraries, the Oakview Public Library notwithstanding. It is a model that works well for homogeneous, middle class communities that know the value of the public library and all its benefits. More importantly, it makes broad assumptions about literacy and readership. Such a model for library service, however, cannot possibly be expected to work in poverty-ridden communities, urban or rural, or in communities that have historically been denied access to books and libraries, either through segregation or miseducation, or through the lack of qualified staff or appropriate materials and services.

Librarians that operate under the Robinson model are trained to be managers, much like a grocery store manager who must order the latest product and insure that best-selling items for the store customers are kept well stocked. Their professional skills, then, are refined, and they become technocrats and bureaucrats, disconnected from the very communities they serve. They function less as innovative leaders and creative thinkers and more like technocrats, unable to think and operate outside the routine for which they have been trained. Moreover, this model creates divisiveness among branches, pitting library professionals against each other because those who work in the middle class and well-to-do neighborhoods develop an arrogance about their success, based almost exclusively on circulation rates, serving to devalue and downplay the hard work of librarians who work against great odds in the at-risk communities that they serve. Staff funding, also affected by circulation rates, ties a librarian to the branch, preventing them from doing the much needed outreach services needed to develop future library users.

The Charlie Robinson model is so ingrained into the thinking of many library professionals that they are anesthetized to the oppressive practices that result when the model is applied in communities that have little or no history of library use, or in communities that have been deprived of their fair share of books and services. Few understand the consequences of a system that has steadily bought into the treatment of information as a market commodity, for sale to the fastest reader.

For San Antonio members of REFORMA, this model provided a challenge as they struggled to provide a quality collection, including Spanish books, while at the same time working to provide the much-needed outreach services to Spanish-speaking constituents with branch budgets that severely limit resources and staff. In their letter to the editor of *Library Journal*, John Berry, regarding the interview with Charlie Robinson and his associate, the group chided Mr. Robinson for his callous remarks and challenged him to revisit public library history, reminding him of the public library's role as the "university of the poor."[4] Led by the able leadership of noted Latina author Sandra Cisneros, the members of the San Antonio community known as "*Los Cien*" ("the One Hundred," the name derived from a popular activist group of intellectuals in Mexico City) have begun to challenge and question administrative practices and voice their concern over inequities. Recently, a group of high school students from one of San Antonio's poorest school districts experienced first-hand the effects of the deficiencies when they discovered the lack of the core literature of books needed to help them complete their reading assignments for the Accelerated Reader program in their branch libraries.

Action by community groups to bring about change in library systems is long overdue in Latino communities, which continue to sink into the black holes created by a global economy, driven by advances in technology worldwide. The capitalization of information that is taking place is a major factor in the process of "social exclusion" that ignores the needs of information have-nots. Unless organized action by community groups takes place, there is little hope for the public library system as a viable, democratic, equitable institution. Pepe and his family, as all Spanish-speaking children and families in the United States, deserve first-rate library systems responsive to their literacy and information needs systems that help them develop to their fullest potential. They deserve libraries that help them to meet these needs—*en inglés o en español*—and treat them with the dignity and respect they deserve.

Studies

Consider for a moment what we know today about children's reading habits in general. The research tells us that (1) literacy is best developed by voluntary reading as students who read more are better readers and writers and have larger, expanded vocabularies[5]; (2) for children between the second and fifth grades, the time spent reading books is the best predictor of a child's growth as a reader[6]; (3) children in gifted programs are more likely to be prompted by their parents to frequent the public library than are children in regular programs[7]; (4) in the summer, the impact of public libraries on summertime reading activity is greatest among students of lower socioeconomic status[8]; and (5) in 1995, only 28 percent of Hispanic children ages 3–5 visited the public library with a parent or family member in a given month, up four points from 24.5 percent in 1991.[9]

From the 1994 surveys conducted by Reynaldo and Marta Ayala in the *Report Card on Public Library Services to the Latino Communities*, we know that (1) children's services lack Spanish, bilingual or Latino qualified professions (p. 28); (2) the public library is providing below-average services for Latino children at a time when the number of Latino children is increasing and when economic hardships prevent Latino families from purchasing books and other educational materials (p.27); and (3) public libraries serving English-speaking Latinos have made little progress in serving the Spanish speaking non–library user who may be illiterate in both English and Spanish (p. 27).[10]

Although limited, these studies provide us with information by which we can evaluate the impact of library services on Latino children. The dearth of information in the library literature, however, is startling, with a few exceptions such as Schon, Artola and Constantino's new collection.[11] Educators of librarians have been derelict in their duties of responding to the needs of language-minority students. These concerns were expressed at the Trejo Foster Foundation Institute on Hispanic Library Education held in Tucson, Arizona, in 1993. The participants of the round table "Library Services to Children and Young Adults" identified eight major areas affecting the delivery of library services to Spanish speaking children, with staffing, collections, services and programs topping the list of concerns.[12] It will be interesting to see if the 1999 Congress on Professional Education sponsored by the American Library Association addresses the needs and concerns raised by this roundtable.[13]

Given the dismal state of affairs that Latino children and their families find in gaining access to first-rate library services and programs, one wonders if library professionals truly understand the seriousness of the present shortcomings, or if they even understand their own rhetoric. What sort of measures can be put in place to hold administrators accountable for ensuring that they apply their democratic principles equally? Unless public libraries begin to change their models and operate differently, Latino children will be condemned to the same inferior services they have received for most of the twentieth century. Moreover, a lack of fundamental language development skills in young children, necessary for substantive language acquisition, may well contribute to the development of Latino children as one of the many "post-illiterates," defined by Barry Sanders (in his thought-provoking social analysis *A Is for Ox: The Collapse of Literacy and the Rise of Violence in an Electronic Age*) as children dispossessed of "oral and written language."[14]

What Do We Need to Do Different?

So what do we need to do different? We can begin by quantifying and qualifying the information and literacy needs of Latino children. Professionals serving Latino children need the facts that library schools should be substantiating and compiling for us. Where is the research on library use among Latino children? What percentage of Latino children participate in summer reading programs? How many Latino parents know that reading to their child is the single most important activity they can do with and for their child? Where is the proof we can take to city policy makers and funders on why they need to be investing in library programs for children now rather than pouring wasteful monies into juvenile detention programs that provide too little too late? Why is it so difficult for us to prove that becoming good readers may well be a direct result of access to free books and participation in story hour programs that a child has experienced in our public libraries? As long as library professionals operate in the dark, libraries will continue to do business as usual with no new resources and no creative ways or political will to change current practices.

Latino Children Need Programs, Programs, Programs!

Infant and baby programs, Born to Read Programs, toddler programs, pre-school programs, elementary age storytime programs, summer reading programs and year-round reading programs are all essential to prepare a child for the many challenges of the 21st century. In addition, learning programs such as Hands-on-Science, poetry programs, art programs, multicultural programs and even holiday programs in both English and Spanish all help to further develop a child's interest and curiosity. Programs are learning opportunities for children that enhance their literacy experiences and help them to develop their social, emotional and intellectual competencies.

Latino Children Need Outreach Services

If Latino children are not coming to the public library, we must find ways to reach them where they are. If there is one lesson that both Pura Belpré and Gabriela Mistral demonstrated, it is that we must take the story and services to the child, no matter if the child is in the rural farms of California, Ohio, or Florida, or the urban jungles of New York, Houston, or Los Angeles.

Latino Children Need Libraries to Serve as Homework Centers

Homework centers are places to get help after school with core subjects such as math and reading. But these homework centers must also be learning centers where students are taught the skills of research that will enable them to become information literate and skilled investigators and to hone their inquiry skills. The public library must provide that creative space that will allow them to develop their curiosity and discover their talents and interests.

Latino Parents Need Parenting Programs in English and Spanish

Parenting programs are needed that provide information and enable parents to synthesize the vast amount of information that will help them to rear their children to be successful students and citizens. Thus, information on child development, early brain development, oral language development and language acquisition, the literacy development of young children, and the vast array of parenting information is essential for success as educated and informed parents.

Latino Families Need Quality Learning Experiences Through Well-Designed Family Literacy Programs—En inglés y en español

These programs should use children's literature as the center of the curriculum and should serve to model story reading in the home. In addition, programs must provide meaning and context, incorporating cultural programs that go beyond music and dance to include the history of Latinos in that particular community, along with civil rights and immigration history of Latinos as a whole.

Latino Children Need Competent, Qualified, Bilingual Children's Librarians and Managers

These professionals must be able to communicate with their constituents and provide the best quality services possible; in short, they should meet all the standards and qualifications set out in the ALSC document "Competencies for Librarians Serving Children in Public Libraries." These professionally trained bilingual librarians must plan and collaborate with social service agencies, schools, churches and other neighborhood groups. Moreover, they must be able to manage, conduct and supervise programs such as Born to Read Programs and community-wide library literacy celebrations such as *Día de los Niños: Día de los Libros,* celebrated on April 30. To do this, they must have the organizational and managerial skills to launch community-wide bilingual reading initiatives that target Latino families. In addition, Latino children need bilingual community outreach workers who can act as library assistants, working closely with bilingual librarians.

LATINO CHILDREN NEED TO VIEW PUBLIC LIBRARIES AS FRIENDLY, USEFUL PLACES

They need to know how a library is organized, what the rules are, how to find information in a timely fashion and how to use their research skills. They also need to learn to use online services effectively. By taking full advantage of the public library, Latino children can become better information seekers, readers, students and citizens.

LATINO CHILDREN NEED ADVOCATES IN THE PUBLIC LIBRARY

Latino families need library professionals who are less proprietary and more sympathetic to local needs. These librarians need to remind themselves of their role as public servants. Library professionals must be willing to create new models and community partnerships that incorporate the needs of the community with best practices. This will entail re-thinking, re-designing and transforming local branch libraries from empty reading rooms into learning laboratories, much like models such as The Family Place.

LATINO CHILDREN AND THEIR FAMILIES NEED COMPREHENSIVE PROGRAMS

Child development funders must be convinced that library services and programs are as critical to the future of Latino children as are Head Start programs, WIC programs and other early child care intervention programs. Programs such as those funded by the Lila Wallace–Readers' Digest Fund may well be the last, best hope for branches in under-served Latino communities.

Conclusion

As public services librarians we must be willing to challenge systems and institutions, our own public libraries included, that treat poor people as second class citizens. If we have learned anything in this century it is that as an institution, we have not done a very good job of serving the needs of Spanish-speaking children and their families. Let us resolve that the little *Pepes* being born today are not left out of the public library literacy equation. In the 21st century, we must move beyond equal access and focus on quality and equal services for all children so that they achieve their fullest potential and blossom into bright, hopeful, healthy, intellectual, responsible, and productive citizens.

Notes

1. Pepe is a nickname for José, the most popular newborn baby boy's name in Texas and California. See the *Houston Chronicle.* "Jose most popular name in Texas and California." January 14, 1999. "Oakview" is a fictitious name used for an actual library system.

2. Kevin Henkes, *Lily's Purple Purse* (New York: Greenwillow, 1996).

3. Nancy Pearl, " Gave 'Em What They Wanted," *Library Journal* 121 (September 1, 1996): 136–138. [An interview with Charlie Robinson and Jean Barry Molz.]

4. Jennifer Till, "Appalled at Charlie," Letters, *Library Journal* 122 (January, 1997): 10.

5. S.D. Krashen, "Introduction: Why Consider the Library and Books?" in *Literacy, Access*

and Libraries Among the Language Minority Populations, ed. Rebecca Constantino (Lanham, Md.: Scarecrow, 1998), pp. 1–15.

6. R.C. Anderson, P.T. Wilson and L.G. Fielding, cited in Sandra Pucci, "Supporting Spanish Language Literacy: Latino Children and School and Community Libraries," in Constantino, p. 19.

7. S. Swanton, "Minda Alive: What and Why Gifted Students Read for Pleasure," cited in Sandra Pucci in Constantino, p. 23.

8. B. Heyns, *Summer Learning and the Effects of Learning,* cited in Sandra Pucci in Constantino, p. 23.

9 U.S. Department of Education, National Center for Education Statistics, National Household Education Survey (NHES), 1991 (Early Childhood Education File) and 1995 (Early Childhood Participation File) available on world wide web at *http://nces.ed.gov/Pubs/ce/c9702a01.html.*

10. Reynaldo Ayala and Marta Stiefel Ayala, *Report Card on Public Library Services to the Latino Community* (Calexico, Calif.: REFORMA, 1994).

11. A. A. Allen, "The School Library Media Center and the Promotion of Literature for Hispanic Children," *Library Trends* 41 (Winter 1993):437–61; Isabel Schon, Kenneth D. Hopkins, and Isabelle Main, "Books in Spanish for Young Readers in School and Public Libraries: A Survey of Practices and Attitudes," *Library and Information Science Research* 9, 1 (January 1987): 21–28; and Constantino, as cited in footnotes 5, 6, 7 and 8 above.

12. This was an important component of the first Trejo Foster Institute on Hispanic Library Education and included a panel consisting of the author, Oralia Garza de Cortés, Gina Macaluso Rodriguez, and Helen Maul.

13. For further information see *http://www.ala.congress.*

14. Barry Sanders, *A Is for Ox: The Collapse of Literacy and the Rise of Violence in an Electronic Age* (New York: Vintage Books, Random House, 1994).

Poetry of the African Diaspora: In Search of Common Ground Between Anglo and Latin America

Sonia Ramírez Wohlmuth
and Henrietta M. Smith

In our capacity as librarians and information specialists we are often called on to help locate resources for inclusion in curricula, programs or presentations which have as their theme the appointed days of celebration throughout the year. In addition to days of religious significance and national import, these days of observance have now extended to month-long recognition of the two major ethnic groups in the United States — Americans of African origin and Americans of Hispanic origin. Although the acknowledgment of the history of these peoples and the relationship of that history to the development of the United States at large is long overdue, the separation into two separate events may have an adverse affect. The history of the United States is not a composite of many separate histories but a single complex history with events occurring simultaneously in different planes — separated by geography or other factors. However, at crucial points there is a confluence of events, and it is no longer possible to treat as separate and self-contained the history of Africa, the history of Spain and its colonies, and the history of Anglo-America.

We propose to review here these points of intersection and have selected as a medium the poetry of peoples of African descent in the Americas. Poetry provides a vehicle not only for narration but also for lyric expression of attitude and emotion. Furthermore, poetry is well suited to performance, which renders it particularly useful for classroom presentation or other types of programs.

It is helpful to examine briefly the historical background of contacts between Africa and Europe. In the case of Iberia, the contact with sub–Saharan Africa is very old and probably the result of early Portuguese explorations. There are references to African servants in Spain in the Middle Ages and the renaissance. Therefore, as Spain extended its realm of influence to the Americas, it is natural that African presence should become part of that expansion. It is popularly believed that there was at least one mariner of African origin among Columbus's crew on the first voyage. Small numbers of slaves were probably introduced in the Caribbean as early as the first decade of the sixteenth century.[1] Among the survivors of Alvar Núñez Cabeza de Vaca's ill-fated voyage of 1527, described in his *Naufragios,* was an African servant, Estebanico. He and other members of the expedition were among the first explorers of the territory that is today Florida.[2]

Throughout the sixteenth century the slave trade continued on a relatively modest scale in the Spanish colonies through special licenses which did not emanate directly from the Spanish crown. This changed in 1595 when the first *asiento* was granted to Gómez Raynel. Vedoya calculates that during this period of 67 years, as many as 163,000 African slaves may have been brought to the Spanish colonies.[3] It is noteworthy that nearly a century passed between the introduction of the first slaves in Spanish America and the arrival of slaves to the English colonies in the form of 20 indentured servants brought to Jamestown in 1619.[4] The economic development of agriculture on a large scale in both the English and Spanish colonies necessitated a constant supply of labor from Africa. Vedoya's computation of the total number of slaves brought to Spanish America through extant documentation and inference (of slaves brought as contraband, and those not included in the headcount of authorized trade because they did not meet the minimum height requirement) is summarized in the table below.[5]

Time Period	Number of Slaves
1503–1595	163,000
1595–1787	488,300
Period not covered by *asientos* (58 years)	311,352
Adjustment for uncounted children	146,490
Slaves brought as contraband	2,085,742
TOTAL	3,194,884

Curiously, the slave trade was abolished before the institution of slavery itself. By 1800 the importing and exporting of slaves to or from the territorial United States had been prohibited, but the institution of slavery lingered in the United States until 1865, when it was outlawed by the 13th Amendment and in Latin America until 1888, when Brazil abolished slavery.

The search for literary expression from African voices at the time the slave trade was active will remain, sadly, unfulfilled. There is no African counterpart to El Inca Garcilaso de la Vega, son of the Spanish conquistador Sebastián Garcilaso de la Vega and an Inca princess. El Inca Garcilaso, educated in Europe, authored the *Comentarios reales*, a history of his mother's people, the Inca. During the Spanish Baroque, African themes emerge as leitmotif, usually as a comic interlude in drama, poetry or narrative. The African servant who deforms language and entertains through songs and chants became a stock character of popular theatre. There are also examples of dialect poetry which supposedly reflect the linguistic modalities of African slaves and servants. This poetry is most often humorous or satiric, but there are examples of devotional poetry as well. The catalog of *villancicos*, or ballads, of the Biblioteca Nacional, has a thematic index which registers over three hundred references to "negros" or "*guineos.*"[6] This excerpt from the Mexican poet Sor Juana Inés de la Cruz, herself the owner of a domestic slave who accompanied her to the convent, is typical. The *villancico*, in form of a dialog between an African servant and an unidentified interlocutor, was composed for a performance on the Day of the Immaculate Conception. The servant is first told to leave because, being black, he is out of place in a celebration of purity. The servant responds sagely that the devout soul knows no color.

> Aunque Neglo, blanco
> somo, lela, lela,...[7]
>
> [Although black, we are
> white — lela, lela,...
> — Tr. S.R.W.]

Although the deformation of language is caricature-like, the next lines "que il alma rivota blanca sá/no prieta" [for the devout soul/is white, not black] are a reminder that the Vatican, after much discussion following the discovery of new peoples in the Americas, had declared that all living beings endowed with reason were possessed of souls. The logical conclusion that these new peoples were therefore equal, however, did not follow. In the example from Sor Juana above it should be noted that when finally given an opportunity to speak at the end of the poem, the black servant reverts to the nonsense verse, imitative of his native language, "¡Zambio, lela, lela!" Clearly, his role is that of court jester.

The classic Spanish novel of the picaresque, *Lazarillo de Tormes*, composed anonymously in the mid-sixteenth century, contains an oft-cited passage in which Lazarillo's half brother, who has never seen dark-skinned people before, recoils in fear when he sees his father, a servant of African origin, for the first time. He identifies him with "el coco," the bogeyman of traditional children's lore. Lazarillo, with his precocious wisdom, notes "(¡Cuántos debe de haber en el mundo que huyen de otros porque no se ven a sí mismos!" [How many must there be in this world who flee from others because they do not see themselves].[8] Children of mixed parentage were not uncommon among the servant class. This historical reality is the basis of Elizabeth de Treviño's historical novel, *Juan de Pareja*. The first person narrator describes his unhappy lot as a slave:

> My mother was a beautiful Black woman. My father was white. My mother's hands were beautiful and moved like two dark birds. I have learned with the fatalism of slave children, not to be surprised when my mistress slapped me with the closed fan, a sharp rap that sent sudden pain along my hand and made tears sting under my eyelids.[9]

During the more than three centuries in which slavery was sanctioned by law, there is little testimony of the life and artistic expression of the slave. Many early examples of poetry by authors of African origin are imitative of European currents and tell us little about the lives of slaves and freedmen. The abolition of slavery brought major changes in the quality of life for Americans of African origin, including the freedom to learn to read and write. The voice of the African diaspora could finally be heard.

A sense of one's own history is a vital component of personal well-being. The search for lost parents or siblings becomes a life-consuming quest for many. Yet, for Americans of African descent, family history is largely unknown even when separation of families is not provoked by circumstances of birth or actions of war. Those who work in public library settings will often have the opportunity to assist patrons with genealogical queries. Do we know how to respond when that patron is African American, or Hispanic of African ancestry? How can we help young people who come to us for aid with the apparently innocuous assignment of researching their family history? What response can the child of African ancestry counter to his or her classmates' stories of family emigration to find religious or political freedom, or economic opportunity? After all, Africans were also emigrants, albeit victims of a forced exile.

The first texts we will examine provide partial answers to these queries. Any discussion of African presence in the New World must begin with a recognition of the institution of slavery. By and large, all Africans who entered the Americas in the 300-year period between the early sixteenth century and the end of the eighteenth century came in bondage. Slavery had these immediate and devastating effects on those who came as human cargo: (1) loss of family structure, (2) loss of linguistic/ethnic identity, and (3) loss of personal and community history. As a consequence, succeeding generations had no sense of family history, as many never knew their parents, grandparents, siblings; the mother tongue passed from one generation to the next became the master's tongue; Christianity replaced other cosmological views; and memories of homeland faded.

The Cuban poet Nicolás Guillén (1902–1982), who referred to himself as "mulato," became an eloquent spokesman for the many like him in the Caribbean who needed to know more about their "*other* family history." His "Balada de los dos abuelos" / "Ballad of the two grandfathers" has become a standard piece in anthologies of Latin American poetry. However, the tentative optimism of "Balada de los dos abuelos," where the poet reconciles his mixed ancestry, is counterbalanced by other poems by Guillén which beg the question, Who am I? as in this passage from "El apellido."[10]

> ¿Sabéis mi otro apellido, el que me viene
> de aquella tierra enorme, el apellido
> sangriento y capturado, que pasó sobre el
> mar...?
>
> [Do you know my other surname, the one
> which comes from that enormous land, the
> bloodied and captive surname that came
> over the sea...?
> —Tr. S.R.W.]

Guillén's image of personal history lost in the trans–Atlantic journey from freedom to slavery is mirrored in Joyce Carol Thomas's "Family Tree":

> I step into this green forest—
> Purple with growing roots
> This forest down by the blue-green
> water that first separated us...
> I look across water
> And cry for our trembling FAMILY TREE.[11]

The loss of family name, family history, and consequently identity with a larger community or nation is also the subject of James Baldwin's essay "Stranger in the Village." He notes that the descendent of the North American slave "is unique among the black men of the world in that his past was taken from him, almost literally, at one blow. One wonders what on earth the first slave found to say to the first dark child he bore. I am told that there are Haitians able to trace their ancestry back to African kings, but any American Negro wishing to go so far will find his journey through time abruptly arrested by the signature on the bill of sale which served as the entrance paper for his ancestor."[12]

The theme of slave ancestry and loss of freedom is expressed by Regino Pedroso, a compatriot of Guillén in "Hermano negro."

Y fuiste esclavo;
sentiste el látigo
encender tu carne de humana cólera....[13]

[And you were a slave;
you felt the lash
inflame your flesh with human ire....]

Beyond the Caribbean one finds similar expressions. Nicomedes Santa Cruz, the Peruvian ethnologist and musicologist is also a poet. His "Ritmos negros del Perú" [Black rhythms of Peru] begins with a reference to the origins of Afro-Peruvian music and continues with a more personal history:

De Africa llegó mi agüela
vestida con caracoles,
la trajeron lo'epañoles
en un barco carabela.[14]

[From Africa my grandmother came
adorned with shells,
the Spaniards brought her
by ship in a caravel.
—Tr. S.R.W.]

The outpouring of music and song as a response to oppression is found also in Sterling A. Brown's "Strong Men":

They broke you in like oxen,
They scourged you,
. . . .
You sang....[15]

Slavery as an institution of oppression and dispossession is also reflected in "Enslaved," the work of one of the first major poets of the Harlem Renaissance, Claude McKay, of Jamaican origin.

Oh when I think of my long-suffering race,
For weary centuries despised, oppressed
Enslaved and lynched, denied a human
place...[16]

The indomitable spirit present in Brown's poem is a a dramatic contrast with McKay's internalization of the cruel fate history has dealt his ancestors. Henrietta M. Smith recalls an anecdotal account of Augusta Baker, renowned librarian, storyteller, and pioneer in advocating "positive images of the black child" in literature for children, in which Baker commented that she had once asked Claude McKay to write some children's poetry. His negative response was based on his belief that poetry for children should be full of joy and hope, and he saw no hope for the black child in America. Perhaps that is why he introduces the idea of a black homeland. References to Africa, a land ravaged by the greed of European merchants, appear in multiple form among poets on both sides of the linguistic divide in the Americas. A cursory examination *The Norton Anthology of African American Literature* produces the following list in English: Frances E. W. Harper (1825–1911), "Ethiopia"; Paul Laurence Dunbar (1872–1906), "Ode to Ethiopia"; Claude McKay (1889–1943), "Africa"; Gwendolyn B. Bennett (1902–1981), "Heritage"; Countee Cullen (1903–1946), "Heritage"; Melvin B. Tolson (1900–1966), "Libretto for the Republic of Liberia."

Similarly, one finds in the Spanish anthology *Antología de la poesía negra americana* such poems as "Canto al Afric," by the Argentine poet Casildo G. Thompson, and "Canto a Etiopía," by Uruguay's Carolos Cardoza Ferreira. This anthology, which contains black poetry of the Americas (United States, the Caribbean, Central and South America), also has a Spanish version of Dunbar's poem cited above. It is noteworthy that the authors listed are not contemporary; the impetus for returning to Africa has been lost in favor of forging a new identity which is neither African nor European nor American.

In returning to the role of the librarian as reader's advisor, this search for a sense of ancestry, of one's personal family history, is an area where we can clearly provide guidance. It is important to recognize that the needs of a Spanish-speaking child of African ancestry from the Caribbean or the coastal areas of Central America (Honduras, Nicaragua, Panama) and South America (Venezuela, Colombia, Ecuador, Peru) are very different from those of a child of mestizo heritage from Spanish America. The glories of Tenochtitlán, Copán, or Machu Picchu do little to contribute a sense of self-worth to a child who knows that these marvels do not represent his or her past. The question of self-identity is paramount and can only be resolved through direct confrontation of the issue of race, a difficult subject to discuss, perhaps even more so in a public setting.

Again, we will turn to poetry to show young people of color that they are not alone in their search for a sense of self, an ancestral repertory, and a link to the historical past of a racial, national, or ethnic group which will give them pride in their African roots. In the texts which follow we see a clear evolution from the white aesthetic to the idea of "negritude," the affirmation that black is indeed beautiful. The white aesthetic favored those features which more closely resembled caucasian features. In geographic areas where there had been intermarriage, physical appearance became a source of envy and mistrust, even among family members, where there was a range of skin hues and hair textures. Many of the poems which treat this subject are highly charged emotionally and reflect the bitterness and hurt of the poetic narrator; others are mocking, self-deprecating, and humorous although there are often tears behind the laughter.

The idea of looking white or passing for white has received considerable treatment in the literature of both the Spanish-speaking world and the English-speaking world. Hoyt Fuller's essay "Towards a Black Aesthetic," written in 1968, summarizes the dilemma of peoples of color to find a new aesthetic, a new world view which does not involve a comparison, implicit or explicit, with the values of western Europe.

> After centuries of being told, in a million different ways, that they were not beautiful, and that whiteness of skin, straightness of hair, and aquilineness of features constituted the only measures of beauty, black people have revolted. The trend has not yet reached the point of an avalanche, but the future can be clearly seen in the growing number of black people who are snapping off their shackles of imitation and are wearing their skin, their hair and their features "natural" and with pride.[17]

As an artist whose own family history included African and European ancestry, Nicolás Guillén often addresses the issue of racial identity. The theme is evident, for instance, in "Balada de los dos abuelos" [Ballad of the Two Grandfathers], referred to above, and in this more subtle expression of the necessity to maintain a façade of racial purity, "El abuelo."

Ah mi señora! Mírate las venas misteriosas,

. . . .

que ya verás inquieta junto a la fresca orilla

. . . .

el que rizó por siempre tu cabeza amarilla.[18]

[Oh, my lady! Look at your mysterious veins,

. . . .

for then you will see next to the cool shore,

. . . .

the one who curled your golden hair forever.
—Tr. S.R.W.]

The dilemma of identity is also the theme of "Cross," by Langston Hughes. Alternately bitter toward and forgiving of his parents, who crossed the color line, the speaker is unable to resolve his own destiny.

Weighing his white father's death in a luxurious house against his mother's death in a shack, he bitterly puts the question to Fate:

> I wonder where I'm gonna die
> Being neither white nor black.[19]

In addition to these pensive compositions, there are more light-hearted expressions of the concern with color and appearance. From Guillén's book of popular poetry, *Motivos de son*, in which many of the poems are written in dialect, "Mulata" is representative:

> mulata, ya sé que dice
> que yo tengo la narice
> como nudo de corbata...[20]
>
> [Mulata, I already found out
> that you see that I have a nose
> like the knot of a necktie.
> —Tr. S.R.W.]

The question of racial identity is not restricted to the Caribbean, however; it is found in all regions where there were slave populations. "Romance de la niña morenita" [Ballad of the Little Dark Girl] by Ecuadoran poet Abel Romeo Castillo, is a particularly poignant expression of the negative effects of racial discrimination as the subject of the poem is a child.

> No era ni blanca ni rubia.
> . . . .
> Y sin saberlo por qué
> al pensarlo entristecía....[21]
>
> [She was neither white nor blonde.
> . . . .
> And without knowing why
> when she thought about it, it made her sad....
> —Tr. S.R.W.]

In her poem "For Sistuhs Wearin' Straight Hair," Carolyn M. Rodgers addresses another concern which comes from the white aesthetic—hair texture:

> me?
> i never could keep my edges and kitchen
> straight....[22]

It has often been suggested that there is a more open attitude toward race in Latin America, that the mixing of the races has gained greater acceptance. However, the texts viewed here seem to cast doubt on that claim. Furthermore, historically, there has been a great deal of deliberation on the question of race. Among the more intriguing genres of Mexican colonial art are the "pinturas de castas," or portraits of the different castes, which were racially determined. The major classifications of the offspring of mixed couples were as follows:

(1) Spaniard with a black woman—Mulatto
(2) *Mulato* with a Spanish woman—Morisco
(3) *Morisco* with a Spanish woman—Salta atrás
(4) *Salta atrás* with an indigenous woman—Chino
(5) *Chino* with a mulatto woman—Lobo
(6) *Lobo* with a mulatto woman—Gíbaro
(7) *Gíbaro* with an indigenous woman—Albarrazado
(8) *Albarrazado* with a black woman—Cambujo
(9) *Cambujo* with an indigenous woman—Sambaygo
(10) *Sambaygo* with a mulatto woman—Calpan mulata
(11) *Calpan mulata* with a sambaygo—Ténte en el aire
(12) *Ténte en el aire* with a mulatto woman—No te entiendo
(13) *No te entiendo* with an indigenous woman—Hay te estás [23]

The mere existence of these multiple classifications is proof that there was great consciousness of race. Furthermore, one's racial category, registered in infancy as part of baptismal records or other official documents, determined whom one could marry, what offices men could hold, and whether or not a man had the right to bear arms. It is no wonder, then, that "pasando por blanco" (passing for white) became desirable, even if it meant repudiating one's family and origins. While it is important for young people to know that these facts — painful as they may be — are part of their legacy, it is equally important to find affirmations of pride and confidence from those who have accepted this patrimony and do not draw back from their African roots. Jackson, in his study, *The Black Image in Latin American Literature,* includes this passage — and accompanying translation — from "Canción del niño del incendio" [Song of the Child of the Fire], from the Ecuadoran poet Nelson Estupiñán Bass, in which the poet proclaims with pride his race.

> negro vengo negro voy,
> negro bien negro nací,
> negro negro he de vivir,...
>
> [I am black coming and going,
> I was born very black and
> black I must live,...][24]

Women's voices have been an especially important part of the Black Arts movement in English-speaking North America. Mari Evans' "I Am a Black Woman" employs a self-asserting, deictic aspect in which the poetic "I" draws attention to himself or herself as an example, a model. These poetic styles are particularly apt for young people who will enhance their own self-image by assuming the identity of the poetic voice in reading or reciting these verses.

> I
> am a black woman
> tall as a cypress

Sandra María Esteves is representative of the Nuyorican poets whose work reflects the struggle for acceptance in a society which views the Puerto Rican as both non-white and foreign. In "A la Mujer Borrinqueña," the speaker declaims with pride her dual heritage — African and Latina.

> I am a Puerto Rican woman born in el barrio
> Our men ... they call me negra because they
> love me
> and in turn I teach them to be strong.[25]

We have relied on poetry as an approximation of cultural values and cultural aesthetic. These expressions cover the entire emotional spectrum. However, for young people, the humorous and exhortatory tone of Jayne Cortez's poem "How Long Has Trane Been Gone" seems especially appropriate as she suggests that black people need to look to their own history for inspiration, and she calls on blacks to establish

> Black Hall of Fame
> so our children will know
> will know & be proud....[26]

This call for black pride invites reflection on the progress toward racial harmony. In the search for a black identity is there also a call to unity, a recognition that beneath the skin we are all of one race? Michelle Cliff's upbeat poem "Within the Veil" touts one basic, optimistic message: "We got to love each other. That is what is known as the bottom line."[27]

The poetic trajectory of the African diaspora glimpsed here covers a gamut of emotions. These poetic outpourings of a people oppressed by slavery will help young people come to terms with their own conflicting feelings. These poets, in the language adopted from their masters — English or Spanish — have given us a testimony of slavery and its aftermath. However, an underlying current is the belief that the journey to the new world has made of Africans and their descendants legitimate immigrants. They have a rightful place in this continent. Langston Hughes' well known "I, Too," with its compelling imagery of coming together at the table, represents the best hope of America. In a closing tribute to the poets of the "other America," a few lines from the artful translation of "I, Too" by the Cuban poet Emilio Ballagas are appended.

> verán que soy hermoso
> y se avergonzarán.
> Yo también soy América.[28]
>
> [They'll see how beautiful I am
> And be ashamed —
> I, too, am America.][29]

Notes

1. Juan C. Vedoya, *La expoliación de América* (Buenos Aires: Ediciones La Bastilla, 1973), pp. 114-115.
2. Samuel Gili Gaya, ed., *Historiadores de los siglos XVI y XVII* (Madrid: Instituto-Escuela, 1925), p. 194.
3. Vedoya, p. 118.
4. Henry Louis Gates, Jr., and Nellie Y. McKay, *The Norton Anthology of African American Literature* (New York: W. W. Norton, 1997), p. 2612.
5. Vedoya, p. 140.
6. *Catálogo de Villancicos de la Biblioteca Nacional* (Madrid: Biblioteca Nacional, Ministerio de Cultura, 1992), p. 334.
7. Juana Inés de la Cruz, "Villancico VIII," in *Obras completas* 2:217.
8. *Lazarillo de Tormes*, in *Novela picaresca española* 2 (1975): 80.
9. Elizabeth Borton de Treviño, *Juan de Pareja* (New York: Bell Books, 1965), pp. 3, 5.
10. Nicolás Guillén, "El apellido," in *La paloma de vuelo popular* (Buenos Aires: Losada, 1958), p. 117.
11. Joyce Carol Thomas, "Family Tree," in *Broomwheat Tea: Poems* (New York: HarperCollins, 1993).
12. James Baldwin, "Stranger in the Village," in *The Norton Anthology of African American Literature*, Henry Louis Gates, ed. (New York: W.W. Norton, 1997), p. 1676.
13. Ildefonso Pereda Valdés, ed., *Antología de la poesía negra americana* (Montevideo: Biblioteca Uruguaya de Autores, 1953), p. 163.
14. Nicomedes Santa Cruz, "Ritmos negros del Perú," in *Poesía peruana: Antología general*, vol. 1, *Poesía aborigen y tradicional popular* (Lima: Fundación del Banco Continental para el Fomento de la Educación y Cultura, Ediciones Edubanco, 1984), p. 432.
15. Sterling A. Brown, "Strong Men," in Gates, p. 1215.
16. Claude McKay, "Enslaved," in Gates, p. 986.
17. Hoyt Fuller, "Toward a Black Aesthetic," in Gates, p. 1813.
18. Nicolás Guillén, *Sóngoro cosongo, Motivos de son, West Indies Ltd. y España* (Buenos Aires: Losada, 1952), pp. 71–72.
19. Catherine Clinton, ed., *I, Too, Sing America: Three Centuries of African-American Poetry* (Boston: Houghton Mifflin, 1998), p. 9.
20. Guillén, *Sóngoro cosongo*, 41
21. Abel Romeo Castillo, "Romance de la niña morenita," in *La poesía negroide en América*, Rosa E. Valdés-Cruz, ed. (Long Island, NY: Las Américas, 1970), p. 210.
22. Carolyn M. Rodgers, "For Sistuhs Wearin' Straight Hair" in Gates, p. 2010
23. "Negros," in *Enciclopedia de México*, vol. IX (Mexico City: Enciclopedia de México, 1978), pp. 738–742.
24. Nelson Estupiñán Bass, "Canción del niño del incendio," in *The Black Image in Latin American Literature*, Richard L. Jackson, ed. (Albuquerque: University of New Mexico Press, 1976), pp. 105–106
25. Sandra María Esteves, "A la Mujer Borinqueña," in *The Latino Reader: An American Literary Tradition from 1542 to the Present*, Harold Augenbraum and Margarite Fernández Olmos, eds. (Boston: Houghton Mifflin, 1997), p. 384.
26. Jayne Cortez, "How Long Has Trane Been Gone," in Gates, p. 1959.
27. Michelle Cliff, "Within the Veil," in Gates, p. 2464.
28. Emilio Ballagas, "Yo, también," in Valdés-Cruz, p. 223.
29. Langston Hughes, "I, Too," in Gates, p. 1258.

References

Arozarena, Marcelino. *Canción negra sin color.* Havana: Ediciones Unión, 1983.

Augenbraum, Harold, and Fernández Olmos,

Margarite, eds. *The Latino Reader: An American Literary Tradition from 1542 to the Present.* Boston: Houghton Mifflin, 1997.
Catálogo de Villancicos de la Biblioteca Nacional. Madrid: Biblioteca Nacional, Ministerio de Cultura, 1992.
Gates, Henry Louis, Jr., and Nellie Y. McKay, *The Norton Anthology of African American Literature.* New York: W. W. Norton, 1997
Gili Gaya, Samuel, ed. *Historiadores de los siglos XVI y XVII.* Madrid: Instituto-Escuela, 1925.
Guillén, Nicolás. *La paloma de vuelo popular.* Buenos Aires: Losada, 1958.
Guillén, Nicolás. *Sóngoro cosongo, Motivos de son, West Indies Ltd. y España.* Buenos Aires: Losada, 1952.
Jackson, Richard L. *The Black Image in Latin American Literature.* Albuquerque: University of New Mexico Press, 1976.
Lazarillo de Tormes. In *Novela picaresca española.* Tomo I. 75–208. Madrid: Editorial Noguer, 1974.
"Negros." *Enciclopedia de México*, vol. IX. 738–742. Mexico City: Enciclopedia de México, 1978.
Pereda Valdés, Ildefonso, ed. *Antología de la poesía negra americana.* Montevideo: Biblioteca Uruguaya de Autores, 1953.
Poesía peruana: Antología general. Tomo I: Poesía aborigen y tradicional popular. [Lima]: Fundación del Banco Continental para el Fomento de la Educación y Cultura, Ediciones Edubanco, 1984.
Poesía latinoamericana contemporánea. [Argentina]: Círculo del Buen Lector, 1991.
Valdés-Cruz, Rosa E. *La poesía negroide en América.* Long Island, NY: Las Américas, 1970.
Vedoya, Juan C. *La expoliación de América.* Buenos Aires: Ediciones La Bastilla, 1973.

Editor's note: Translations noted as by "S.R.W." are by this article's coauthor, Sonia Ramírez Wohlmuth.

Collection Development Across the Borders

Haydee C. Hodis

To carry on the educational, informational and recreational activities related to the positive promotion of the Hispanic community, its language and culture, libraries must continue addressing that population's growing demands and needs. The Hispanic community in the United States of America comprises Latinos, Chicanos, Cubans, Puerto Ricans, a mixture of Amerindian, European and African influences — all bound by the Spanish language. The children of these diverse groups, attending early literacy programs, elementary, middle and high schools, are also users of public libraries.

The members of this community reflect a myriad of traditions, experiences and changes. Recent examinations of publications indicate the need to increment and supplement materials, monolingual and bilingual, in print and non-print formats, to support the curricula. Even though national and international markets are responding to these needs, much more needs to be done. The challenge remains for librarians doing collection development to acquire a balanced representation of materials while opening a dialog with distributors and publishers.

Those of us who have acquired a degree of expertise in the selection and acquisition of library materials in the Spanish language can offer a testimonial to the increase and improvement in quality and availability of publications in a variety of formats. This has occurred mainly in the current decade. It is possible now to have at our disposal traditional tools reviewing materials in library journals and periodicals. *School Library Journal*, *Hornbook*, and Isabel Schon's column in *Booklist* are useful for those libraries starting new collections, expanding or updating. The drawback is that the number of titles reviewed are few by comparison. A more comprehensive source is the latest publication by Isabel Schon, *The Best of the Latino Heritage: A Guide to the Best Juvenile Books About Latino People and Cultures.* Other sources include professional newsletters such as REFORMA— the National Association to Promote Library Services to the Spanish-Speaking — whose membership provides guidance and advice when requested; and the American Library Association, Ethnic Materials and Information Exchange Round Table newsletter, which reviews new books in their multicultural columns. Vendors also offer approval plans based on profiles that can be useful for those libraries starting collections or which lack bilingual professionals in their staff. Catalogs provided by vendors with annotated information are another resource that fills some of the gaps.

Spanish magazines, local newspapers, radio programs and the mass media, which impact the daily lives of Hispanics through their Spanish-language channels of information, provide librarians with an important non-traditional tool to learn more about their patrons, their communities, and preferences in music, film and popular titles.

An example of an event that went across regional borders was the death of the popular singer Selena. Her success and popularity in the Southwest caused an immediate reaction in the Northeast, where patrons, young and old, requested information about her life and untimely death. Her biography was produced and distributed on demand and our library had to acquire multiple copies to keep up with local requests. In addition, there was a jump in interest in Tex-Mex music. (See the list of Spanish-language resources at the end of this article.)

Still, nothing can replace periodic visits to bookstores, where the sources are in view and the hands-on experience takes place. Library systems in close proximity to metropolitan areas have a great advantage in selecting and purchasing a variety of materials to fulfill different areas of the collection. An important aspect of this process is building new avenues of communication with distributors and booksellers. For those with extra money in their budgets, these relationships become very beneficial when rebuilding collections, implementing specific grants or replacing materials.

Collection-development policies, with written guidelines and established criteria, are of great importance in maintaining a balanced collection. It should include basic reference tools, strong non-fiction in support of school curricula, and a fiction collection that combines classic and popular materials for the various reading levels. Audio tapes, videos, and music compact discs should all reflect popular taste and name recognition. However, the best collection-development policy is the one that takes into consideration patron needs and remains in tune in areas of recreational reading and entertainment. (See the list of resources at the end of this article.)

Levels and Scope

A basic core collection of Spanish materials for young Hispanics should include various levels of readership starting with the very young and pre-school age, followed by the elementary, middle and high school levels. Strong consideration should be given to acquiring pre-school materials to supplement the needs of families and the emergent literacy movement. A combination of original and translated titles of well-known authors and some new ones adds flavor and substance to the collection for children. A demand for *nanas*, lullabies, Mother Goose rhymes, finger plays in board-book or paperback form, audios and read-along kits are the staple of day-care centers, home-care providers and nurseries. The names of Jose Luis Orozco, Sarah Barch and Lulu Delacre are prominent with this age group.

Also worthy of inclusion are early versions of traditional tales, concept books that include colors, shapes, counting and an assortment of themes that capture experiences from Spain, Latin America and Caribbean countries. The series *Ya se leer / I Can Read*, *Mis primeros libros / My First Books* and the Spanish version of the *Muppet Babies' Big*

Step are popular for the colorful and well-organized presentation.

The picture book scene offers a wide range of options and titles, some of them rooted in the Hispanic tradition, while others cross borders through their universal appeal. A large proportion are translated works of U.S. and English authors as well as writers from other European and Asian countries. It is always important to locate books that reflect the urban setting, where many of the Hispanic children live; the migrant experience; and biracial and working class families that children can identify or learn about. Maria Cristina Brusca, Pat Mora, Lucía González, Alma Flor Ada, Carmen Lomas Garza, Esther Feliciano Mendoza, Francisco X. Alarcon and Tony Johnston are all recommended writers here. Others include Margaret Wise Brown, Eric Carle, Martin Wadell, Don Freeman, Robert Kalan, Lucy Cousins, Marc Brown and the *Pata Pita* series for its emphasis on phonetics.

Bilingual books that serve as the go-between to the monolingual are an essential part of the collection for their dual language format, design and presentation. They have been gaining popularity and have acquired their own place in the juvenile collection. These works are popular with parents, teachers and students for their usefulness in the bilingual classroom and home where adults can reinforce the language skills of children as needed. Adults, on the other hand, can practice and gain confidence as they make use of their acquired language. Denise Agosto, in her article "Bilingual Picture Books: Libros Para Todos," discusses various titles published in the last five years.

For children in the elementary and middle grades, the emphasis is on crossover titles, since the reading skills seem to overlap. Popular fiction is represented by translated series such as *Escalofrios*, or *Goosebumps*, folktales and fairy tales are other forms of recreational reading. *Los Cuentos de Juan Bobo / Tales of Juan Bobo, La cucarachita Martina / The Little Cockroach*, along with translations of the Brothers Grimm and Charles Perrault stories, should be considered. Pura Belpré, the well known Puerto Rican author and librarian, left an important legacy in her work, and her books are important for collections serving Puerto Rican children, in particular. Arthur Dorros, Felix Petri, Lucía González, Cruz Martel, Omar Castaneda, Hilda Perera, Leo Politi and Harriet Rohmer provide a representative selection of the work for this age group.

Cuentos, or "stories," anthologies and classics in paperbacks are some of the titles welcome for students in the upper grades. Works by distinctive authors should be considered, keeping in mind the ethnic origins or the audience and geographical setting. What appeals to young people on the West Coast might not meet with the same favor on the East Coast. Librarians must be aware of these differences before committing dollars to the process. Claribel Alegria, Manuel Alonso, Sandra Cisneros, Laura Esquivel, Esmeralda Santiago, Nicolasa Mohr, Mary Ellen Ponce and Judith Ortiz Cofer are some of the Hispanic authors whose work is being introduced to high school students as part of their reading lists. (A list of non-fiction to be included as part of a core collection may be found at the end of this article.)

Surveying and Connecting

Those of us working with Hispanic youth know all too well that the dropout rate for these high school students is alarmingly high. How are librarians and educators working to reverse this trend? To begin exploring the possibilities, I distributed a brief survey among a sample of bilingual teachers from elementary, middle and high school levels. Their responses revealed a lack of resources in their school libraries to support their curricula; oftentimes they have to purchase their materials. The school library program is not an integral part of their educational program. For those educators at the high school level, the answers were categorical and unanimous. When asked to name the most challenging issues in educating the Hispanic student, they cited low levels of literacy, lack of support from home in school affairs, poor language skills, lack of motivation, few if any life goals, and poor attendance. Another teacher cited the lack of books, lack of connection with sources, and lack of social family connections. A teacher from the elementary (Grade 5) level elaborated: "The most challenging issue in educating the Hispanic youth in the urban setting is motivating both the parents and the children to want to be successful.... The future is not looked at as something rewarding and positive, nor is education a very viable solution."

They all offered ideas for working in partnership with the public library and connecting with their school librarian. They also mentioned seeking funds to develop tutorial programs and explore mentoring. To create links between the school, home and library, said another teacher, would afford the opportunity to teach the parent and child why and how to set up goals. Librarians working in schools offering bilingual programs indicated that they do not administer the budget.

Bibliography

Books

Güereña, Salvador, and Vivian M. Pisano, eds. *Latino Periodicals: A Selection Guide.* Jefferson, N.C.: McFarland, 1998.

Muse, Daphne., ed. *The New Press Guide to Multicultural Resources for Young Readers.* New York: The New Press, 1997.

Schon, Isabel. *The Best of the Latino Heritage: A Guide to the Best Juvenile Books About Latino People and Cultures.* Lanham, Md.: The Scarecrow Press, 1997.

Articles

Agosto, Denise. "Bilingual Picture Books: Libros Para Todos." *School Library Journal* (August 1997): 38–39.

Amato, Anthony S."From the Desk of the Superintendent: 'We Will Never Be Last Again.'" *The Hartford Courant,* 24 Feb. 1999, A–15.

Bodipo-Memba, Alejandro. "Wage Gap Widens in 'English Only' States." *The Wall Street Journal* 26 Feb. 1999, A-2.

Freiband, Susan J. "Developing Collections for the Spanish Speaking." *RQ* (Spring 1996): 330–42.

Kulenik, Patricia L. "Communicating with Administrators Try a Survey." *The Book Report the Journal for Junior and Senior High School Librarians* (May/June 1998): 13–15.

Shapiro, Michael. "What About the Library Market?" *Publisher's Weekly* (August 1997): 47.

Tarin, Patricia A. "Books for the Spanish-Speaking Si Se Puede." *Library Journal* (July 1987): 25–29.

Taylor, Sally. "Mexico: A Growing Book Industry in Search of Readers." *Publisher's Weekly* (September 1998): 16–19.

Wilson, Patricia Potter, and Angus J. McNeil. "What's Keeping Principals from Understanding Libraries?" *School Library Journal* (September 1998): 114–116.

Organizations

REFORMA, National Organizations of Librarians Serving the Hispanic Community *http://latino.sscnet.ucla.edu/library/reforma/refonews.htm*

Center for the Study of Books in Spanish for Children and Adolescents *http://www.csusm.edu/campus_centers/csb* Director: Dr. Isabel Schon

Ethnic and Multicultural Information (EMIE) Bulletin Exchange *http://www.union.edu/PUBLIC LIBRARY/guide/mc_menu.html*

Selected List of Distributors of Materials for Children and Young Adults

Arte Publico Press
Pinata Books
University of Houston
Houston, Tx 77204-2090
800-633-ARTE
Fax: 713-743-2847

Bilingual Educational Services, Inc.
2514 South Grand Avenue
Los Angeles, CA 90007-9979
213-749-1820
800-448-6032
Fax 213-749-1820
www.besbooks.com
e-mail: Sales@besbooks.com
President: Jeff Penichet

The Bilingual Publications Co.
270 Lafayette Street
New York, NY 10012
212-431-3500
Fax 212-431-3567
e-mail: Linda Goodman@juno.com
President: Linda E. Goodman

Curbstone Press
321 Jackson Street
Willimantic, CT 06226-1738
860-423-5110
Fax: 860-423-9242
e-mail: curbston@connix.com
http://www.connix.com/~curbston/

Descarga
328 Flatbush Ave. Suite 180
Brooklyn, NY 11238
718-693-2966
Fax: 718-693-1316
Specialties: Recordings and videos

Educational Record Center, Inc.
3233 Burnt Mill Drive, Suite 100
Wilmington, NC 28403-2698
910-251-1235
800-438-1637
Fax Toll Free: 1-888-438-1637
e-mail: Descarga@aol.com

Giron Spanish Book Distributors
1443 West 18th Street
Chicago, Ill 60608
312-226-1406
Fax: 312-7381997

Ingram Book Company
One Ingram Blvd.
P.O. Box 3006
La Veigne, TN 37086-1986
800-732-8173

Lectorum
A Subsidiary of Scholastic Inc.
111 Eight Ave.
New York, NY 10011-5201
212-929-2833
Fax: 212-727-3035
http://www.lectorum.com
Representative: Carmen Rivera Ext. 220

Libros Latinos
P.O. Box 1103,
Redlands, CA 92373
909-793-8424
800-MI-LIBRO
Fax: 909-793-8423
e-mail: Libros@concentric.net

Libros Sin Fronteras
P.O. Box 2085
Olympia, WA 98507-2085
800-454-2767
360-357-4332
Fax: 360-357-4964
e-mail: Libros@win.com
www.win.com/libro
Owner/Director: Michael Shapiro

Madera Cinevideo
525 East Yosemite Avenue
Madera, CA 93638
209-661-6000
800-828-8118
Fax: 209-674-3650

Mariuccia
Iaconi Book Imports, Inc.

970 Tennessee Street
San Francisco, CA 94107
800-955-9577
Fax: 415-821-1596
e-mail: mibibook@IX.net.com
http://www.mibibook.com

Multi-Cultural Books and Videos, Inc.
28880 Southfield Road, Suite 183
Lathrup Village, Michigan 48076
800-567-2220
e-mail: multicultural @win.com.net
http://www.multiculbv.com
President: Rakesh Kumar

Live Oak Media
P.O. Box 652
Pine Plains, NY 12567
518-398-1010
Fax: 518-398-1070

National Textbook Co.
4255 West Touhy Ave
Lincolnwood, IL60646
847-679-5500
Fax: 847-674-5390

Ninos
P.O. Box 1603
Secaucus, NJ 07096-1603
800-634-3304
Fax: 1-201-583-3644

Santillana Publishing Company, Inc.
2105 NW, 86th Avenue
Miami, FL
305-591-9522

Puerto Rico

Editorial de la Universidad de Puerto Rico
Apartado 23322
San Juan, Puerto Rico 00931-3322

Instituto de la Cultura Puertorriquena
Apartado 9024184
San Juan, Puerto Rico 00902-4184
787-724-4215 and 724-4295
Fax: 787-723-0168

Isla
Puerto Rican Treasures from Caribe Direct
P.O. Box 9112
San Juan, PR 00909-0112
1-800-575-4752

Libros de Barlovento
Rene Grullon
San Juan, Puerto Rico 00902
Phone/Fax: 809-250-1868
e-mail: rgrullon@Caribe.net

Ediciones Huracan
Ave. González # 1002
Rio Piedras 00925
Puerto Rico
(787)763-7407
Fax: 787-763-7407

Mexico

Casa Autrey, S.A. de C.V.
Division Publicaciones
Av. Taxquena 1798,
Col. Paseos de Taxquena
Delegacion Coyoacan
C.P. 04250
624.0100
Fax: 624-0148

Fondo de Cultura Economica
Carretera Picacho — Ajusco # 227,
Col. Bosque del Pedregal
Del Tlalpan
DF 14200
Mexico
(5)227-4652
Fax: (5)227-4659
e-mail: ventas@fce.com.mx

Editorial Diana, S.A. de C.V.
Roberto Gayol # 1219,
DF 03100
Mexico
(5) 575-0711, 559-2700
Fax: (5) 575-3211/1818
e-mail: 4sales@diana.com.mx
http://diana.org.org.mx

Editorial Trillas, S.A. de C.V.
Av. Rio Churubusco # 385
Col. Gral. Pedro Maria Anaya
Del. Benito Juarez DF 03340
(5) 688-8388
Fax: (5) 604-1364

Editorial Patria
Renacimiento # 180
Col. San Juan Tlihuaca,
Del. Azcapotzalco
DF 02400
Mexico

(5) 561-8333/9299
Fax: (5)561-5231
e-mail: info@patriacultural.com.mex

VENEZUELA

Ediciones Ekare, A.C.
Av. Luis Roche, Edificio Banco del Libro
Altamira Sur
Caracas, Miranda 1062
Venezuela
582-263-0080/91
Fax: 582-263-3291
e-mail: books@ekare.com.ve
Contact: Maria C. Serrano

Selected Listing of Serials for Teens

Como Ves
El Sol
Eres
Geomundo
Latina Magazine Bilingue
Lowrider
Mi Vida Loca: A Magazine by Raza and for la Raza
National Geographic in Spanish
15 a 20
Saludos Hispanicos
Teen Angels

For Children

Colibri
Chispa
Turey, El Taino

Spanish Book Fairs

NATIONAL

Los Angeles Times Book Fair
April 24-25, 1999
UCLA Brentwood campus.
Fax: 213-237-5342
e-mail: festival.books@latimes.com

The Latino Book and Family Festival
Spring 1999: San Jose, Calif.
Summer 1999: Chicago.
Fall 1999: Houston, Texas
Contact: Kirk Whisler
e-mail: mexico@deltanet.com.

Miami Book Fair International
Miami-Dade Community College
Wolfson Campus
Fax: 305-237-3645

INTERNATIONAL

20th Feria Internacional del Libro — Mineria
March 12-21, 1999
AP 20-515, Mexico DF 01000
phone: 52-5-512-8723
Fax: 52-5-512-8956
e-mail: feria@tolsa.mineria.unam.mx

Bogota Feria Internacional del Libro
April 8-23, 1999
CORFERIAS
Carrera 40, No. 22C-47
P.O. Box 6843
Santafe de Bogota, D.C. Colombia
phone: 57-1-337-7676
Fax: 57-1-337-7272 or -7271
e-mail: camlibro@latino.net.co

24th Buenos Aires Feria Internacional del Libro
April 16-May 5, 1999
Avda Cordoba 744,
Pb 1, 1054 Buenos Aires, Argentina
phone: 54-1-322-2165
Fax: 54-1-325-5681
e-mail: fund@libro.stalink.net
Web site: *www.el-libro.com.ar*

Sao Paulo International Book Fair
plus SILAR 99
April 21-May 2, 1999
Expocenter Norte, Sao Paulo
Camara Brasileira Do Livro
Av. Ipiranga, 1267 10th andar
Sao Paulo, SP, Brazil
phone: 55-11-225-8277
Fax: 55-11-229-7436
e-mail: cbl@cbl-net.com.br
Web site: *www.cbl-net.com.br*

Feria Internacional del Libro de Guadalajara (FIL)
November-December 1999
A.P.39-130 Guadalajara 44190 Jalisco Mexico
phone: 52-3-610-0331
Fax: 52-3-812-2841
e-mail: msierra@udgserv.cencar.udg.mx or daucc@cun-yvm.cuny.edu

Part IV : Planning and Evaluating

Implementing New Services

James O. Carey

Overview

Strategic planning has become a very popular management tool for getting branch libraries, school media centers, and their parent organizations in touch with their constituents and on a productive path. Strategic planning is an excellent means of bringing an organization's good intentions front and center in the eyes of the people who work within that organization and the customers or patrons that the organization serves. Unfortunately, strategic planning sometimes takes so much time, energy, diplomacy, and money that the whole effort bogs down before those good intentions become useful outcomes. The purpose of this article is to review briefly some of the critical steps in the early stages of strategic planning, and then to focus on the action planning steps that can turn good intentions into useful outcomes. The article concludes with some brief comments on program implementation and evaluation.

Strategic Planning and Continuous Improvement

Before continuing, it will be useful to enumerate the steps in a typical model of strategic planning. Figure 1 (next page) is a fairly standard listing of strategic planning activities that will be referenced throughout the rest of this article.

Figure 1 includes an implementation step and a feedback line to indicate that strategic planning is an iterative process in which the results of evaluation are used to inform earlier planning stages and guide revisions and corrections in the current course of action. This iterative planning process is what we think of as the "continuous improvement" cycle in managing the productive efforts of an organization. The thinking is that to be most effective, libraries must determine needs, plan and implement programs to meet the needs, and then evaluate the outcomes of programs to determine whether the original needs have been met. If needs are met, then all is well and the library consolidates its progress and moves on to address new challenges. If needs have not been met, then results of evaluation are used to figure out why, make corrections, and redouble efforts to solve the problem. Figure 2 is a diagram of the continuous improvement process. Continuous improvement is an outcome of good strategic planning, but for practical purposes it can almost be thought of as synonymous with strategic planning.

One caveat about strategic planning is

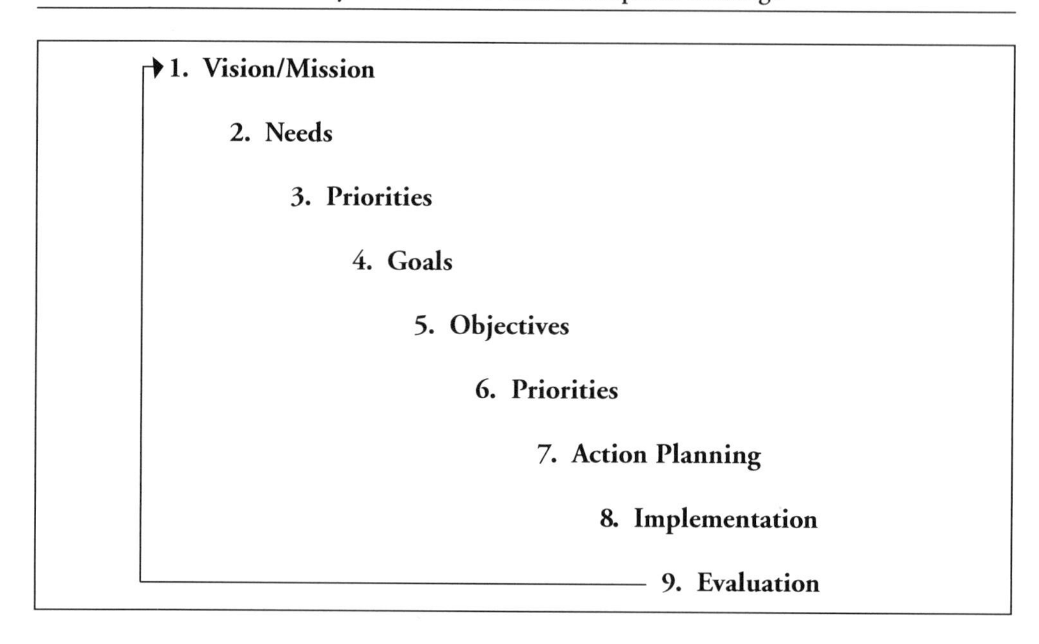

Figure 1. Model of typical steps in a generic planning process.

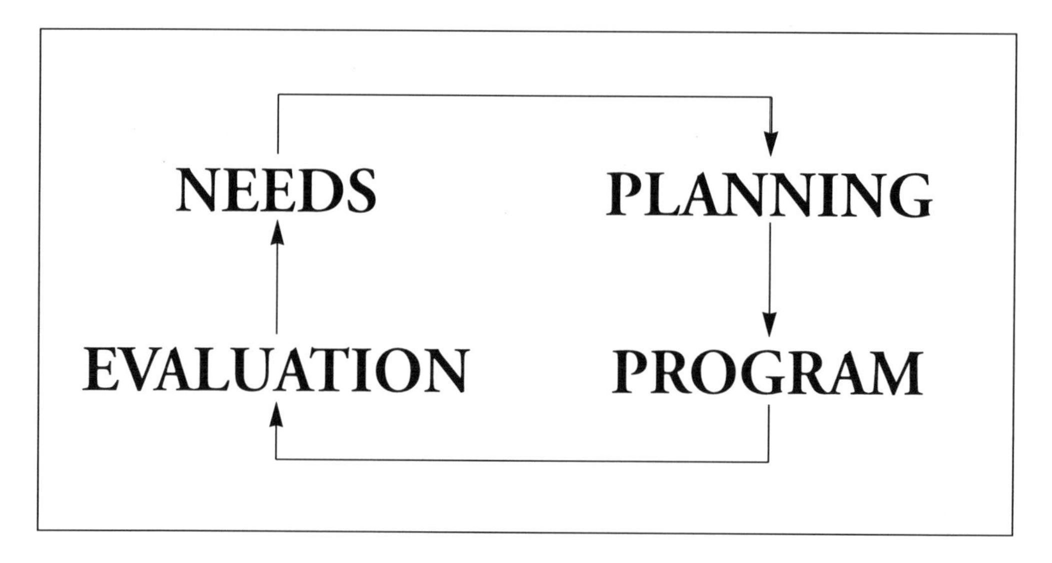

Figure 2. Continuous Improvement Process.

that to be truly effective the process must include those who work at the level of service delivery and those to whom services are delivered. Strategic planning must be a process that includes the interests of the entire community. This is particularly true in larger library systems or school districts where portions of a population have traditionally been underserved. If the participants in a strategic planning process are drawn only from higher levels of management, the library board or school board, and influential members of the political establishment and the community, then the results of the planning process will reflect the perspectives and interests of those participants. Granted, the views of many administrators and politicians are heart-felt and well intentioned; the problem is that as the level of responsibility increases, the knowledge of front-line operations and services decreases.

There was a time when providing equitable access meant unlocking the door of the library or media center and allowing all who approached to enter. This self-selecting approach to patron identification automatically creates under-representation of Hispanic and other minority segments of the population who have no tradition of library use. Equitable access more properly means the identification of all populations in a service area and the development of programs for taking services to patrons or bringing patrons to services. The point to be made here regarding strategic planning is that to have the desired effect on services, the planning process must include representation from all segments of the population and from those employees who are responsible for the day-to-day delivery of services. In cases of large library and school systems, the best approach to ensuring a planning process responsive to underserved portions of the community may be to institute strategic planning at the branch library or media center level. That is hard to do when there may be only a couple of professionals on staff, but in such cases clusters of three to five branches or media centers can be formed for planning based on geographic and service interests.

Early Stages of Strategic Planning

Most of us have been involved in a strategic-planning process at one time or another, and the steps we probably remember most are numbers one through five in Figure 1. This is the "good intentions" part of planning where we decide what we are all about and what we should be doing. Although these early steps are not the focus of this paper, some brief paragraphs follow on each step just to ensure that we have a common understanding of their meaning.

Step 1: Vision and Mission

Statements of a vision and mission have made their way over the past 20 years from private enterprise into public-sector service agencies. A *vision* is an optimistic, ideal view of the role and function of a library in its community, and often includes several statements of how the library wishes to be perceived. One statement of a library's vision could be, "The South County Branch Library will be the first choice of an informed citizenry for the free exercise of their rights to access information that will enhance the quality of their lives." A *mission* statement is more action-oriented than a vision. It provides general guidance for what the library should be doing. A mission statement could be as straight forward as, "The mission of the South County Branch Library is to collect, organize, and provide equitable access to recreational, educational, informational, and cultural resources to meet the changing needs of residents of all ages, and ethnic, cultural, and economic backgrounds." Vision and mission statements are useful for the view that they provide of our reasons for existing and our responsibilities as service agencies.

Step 2: Needs

Needs-assessment can be a long and complex process, involving all levels of a library's operations, programs, and service areas. At its heart, however, needs-assessment is a fairly simple concept. First, we establish a *desired status*; that is, a concept of what we want our library to be with regard to its internal operations and its collections, programs, services, and community impact. We establish this desired status by such activities as reviewing professional standards, looking at model programs in other libraries, looking at our vision and mission, and surveying the community. The next step in needs-assessment is to determine our *current status* on the items that have been specified in the desired status. This is accomplished with a scan of the library, its services, and the community. Then, to arrive at statements of needs, we compare the desired status with the current status and determine differences between where we are and where we want to be. Table 1 provides an example of these steps in needs assessment. It is clear in the example that a gap exists between the library's desired service standards for Hispanic youth and the actual standard of service being provided. When a gap exists between current and desired levels, a need has been identified.

Desired Status	All patrons should feel "ownership" in the library and experience an open, friendly, welcoming, receptive atmosphere.
Current Status	A survey of Hispanic youth in the South County Branch Library's service area indicates that they feel no identification with or affinity for the library as a physical place or as a provider of useful services.
Needs	1. Improve services to Hispanic youth. 2. Improve the perceptions that Hispanic youth hold of the library and its services.

Table 1. An Example of Needs Assessment

Step 3: Priorities

Only a brief comment will be made here about setting priorities because this step appears later in the discussion of step six. In setting priorities at this stage, the staff decides which needs will be carried forward in the strategic-planning process. It takes lots of time and effort to work through all of the planning steps. If it can be determined up front that there is just no way that funds are available to meet some needs this year, or other needs could be put off for later consideration, then it makes sense to table them. Remember, however, that "table" should not mean "forget." Planning should be for continuous improvement, and legitimate needs that have been documented should not be placed in the back of a file drawer and ignored forever.

Steps 4 and 5: Goals and Objectives

We are all familiar with goals and objectives, so just a reminder is needed here of some of the characteristics that distinguish the two.

When speaking of goals, we are

describing desired outcomes for the library that

- Are derived directly from the needs identified in step two
- Are long range — to be accomplished in two to five years
- Are optimistic
- Guide the direction of a management process or a program of service

When speaking of objectives, we are describing desired outcomes for the library that

- Are derived directly from one of the goals stated in step four
- Are short range — to be accomplished within a year
- Are realistic — can really be obtained
- Are measurable — results can be observed
- Specify the outcomes of a management process or a program of services

Table 2 follows the example begun in Table 1 and illustrates an appropriate goal and objectives. You will see that the goal is derived directly from the need, almost a rephrasing of the need with a few additional details. The objectives explain how the goal will be accomplished by enumerating very specific programmatic outcomes.

Need	1. Improve services to Hispanic youth.
Goal	1. Increase circulation of Spanish-language titles and English-language titles on Latino culture and traditions.
Objectives	1.1. The number of children's fiction titles in Spanish that are checked out this year will be 50 percent higher than last year.
	1.2. The number of English-language titles on Latino culture and traditions that are checked out this year will be 50 percent higher than last year.
	1.3. Etc.
Need	2. Improve the perceptions that Hispanic youth hold of the library and its services.
Goal	2. Over the next two years change perceptions of the library among Hispanic youth from average negative to average positive.
Objectives	2.1. Create an atmosphere in the South County Branch Library with which Hispanic youth can identify.

Objectives ***(cont.)***

a. Within the next month, change signage from English to bilingual.
b. Within the next six months, train children's, youth services, and reference librarians in awareness of Latino culture.
c. Within the next year, train children's, youth services, and reference librarians in conversational Spanish words and phrases appropriate for a library setting.
d. Hire a bilingual librarian in children's services
e. Etc.

2.2. Develop relationships with other public and private agencies that serve Hispanic youth in the South County Branch Library service area.

a. Within the next six months, establish working relationships with media specialists for publicizing South County's programs in all public and private schools in the service area.
b. Within the next six months, establish working relationships with youth group and club leaders who have contact with Hispanic youth for publicizing South County's programs in clubs and other organizations in the service area.
c. Etc.

2.3. Etc.

Table 2. An Example of Goals and Objectives

Action Planning Stages of Strategic Planning

This is the point in strategic planning where we often feel pleased (and relieved) to have made it this far. After all, there is a set of relevant, progressive goals and objectives on paper. Time to take a break, relax a bit, and distribute our work to appropriate department heads and employees and watch our operations improve and the new programs and services begin, right? Wrong. This is a critical point in the process where additional planning steps must be taken or the momentum will stall and our good intentions will never become the useful outcomes that we envision.

Step 6: Priorities

Taking time to set priorities among the goals and objectives will ensure that we make both quick and lasting impact. Trying to attack needs on all fronts simultaneously is frustrating and counterproductive, because there are seldom sufficient resources and energy to accomplish everything at once. Only small, slow changes are likely in any one effort, and people soon lose their focus and enthusiasm for change. A preferred path is to set priorities, focus energy, and demonstrate impact. People then see progress and enthusiasm build. There are three rules of thumb for setting priorities.

• First, be practical. Set high priority on objectives that can be met with minimum effort and expense. These are often little things that fall into the "Why didn't I think of that before?" category. For example, Objective 2.1.a in Table 2, should be around the top of a list of priorities because it could be achieved in a small library over a weekend for hundreds — rather than thousands — of dollars.

• Second, be political. Set high priority on objectives that represent *legitimate, deeply* felt needs among members of the community (your patrons), management (your boss and central administration), and the parent agency (library board, school board, county government). This is not to be confused with creating projects to satisfy the whims of a local politician or a strong public interest group. Remember that you have already developed legitimate objectives through a careful planning process; now there are good reasons to give priority to solving needs that will win the favor of those who control your working conditions or your funding. For example, if an influential county commissioner has had a longstanding interest in cooperation among school and public libraries, then Objective 2.2.a in Table 2 should be high on your list of priorities.

• Third, be efficient. Set high priority on urgent needs that will have high impact. Figure 3 (next page) is a graphical representation of how to combine the considerations of urgency and impact. For example, you might judge Objective 1.1 in Table 2 to be of fairly high urgency and very high impact and place it where it appears in Figure 3. On the other hand, because of your knowledge of the Hispanic community you might judge Objective 1.2 in Table 2 to be of fairly high urgency but rather low impact, and place it accordingly in Figure 3. By working through your objectives and noting each on this graphic display, you can get a quick look at high priority objectives (grouped in the top left corner), medium priority objectives (grouped around the dotted line), and low priority objectives (grouped in the bottom right corner). Once priorities are set, you are ready to begin action planning.

Step 7: Action Planning

The step where people, tasks, and timelines are brought together is called action-planning. Sometimes the objectives you have written are ready to take forward into action-planning and sometimes they are not. Take a look at Objective 2.1.a in Table 2 and note that the only decision you need to make before proceeding with your sign project is whether to make them in-house or to hire someone from outside to do it for you. You would probably make a quick, informal decision and then move on into an action plan to get your new signage done. Now compare that objective with Objective 2.1.b. There is a big difference in the number of decisions that need to be made before you can carry out the objective. You know that you want to train librarians in cultural awareness, but just how are you going to do it? How long will the training

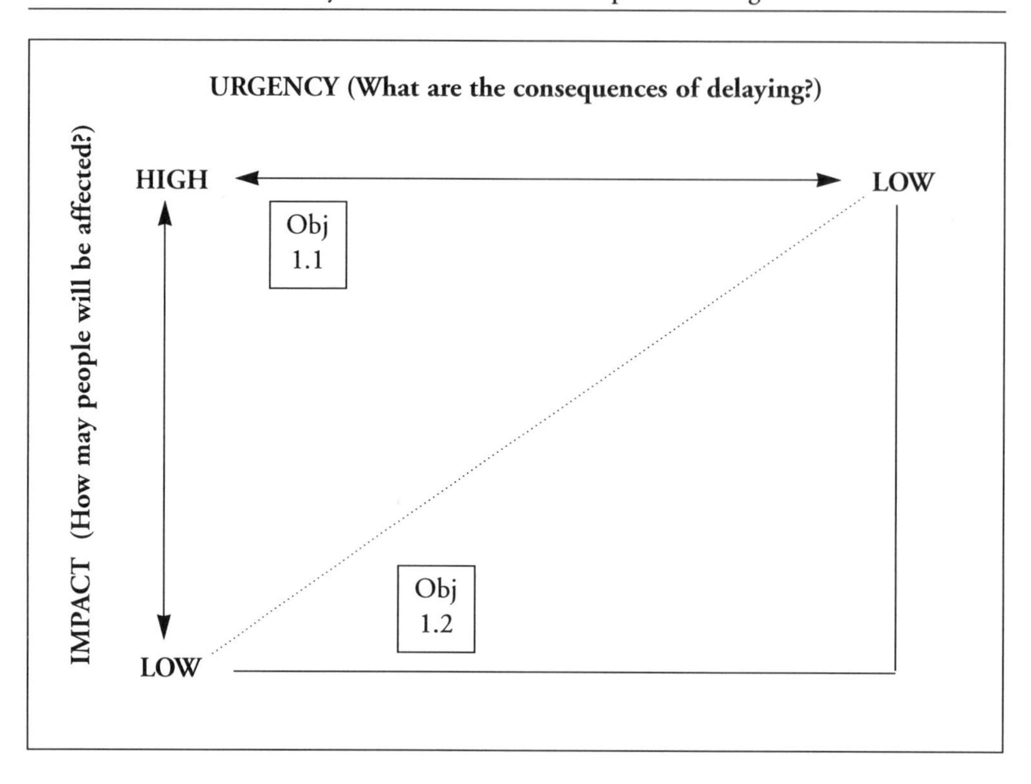

Figure 3. Graphical Representation of Urgency and Impact.

last? Will you develop the training yourself, or send librarians to the junior college for a course, or hire a consultant, or get someone from the central office, or the regional consortium? When you have an objective that raises lots of questions about implementation, you need to take a substep under action-planning that is called "means and methods analysis." The substep is also called "solution strategies," but it is really logical problem solving that we use every day as we go about our normal business. The steps are

- Define the need or problem (this has already been done through needs-assessment and writing goals and objectives).
- Describe the setting in which the objective(s) will be accomplished, paying particular attention to resources that will support your solutions and constraints that may block or limit your range of solutions.
- List possible solutions for accomplishing your objective (usually a good small-group brainstorming task).
- Analyze the alternative solutions, paying attention to resources and constraints.
- Select the best solution, or a combination of solutions, or assemble pieces of several solutions that will accomplish the objective.

After finishing this substep, action-planning can be finished by listing the tasks that must be completed, assigning responsibility for each task to a specific person or committee, and establishing time lines for completion of each task. Effective, timely completion of a project or program is a direct result of the commitment of the people involved, and one good way to secure commitment is by writing names next to tasks and timelines on a planning document that is distributed to all people working on the project. A Gantt chart is a planning document that gets all of this information on a single sheet of paper. It can be a great project organizer and project management tool. Included at the end of this article is a sample of a Gantt chart that was prepared for Objective 2.1.b from Table 2. The assumption is that a decision was made to develop and deliver the cultural sensitivity training using in-house personnel.

The Implementation and Evaluation Stages of Strategic Planning

STEP 8: IMPLEMENTATION

The implementation step is the carrying out of the action planning completed in Step 7, but progress must be monitored and the projected time and budget projections must be compared with actual accomplishments. This description of implementation is, of course, vastly oversimplified, because implementation includes everything from creating an administrative structure to developing a management style. Two summary points are that implementation should be faithful to the objectives developed in strategic planning, and the evaluation approach described below can be employed during implementation to gather information for keeping things on track.

STEP 9: EVALUATION

Needs, goals, and objectives are all about differences between where we are now and where we want to be. When we plan, develop and implement new or improved programs of services, we are attempting to decrease or eliminate those differences. Evaluation is the process of gathering the information that we need to make decisions about how much change we have made, and whether the change has been beneficial. Following the Gantt chart at the end of this article is a sample project evaluation planning chart for organizing the questions that will be asked, the types and sources of information needed to answer the question(s), the methods and instruments for collecting information, and the methods for analyzing and reporting the results. The whole purpose for evaluation is to generate information that will feed back into the strategic-planning process where we will again assess needs to see whether our programs and services have had the desired effect.

Summary

It is easy to get frustrated with the process of strategic planning because it really is higher-order problem-solving activity where there are no simple right and wrong answers. The results of each strategic-planning effort are unique, incorporating the thinking of all participants and partners in the library enterprise. If you take the time to figure out where your programs and services are going, you will have the concomitant satisfaction of being able to figure out when you have arrived. That satisfaction with planned programs that are on track and producing results is far superior to the alternative of getting this week's crisis under control only to wonder when next week's crisis will strike.

A more complete treatment of strategic planning in library settings may be found in the Himmel and Wilson book from ALA Publications.[1]

Note

1. Ethel Himmel and Bill Wilson with the ReVision Committee of the Public Library Association, *Planning for Results: A Public Library Transformation Process* (Chicago: American Library Association, 1998).

South County Branch Library

Project Planning Gantt Chart

Objective 2.1.b: Within the next six months, train children's, youth services and reference librarians in awareness of Latino culture.
Strategy: Design and develop training in house using staff personnel.

Tasks	Responsible Personnel	Timeline in Months					
		1	2	3	4	5	6
Review need for training	Mary	■					
Analyze learners	Mary and Carlos	■					
Analyze content	Mary and Carlos	■					
Write learning objectives	Mary and Carlos		■				
Plan teaching/learning strategies	Mary and Linda		■				
Prepare draft instructional materials	Linda		■	■			
Try out instructional materials with 1 learner	Mary and Linda			■			
Revise materials as needed for effectiveness	Linda			■	■		
Produce final instructional materials	Linda				■		
Publicize workshop series	Sonia		■	■	■		
Schedule and reserve workshop facilities	Sonia	■					
Conduct workshop series	Mary, Carlos, and Linda					■	
Evaluate results of workshop series	Mary and Carlos						■
Plan followup as needed	Carlos						■

South County Branch Library

Project Evaluation Planning Chart

Objective 2.2.a: Within the next six months, establish working relationships with media specialists for publicizing South County's programs in all public and private schools in the service area.

Statement of the Need, Goal, or Objective	2.2.a. Within the next six months, establish working relationships with media specialists for publicizing South County's programs in all public and private schools in the service area.
Evaluation Question or Questions	1. What % of Latino Youth in the schools are aware of our services? 2. Are media specialists who serve Latino Youth in the schools aware of our services? 3. Are our publicity materials displayed prominently in locations accessible to Latino Youth in schools?
Audience(s) for Evaluation Reporting	1, 2, 3. System Director, Unit Staff, Public Schools, Community Organizations
Types and Sources of Information Needed to Answer the Question(s)	1. Perceptions of Latino students in the schools 2. Perceptions of media specialists in the schools 3. Personal observation
Methods and Instruments for Collecting Information	1. Survey 1-b. Phone interview of media specialists 1-c. Site visit with notes
Methods for Analyzing and Reporting the Results	1. Mean and range displayed in Excel graph 2. Tally of responses with notes about content of anecdotal comments 3. Descriptions of locations and traffic patterns

Subject Access to Fiction: A Case Study Based on the Works of Pat Mora

Elaine Yontz

When I'm trying to persuade my students that service to people of Hispanic heritage will be a strong concern in their professional lives, no matter what kind of library work they do and no matter where in this country they do it, I could refer to the United States Census Bureau's *Current Population Reports*, which shows that residents of Hispanic origin steadily increased, in both real numbers and percentage of the population, every year from 1980 through 1996 and that the increase is projected to continue in each year through 2050.[1] But what I usually do is tell them some true stories.

One of the stories took place in Chiefland, Florida, in the summer of 1997. Chiefland, with an approximate population of 1,989,[2] is situated in north-central Florida, about one hour's drive from several equally obscure places. In spite of the absence of such amenities as a movie theatre or a Red Lobster Restaurant, Chiefland is a tri-county trading center, largely because of the presence of a Wal-Mart SuperStore. I was in Wal-Mart in Chiefland on a day when I was desperate for a paperback book. I approached a woman in an employee's uniform who was stocking shelves in Cosmetics and asked, "Where are the books?" She looked at me quizzically. Assuming that I must have mumbled, I repeated my question more distinctly and a little louder. Fortunately another customer was close by and able to direct me to the books, because the employee could not speak enough English to understand or answer my question. Shortly after that I started to notice the bilingual signs in the grocery-stores in such Florida towns as Archer and Bronson, places even less cosmopolitan than Chiefland. I'm convinced that if this is happening in Chiefland, Archer, and Bronson, it will happen wherever my students find their jobs.

The provision of bibliographic access to library materials is one of the vital public services of a library. Needed materials which cannot be found by patrons or by the librarians who help them represent a waste of valuable resources and do not, for practical purposes, even exist. Most libraries today attempt to provide cost-effective bibliographic access to materials by using catalog records from bibliographic utilities or other nationally accessible databases. The number and appropriateness of the access points provided on these catalog records have serious implications for patron service in libraries of all types and sizes in all parts of the United States.

As a method for investigating the current effectiveness of subject and genre access to fiction which would be of interest to Hispanic youths, I imagined myself to be an elementary-school media specialist in Chiefland, Florida, an Anglo librarian with little knowledge of Spanish, newly faced with the need to locate materials for Hispanic students. The works of Pat Mora would be very valuable to such a librarian. I examined the bibliographic records for Mora's writings which appear in the two databases I think my alter ego would consult first. One is SUNLINK, the union catalog of Florida's K–12 public school media centers.[3] The other is the union catalog of Florida's State University System, the Library User Information Service (LUIS).[4] SUNLINK is produced by Brodart Automation, which uses the Library of Congress database as its primary resource.[5] Records in the LUIS database come from the Online Computer Library Center (OCLC), and complete Library of Congress records are chosen for use when available. Since both of these databases rely heavily on Library of Congress cataloging, the records found can be assumed to be comparable to the records provided by other vendors or bibliographic utilities and thus offer a useful reading on the quality of cataloging which is available for use nationally.

Findings

Three systems for controlled-vocabulary subject access are used on the records. Library of Congress Subject Headings (LCSH), found in the "big red books," is one system. The LCSH is designed for research libraries used by adults. However, this system is widely used for other kinds of collections as well. Many libraries and groups of libraries find that the cost-effectiveness of using Library of Congress cataloging records without doing local editing outweighs the disadvantage of using a subject system which is not ideal for their needs. Topical LCSH headings appear in MARC field 650 with a second indicator of zero.

The second system for subject access is the Annotated Card Program. The AC Program is maintained by the Library of Congress and is intended for collections used by children. The AC Program is described at the beginning of volume one of each edition of the LSCH "red books" and in Joanna Fountain's *Subject Headings for School and Public Libraries: An LCSH/Sears Companion*.[6] Topical AC headings appear in MARC field 650 with a second indicator of one.[7]

A third system is Bilindex, a "bilingual Spanish-English subject heading list" the provides "Spanish equivalents to Library of Congress subject headings." Edited by Robert Cabello-Argandoña, this list was first published in paper in 1984. The FirstSearch database reports several paper and digital supplements published by Floricanto Press.[8]

Twenty-seven editions of works by Mora were found in SUNLINK and LUIS. The titles included fiction, poetry, sound recordings, videos, and a kit. No uniform subject search will retrieve all the records by Mora, however. Five records, over one-fifth of the total, included no controlled subject headings which indicate relevance to Hispanic readers.

Twelve unique subject headings from LCSH or AC which relate the works to Hispanic interests were discovered. The most often used is "Mexican Americans," which appears on seven records. The AC heading "Spanish Language Materials — Bilingual" is used on six records. Other headings used more than once are "Mexico" (three occurrences), "Folklore-Guatemala" (two occurrences), and "Spanish Language Materials," an AC heading for monolingual Spanish works (three occurrences). Headings which appeared one time apiece were "Mexican American Women," "Children's Poetry,"

"American-Translations into Spanish," "Posadas" (Social custom), "Spanish Language–Readers," and "Southwest, New."

Five instances of spurious headings, which appear to represent a misunderstanding of either LCSH or AC practice, were also found. "Spanish Language—Bilingual" appeared on four records. This seems an obvious attempt to use the valid AC heading "Spanish Language Materials—Bilingual." But what a difference a word makes to the computer. This kind of omission will prevent titles on the same subject from indexing together when a controlled-vocabulary search is used. The other doubtful heading, "Bilingual Books—English-Spanish," was a creative rendering which I could find validated nowhere.

Two records included Bilindex headings. Both of these records were created at the Library of Congress and enhanced by the Chicago Public Library. Since no other LC records in the study included Bilindex headings, these additional access points were evidently added by Chicago Public. Mower's report that LC does not using Bilindex and that Chicago Public is among the libraries that do would appear to be validated here.[9] The Bilindex headings used are "Cumpleanos-Novela," "Mercados-Novela," "Mexico-Novela," "Contar," "Cuentos en rima," "Materiales en espanol," "Materiales en espanol—Bilingue," "Desiertos-Poesia," and "Poesia estadounidense."

Eight incidents of multiple editions of the same book were found. The subject cataloging for different editions of the same book was consistent in only three of the eight cases. In one case, the records for two different editions of the same book had no subject fields in common.

Another possibility for subject access in catalogs that support keyword searching of this field is MARC field 520, the Summary Note. Twenty-six of the 27 records included a 520 field. Twenty-two of these 27 included terms in the 520 field which might be found by a determined Anglo searcher. These terms included "Bilingual" (five occurrences), "Chica" (four occurrences), "Chicana," "Posadas," "Mexican," "Mexico," "Mexican-American" (two occurrences), "Migrant" (two occurrences), "Southwest," "Spanish" (two occurrences), and "Tio" (two occurrences).

Discussion and Recommendations

My alter ego in Chiefland may have some trouble finding Mora's works. No single subject-searching strategy will retrieve all the records, or even most of them. Also striking and distressing is the lack of any Hispanic-related subject headings on some records and the inconsistent subject cataloging on different editions of the same title.

Much of the cataloging available through vendors and bibliographic utilities is created at the Library of Congress. Some of the attributes of the cataloging produced there are logical consequences of LC's priorities and organization. The Library of Congress has a primary patron base, which is Congress, and service to that patron base is LC's first priority.[10] To help other libraries is part of LC's mission, but their main focus, appropriately, is on their primary constituency. Another factor is that LC is a big place. Cataloging is done in many different departments. Works by the same author, even different editions of the same title, may be handled by different groups of people.

To lobby for a certain amount of consistency in the cataloging produced for national use is reasonable. Likewise, we should encourage utilities and vendors to catalog with more sensitivity to special populations. As service to patrons of Hispanic heritage becomes more important to all types of libraries throughout the United States, perhaps we will see some improvements.

On the other hand, it is unlikely that distant catalogers will ever produce records which are ideal for each local catalog. Gregor and Mandel and Chan have discussed the elusive nature of inter-indexer consistency.[11] Individual librarians must accept ultimate responsibility for the quality and effectiveness of their catalogs. This is a patron service that can be provided only at home, by someone who knows and cares about the local situation. This is the reason that all librarians must know the basics of troubleshooting and editing a MARC catalog.

So how would I suggest that my Chiefland media specialist make her collection and catalog more useful to her Hispanic patrons, now? The current subject accessibility will help her find a few appropriate titles, which will give her ideas for authors and publishers to try. As she finds and acquires these titles, she should add one or more access points to each catalog record to insure consistent accessibility in the school catalog. The LCSH heading Hispanic Americans might be a good choice. Alternatively, she might decide to put a phrase of her own making into MARC field 690, the tag for Local Subject-Added Entry, into a Target Audience field (521), or into a 520 field. I would invite her to go to the Huddle House for coffee, and I'd show her on a napkin how simple these fields are to formulate: 650: 0: =a Hispanic Americans; 690: : =a Hispanic topics; 521: : =a Hispanic students; 520: : =a Hispanic topics.

I'd tell her that having a consistent access point which she controls will insure that she and her patrons can locate these items quickly. I'd also be sure she understood that this kind of editing can be done by anyone who can read, think, and type. I know of a media center for which parent volunteers working under the direction of the librarian put a consistent 520 field on every record in the catalog. It can be done.

I'll end this article with another story I tell my students when I'm trying to help them see that service to people of Hispanic heritage has something to do with them, whoever they are. In the fall of 1994, during a morning plane trip to a conference, I was reading Joel Garreau's *The Nine Nations of North America*, specifically his chapter on MexAmerica, which says, "the Southwest is now what all of Anglo North America will soon be — a place where the largest minority will be Spanish-speaking."[12] I arrived at my small hotel and got into my room before the maids had finished cleaning. There was a Spanish-language station on the radio, and the maids spoke no English. And where do you think I was? Miami? Or perhaps San Antonio, Santa Fe, New York, or Los Angeles? Not at all. I was in Milwaukee, in the heart of North America. If service to Hispanic patrons is not yet a major concern of your library, it will be soon. Providing effective subject access to materials aimed at children and young adults of Hispanic heritage should be a part of your palette of care and concern for this special, growing population.

Notes

1. United States Bureau of the Census, "No. 19. Resident Population, by Hispanic Origin Status, and Projections," Current Population Reports, P25-1095 and P25-1130; and Population Paper Listing PPL-57. 1997, *http://www.census.gov/population/www/* (11 Feb. 1999).

2. Susan S. Floyd, ed., "1998 Florida Statistical Abstract" (Gainesville, Fla.: University of Florida Bureau of Economic and Business Research, 1998): 15.

3. Florida Department of Education, "Welcome to SUNLINK on the World Wide Web," *http://sunlink.brodart.com/* (14 Feb. 1999)

4. Florida Center for Library Automation, "WebLUIS," *http://webluis.fcla.edu/cgi-bin/cgiwrap/fclwlui/webluis* (14 Feb. 1999).

5. Brodart Automation, "Retrospective Conversion," *http://www.brodart.com/auto/aretr.htm* (14 Feb. 1999).

6. Joanna Fountain, *Subject Headings for School and Public Libraries: An LCSH/Sears Companion* (Englewood, Col.: Libraries Unlimited, 1996).

7. A discrepancy in subject cataloging occurs when attempting to differentiate between subject and genre. Subject headings deal with "aboutness," while genre terms tell the type of material. Although a specific MARC field, the 655, has been defined for genre terms, genre terms are still found in field 650 in many catalogs. This is true for the records examined in this study.

8. See Robert L. Mowery, "Spanish Subject Headings in ILLINET Online," *Illinois Libraries* 77 (Winter 1995): 32–34. Attempts to ascertain the current status of Bilindex have yielded inconclusive results to date.

9. Mowery, 32.

10. Library of Congress, "The Mission and Strategic Priorities of the Library of Congress, FY 1997–2004," *http://lcweb.loc.gov/ndl/mission.html* (15 Feb. 1999).

11. Lois Mai Chan, "Inter-Indexer Consistency in Subject Cataloging," *Information Technology and Libraries* 8 (December 1989): 349–358; and Dorothy Gregor and Carol A. Mandel, "Cataloging Must Change!" *Library Journal* 116 (April 1, 1991): 42–47.

12. Joel Garreau, *The Nine Nations of North America* (New York: Avon Books, 1982): 210–211.

HISPANIC DEMOGRAPHICS AND IMPLICATIONS FOR MEDIA SERVICES

Alice Robbin

Equal access to information for everyone and removal of barriers to library and information services are central policy goals of the library profession. Developing effective policy for library services for youth of Hispanic and Latino origin depends on the stock of available knowledge about the characteristics of these communities.[1] As Dyer and Robertson-Kozan state, if we are going to provide services to Hispanic and Latino children, we need to understand their informational and social needs, including their "cultural heritages, various languages, socio-economic backgrounds, socialization patterns, and preferred learning modes of groups within the community."[2] Some of the salient demographic and socio-economic characteristics of children of Hispanic- and Latino-origin in the United States which are correlates and predictors of library use are discussed here.

The first part of this article briefly discusses a theoretical framework on which the information base about children rests, called the "Investments-in-Children" perspective. Part two synthesizes some of the accumulated evidence that contributes to evaluating options and alternatives and developing wise and realistic policy for library services for Hispanic and Latino children. Part three considers why library programs may not have succeeded and calls for action. Concluding remarks offer strategies for examining the library's current mission and its policy on programs and services for Hispanic and Latino young people.

Part One: Modeling System Properties and Their Relationships

The policy goals of equal access to information and removal of barriers to library and information services make two assumptions: (1) structural characteristics of the system impede access to and use of library and information services, and (2) life chances are not equally "distributed" in the population. A conceptual model of the system assumes relationships between principal institutions, such as family, church and

Author's Note: I would like to acknowledge Dr. William Summers, School of Information Studies, Florida State University, for the stimulating conversations on the history of the public library, and my graduate assistant Ms. Diane d'Angelo, who identified and tracked down many more sources than were used in this paper.

other neighborhood and community-based organizations, school and government and the library, and makes hypotheses about the relative contribution of each institution to the library and about interactions and interdependencies between institutions and library use and services.[3]

The policy model on which the goals of the library profession rest makes another assumption, however, which alters the simple, uni-directional causal order of relationships. Implicit in library policy goals is a conception of the library as a critical social change agent, and, thus, an influential institution that can modify the policies and practices of the other social institutions, with a principal effect on the family.

The second assumption about the "distribution of life chances" posits that the properties of individuals in a population vary in several dimensions related to their success (attainment) in accessing information. A theoretical model that guides much of our information base about children rests on a conception of the relationship between choice, investment, and success, called the "Investments-in-Children" perspective.[4] Following Haveman and Wolfe, Figure 1 models the assumed relationships between family background variables, social choices, parental choices, and young-adult choices.[5] Attainment (success) is therefore a function of a complex array of variables.[6]

Children's success, no matter how *success* is defined, rests on investments that parents and society make in their children. Choices that families make and what happens inside families have a direct effect on whether children use libraries. Parents have objectives, options, and constraints.[7] Family income, the time parents have to allocate to their children, their own educational attainment, psychological stability, resiliency, attitudes and values all contribute to the environment in which their children grow up. Because families are the major social agent for producing human capital, the social and economic well-being of the family significantly affects whether other social institutions have sufficient resources to conduct their "business." Children, in their young adult years, are also independent decision makers. They decide whether to stay in school, get pregnant, obtain employment, smoke cigarettes, apply for welfare, and so on. In addition to the family, children are nurtured in the "nest" of neighborhoods that form their community, and this "nest" also influences family life as well as other institutions. Geographic and residential location also contribute, as do parental and social choices about where a family locates.

Society makes choices through government policies about the extent to which the family unit will be supported. Government financing represents a form of "public promises,"[8] investing resources in schooling, preschool child care, family income support, controlling crime and drugs, ensuring employment opportunities for parents, and so on.[9] Government has a direct effect on schools and an indirect effect on the library through the school. The school plays an important role in supporting the concept of the library, principally through the curriculum.

This conception of the determinants of attainment ("success") forms the basis for a large number of data and record-keeping systems that are designed to carry out the constitutional, legislative, and administrative mandates of government, as well as programmatic functions of non-governmental institutions, including the library. Selected data from governmental sources on the characteristics of the Hispanic and Latino population are presented, to illuminate understanding and future decisions about library services for Spanish-speaking children. Data on the demographic, economic well being, health, and educational attainment charac-

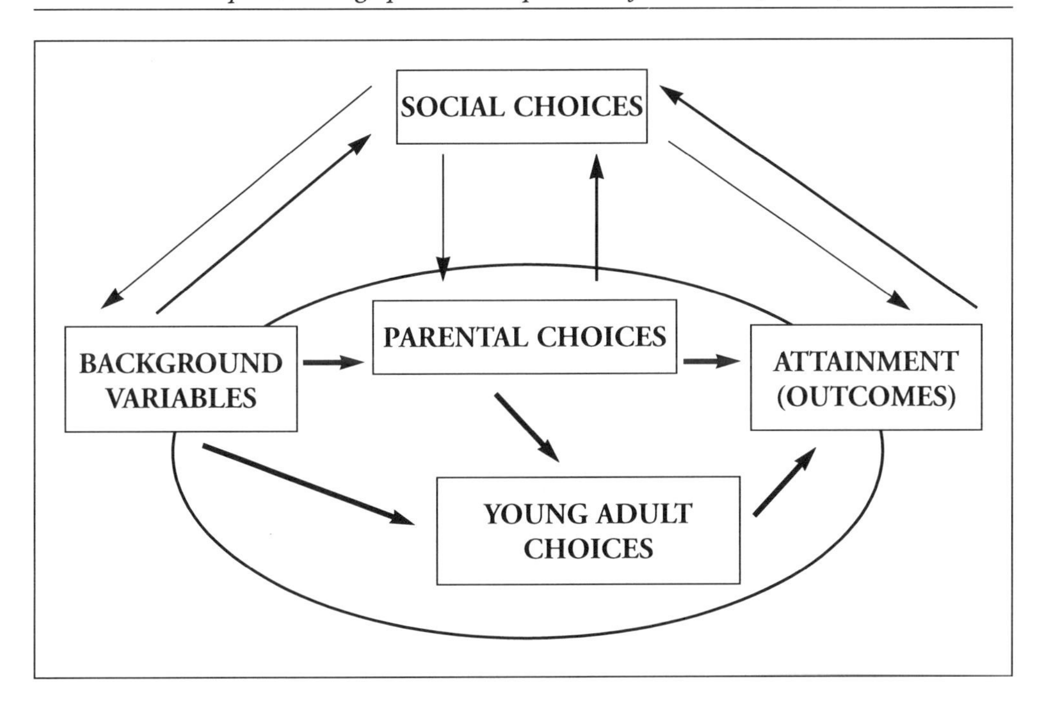

Figure 1. Simple Model Determinants and Correlates of Attainments and Choices of Children and Youth (Investments-in-Children Model)
Source: Robert Haveman and Barbara Wolf, *Succeeding Generations: On the Effects of Investment in Children* (New York: Russell Sage Foundation, 1994).
Key: Heavy lines indicate strong relationships, thinner lines indicate reduced or minimal effects. Ellipse indicates the primary factors that influence outcomes.

teristics of the Spanish-speaking populations are compared to the general population.

Two important caveats must be stated. First, a good deal of the data discussed below were collected nearly 10 years ago, and thus their informational content is somewhat degraded. Nevertheless, more recent data are consistent with the earlier trends. Second, these data reflect population aggregates. There are also significant differences in the Spanish-speaking population that are a function of their country of origin, time of arrival in the United States, generation or cohort, and membership in different ethnic groups. These differences are critical for developing appropriate user services; however, this paper is not designed as a comparative analysis of different ethnic groups, but seeks, instead, to understand the Spanish-speaking population at a national level.

Part Two: Demography and Indicators of Well-Being of Spanish-Speaking Youth[10]

The revised rules for U.S. immigration law after 1965 resulted in an expansion of immigrants from many different countries, but particularly from Asia and the Western Hemisphere. Large-scale illegal immigration began during the 1960s and increased during the 1970s and 1980s, but many of these formerly illegal immigrants acquired legal status under programs authorized in 1986 and 1990.[11] During the 1980s, the United States also experienced large groups of refugees from Western Hemisphere countries, particularly, Cuba and Central America.

More than 25 years of immigration have altered the racial, ethnic, and generational composition of American society. Immigration from Latin and Central America has contributed significantly to population growth.[12] The 1990 Census of Population recorded nearly 22 million people, or almost nine percent of the U.S. population, who identified themselves as "Persons of Hispanic Origin."[13] "Hispanic origin" counted people who identified themselves as Mexican, Puerto Rican, Cuban, and other Hispanics and Latinos of the Caribbean, Central American and South American regions.[14] In 1990, Mexicans constituted the largest group, followed by Puerto Rican and Cuban origin.[15] Distinct differences in socioeconomic and demographic characteristics, immigrant, and incorporation experiences exist among the different Spanish speaking ethnic groups.[16]

The cumulative impact of U.S. immigration will have significant effects on the future racial and ethnic composition of American society.[17] The Spanish-speaking resident population is projected to grow to 12.6 percent of the total population by 2010; to 16.3 percent, by 2020; almost 20 percent, by 2030; and to nearly 25 percent by 2050.[18] Hispanic-origin persons will constitute the largest minority group in the population, and the one that has experienced the greatest increase in population over half a century. This projected growth is due to a population of younger age cohorts that experiences higher than average birth rates. The Hispanic-Latino population is much younger than the population as a whole (median age of the white population is 38.9; the total population, 35.7; and the Hispanic-Latino population, 27 years).[19] Spanish-speaking ethnic groups have the highest fertility rates of all ethnic groups in the population.

Economic Security and Well-Being

The distribution of income and wealth of the Spanish-speaking population differs significantly from the U.S. population as a whole. About 52 percent of the Spanish-speaking households earn under $25,000, compared to about 34 percent of all households.[20] The differential in per capita income in 1989 between the U.S. population as a whole and persons of Hispanic origin is very large: $14,420 to $8,400, U.S. and Hispanic origin populations, respectively.[21]

Furthermore, the differential is more striking when the statistics for the population as a whole above and below the poverty level are examined, particularly for the age cohort 17 years and below. More than 40 percent of Hispanic children under 17 — versus about 36 percent of the total population — now live in poverty, and the percentage of Hispanic children living in poverty has increased since 1980, when it was recorded at 33 percent.[22] Data from 1996 indicate that 40 percent of Hispanic children resided in families under 100 percent of poverty, compared to 10 percent of white, non–Hispanic families.[23]

The large differential in income is also reflected in home ownership, which is an important indicator of income security. About 60 percent of Hispanic families — in contrast to 32 percent of white families — rent rather than own their own home.[24]

Another salient characteristic of

economic well-being is the presence of two-parent households. Family structure significantly influences economic well-being. Table 1 (below) describes the differences between the family structure of the Hispanic and total populations in the 1990 census, and the substantial differences in the presence of children under 18, the number of single-parent family units, and the large differential in the employment status between Hispanic female and male single parents. Nearly 66 percent of married couple Hispanic families have children under 18 years.

Family households	**#Hispanic**	**%Col**	**# Total Pop**	**% Col**
Married-couple family				
With own children under 18 years	2,201,368	65.9	9,328,579	18.0
No own children under 18 years	1,138,326	34.1	42,389,635	82.0
Total Married-couple family	3,339,694	100.0	51,718,214	
Other family				
With own children under 18 years	196,872	48.4	4,075,766	39.3
No own children under 18 years	209,863	51.6	6,305,888	60.7
Total Other family	406,735	100.0	10,381,654	
Female householder, no husband present				
With own children under 18 years	682,929	66.3	4,075,766	39.3
No own children under 18 years	346,717	33.7	6,305,888	60.7
Total Female householder	1,029,646	100.0	10,381,654	
Male householder, no wife present				
With own children under 18 years	196,872	48.4	856,928	29.1
No own children under 18 years	209,863	51.6	2,092,632	70.9
Total Male householder	406,735		2,949,560	
Total Married and Other Family Type	3,746,429		62,099,868	
% Married of Total Pop		72.3		82.3
Total Single Parent Family, no spouse present	1,436,381		13,331,214	

Family households	#Hispanic	%Col	# Total Pop	% Col
% Single Parent of Total Pop	27.7			17.8
% Female of Single-Parent Pop	72.0			77.8
% Male of Single-Parent Pop	28.0			22.1
Total Family (Married, Other, Single Parent)	5,182,810		75,431,082	
Nonfamily households	1,095,965		26,944,154	

Table 1. Household type and Presence and Age of Children. Sources: U.S. Bureau of the Census, "Table P19. Household Type and Presence and Age of Children," "P21. Household Type and Presence and Age of Children (Householder of Hispanic origin)," *1990 US Census Data Database*. C90STF3C1 (Summary Level: Nation). Percentages rounded down below .5 and rounded up above .5. *http://www.census.gov/*

Hispanic children who live in two-parent families experience significantly lower levels of poverty (29 percent) than children in female-householder families with no husband present (67 percent).[25] Nearly 28 percent of Hispanic families are headed by single parents, compared to 18 percent in the total population.[26] Only 27 percent of the children living in female-headed families have a mother employed full time, whereas 42 percent of white children are headed by a fully employed white single mother. In contrast, 66 percent of Hispanic children and 69 percent of white children live in families headed by fully employed white single fathers.

Health Indicators

Health is an important indicator of a child's well being and development. Children living in poverty are significantly less healthy than children whose families are above the poverty line: 65 percent to 85 percent, respectively, are in good health.[27] Nearly 30 percent of Hispanic children under age 18 are not covered by either public or private health insurance.[28]

Low birth-weight places a newborn child at risk, and the consequences for future well-being and learning are deemed significant. The percent of low birth-weight births between 1980 and 1995 was between 5.7 and 6.3 for the white population; between 12.7 and 13.1 for the black population; and between 6.1 and 6.3 for the Hispanic population.[29] However, within the Hispanic population, Puerto Rican (9.4 percent) newborn children are at much higher risk than Mexican-American (5.8 percent), Cuban (6.5 percent) or Central and South American (6.2 percent) newborn children.

Data from the National Immunization Surveys for the period 1994–1996 indicate that a lower percentage of Hispanic children than white, non–Hispanic children ages 19 to 35 months receive vaccinations for the combined series of DPT, polio, and measles: 77 percent of white non–Hispanic versus 69 percent of Hispanic children in 1995; and

79 percent of white non–Hispanic versus 71 percent of Hispanic children in 1996.[30]

Teen pregnancy has long-term consequences for the well-being of the mother, child, and society. Adolescent pregnancy is associated with poverty, female-headed households, low schooling-completion rates, reduced prospects for educational attainment and future employment of both parent and child, low birth weight, and higher infant mortality.[31] Table 2 indicates that pregnancy rates for Hispanic teens have increased dramatically since 1980, although the teen birth rate dropped by 17 percent among non–Hispanic blacks and by more than 9 percent among non–Hispanic whites between 1991 and 1995.[32] Pregnancy rates for Hispanic teens are now two and a half times greater than for white, non–Hispanic teens.[33]

Race/Ethnicity	**1980**	**1986**	**1990**	**1991**	**1992**	**1993**	**1994**	**1995**
Hispanics	82	80	100	107	107	107	108	107
Non-Hispanic Blacks	105	104	116	119	116	111	108	99
Non-Hispanic Whites	41	36	43	43	42	40	40	39

Table 2. Teen Birth Rate (Births Per 1,000 Females Aged 15–19) by Race/Ethnicity. Source: Child Trends, Inc. *http://www.childtrends.org/faag97.htm*

Language, Literacy, and Schooling

Fluency in the dominant language is viewed as critical for incorporation into the cultural, social, and economic life of the majority group. As recorded by the 1990 census, more than 132 million people between 18 to 64 years spoke only English at home.[34] Table 3 reveals that among those who spoke Spanish at home, about 83 percent stated that they spoke English "very well" or "well," whereas about 17 percent said they spoke "not well" or "not at all." Nearly 74 percent of children aged 5 to 17 spoke Spanish at home in 1995.[35]

The Census Bureau constructs a measure of "Linguistic Isolation" to identify households where no one above the age of 17 speaks English.[36] Nearly 31 percent of Spanish-speaking households were identified as linguistically isolated. Linguistic isolation is related to age: the economically dependent members (the very young and those more than 65 years) are the most isolated.

Of the 5.1 percent of children ages 5–17 years who were identified as having difficulty speaking English, 31 percent were Hispanic and almost 42 percent spoke Spanish at home. Part of the explanation for this isolation is that many Hispanic children under the age of six remain at home and do not participate in nonparental child care arrangements or early education programs, which contribute to learning English.[37]

The role of parents in early childhood education and during elementary and high school is correlated with childhood and young adult achievement in school. Hispanic children are far less likely than white,

Persons 5 to 17 years:	**# of Persons**
Speak only English	39,019,514
Speak Spanish:	
Speak English "very well"	2,530,779
Speak English "well"	993,417
Speak English "not well" or "not at all"	643,457
8 to 64 years:	
Speak only English	132,200,180
Speak Spanish:	
Speak English "very well"	6,105,722
Speak English "well"	2,589,195
Speak English "not well" or "not at all"	3,425,937
65 years and over:	
Speak only English	27,381,104
Speak Spanish:	
Speak English "very well"	398,568
Speak English "well"	223,350
Speak English "not well" or "not at all"	434,639

Table 3. Language Spoken at Home by Age and Ability to Speak English (Persons 5 years and older). Source: U.S. Bureau of the Census, "Tables P28. Age by Language Spoken at Home and Ability to Speak English," *1990 US Census Data Database*. C90STF3C1 (Summary Level: Nation). *http://www.census.gov/*.

non–Hispanic children to be read to by a family member: 39 percent to 64 percent in 1996, respectively.[38] Hispanic children between the ages of 3 and 4 are also significantly less likely than white, non–Hispanic young children to be enrolled in early childhood education programs: 37 percent to to 54 percent, respectively, in contrast to black children (63 percent), who are more likely than white, non–Hispanic young children to attend these programs.[39]

Between 1982 and 1996, white, non–Hispanic students "have consistently had higher reading and math scores than either black, non–Hispanic or Hispanic students ages 9, 13, and 17."[40] The gap between Hispanic students and white, non–Hispanic students in the 1996 mathematics achievement scores was about the same across the three age groups (between 21 and 25 points lower for Hispanic children). Hispanic 17-year-olds did, however, somewhat better in mathematics achievement than black, non–Hispanic students.[41] Reading achievement scores of Hispanic children for ages 9, 13, and 17 differed from white, non–Hispanic children consistently across all cohorts, with scale scores that average between 26 and 29 points lower.[42]

Educational Attainment

Perhaps the indicator that provides the most powerful insights about the future of the Hispanic-Latino population is high school completion rates. The Spanish-speaking population is characterized by much lower levels of educational attainment than the population as a whole, which reflects both the level of literacy and educational schooling that has been attained.[43]

Between 1980 and 1996, Hispanic young adults between 18 and 24 years consistently had the lowest high school completion rates of all racial and ethnic groups.[44] Whereas 92 percent of white, non–Hispanic young people graduated from high school in 1996, only 62 percent of Hispanics did so. The Hispanic high school completion rate is also significantly lower than for black, non–Hispanics, of whom 83 percent received a high school diploma.

The Hispanic population has achieved lower levels of schooling at every level of educational attainment through post-graduate training. The dropout rate from high school for Hispanic-origin young adults between 16 and 24 years is nearly one in five.[45] In 1990, more than 31 percent of the Hispanic population 25 years and older had completed only nine years of schooling, compared to about 10 percent of the population as a whole. Only 9.5 percent of the Hispanic population at the time of the 1990 census had attained a baccalaureate or higher degree. For the older population of adults 25 to 29 years, however, recent data from the Current Population Surveys for 1997, indicate that about 18 percent of the Hispanic population had attained a bachelor's degree or higher. Hispanic college graduation rates were, however, half that of the white, non–Hispanic population.[46]

Years of schooling — in particular, being a high school graduate — are highly correlated with employment. Young people who leave high school without a diploma are at greater risk of unemployment than those who obtain a high school degree. Hispanic and Latino high school graduates have 1.4 times the chance of being employed than those who left high school without a diploma.

More recent data from the Current Population Surveys also show that, in 1997, nearly twice as many Hispanic than white young people between the ages of 16 and 19 years were neither enrolled in school nor working (14.2 percent of Hispanic to 7.7 percent of white young adults).[47]

Discussion

These indicators of economic well-being, health, and educational attainment show the current status of Hispanic children is not good. Hispanic and Latino children and young adults are at risk. Their prospects for future success are uncertain.

Although only univariate statistics have been tabulated, the dynamics of family's well-being as it relates to life chances has been extensively studied. This research has demonstrated that these indicators are correlated and are also predictors of success. Research has consistently shown that educational and occupational mobility are direct and indirect outcomes of the socio-economic conditions of family life.[48]

Parents and society (through the governmental institution) make choices that affect the success of children. Background characteristics, such as family stability, residence, and parental characteristics, have independent effects on the child's attainment.[49] Parental schooling and occupational status persistently show their effects on the child's future educational and labor market attainments. Effects of neighborhood and the cost of educational, occupational, and wage discrimination, must be considered, although measurement of neighborhood effects and the costs of discrimination is difficult.[50] The effect of schools on attainment appears small, although some studies have found statistically significant and positive effects.[51] Economic incentives and opportunities offered by the society (government) can alter behavior, but, as Haveman and Wolfe have noted, "the magnitude of their impact is often quite limited."[52] Other factors ("luck") explain between 50 and 60 percent of the variation in outcomes.

Economic security of the family is essential for a host of quality of life issues. Low levels of parental educational attainment predict lower educational attainment of their children, and are related to higher rates of teenage out-of-wedlock births and economic inactivity. Parental separation or dissolution during childhood is likely to influence young adult development and attainments, in particular, teenage pregnancy and completed schooling. The trend in high rates of Hispanic teen pregnancy is of special concern because parenthood places teens at high risk of early school failure, early behavior problems, lower rates of schooling completion, family dysfunction, and poverty.[53]

Family income makes a very large difference in the life chances of children. The experience of poverty is a significant stressor in the life of a child and may have serious long-term effects. Children whose families live in poverty experience more low birth-weight births, higher infant mortality in the first year of life, lower rates of vaccination, and debilitating chronic conditions that limit activities. Growing up in poverty means that children are less likely to graduate from high school, and even less likely to continue education beyond secondary school.

The traditional assimilationist model of immigrant incorporation has assumed that subsequent generations of immigrants are gradually absorbed into the dominant society, as achievement norms are inculcated by the second generation.[54] Thus, Hispanic and Latino immigrant groups should over two or three generations resemble the non–Hispanic groups. But not only is the recent Hispanic and Latino immigrant population on the whole poorer and less literate than other immigrant groups, they manifest lower educational attainment than earlier immigrant groups even after two or three generations.[55] This suggests that we must also look elsewhere, perhaps to the effects of discrimination and lack of equal access to educational and economic opportunities, as part of the explanation of why Hispanic and Latino immigrants have fared so poorly compared to other immigrant groups.[56]

Some evidence appears to support the claims that there has not been equal access to educational and economic opportunities.[57] The public policy decisions that have contributed significantly to the reduced life chances of Hispanic young Americans appear to be nearly all related to education, including literacy.[58] There are, for example, serious disparities in school funding at the national, state, and local level, which result in underfunded schools in urban areas where the majority of Hispanic students and poor children are concentrated.[59] Educational standards are not enforced at the state and local levels.[60] Bilingual education has provided millions of dollars to support schools, but has marginalized rather than mainstreamed Hispanic students and has failed to produce students who achieve English proficiency.[61] The numerical strength of the Hispanic and Latino population has not been and is not currently reflected in national and state legislatures.[62] Under-representation reinforces the marginal status of the Hispanic and Latino population and renders them ineffectual as agents for political change.

Part III: Implications for Library Professionals

Embedded in a large and complex social system, libraries have long reflected and reenforced societal norms and values. Both revisionist and classical conceptions of the role of the library agree that the institution was conceived as a socializing agent and as an agent for social change. Historically, libraries have seen one of their principal educative functions as contributing to the integration of immigrants into the U.S. society, and, thus, playing a central communication function to both articulate and inculcate social norms and values.[63] In other words, libraries developed services designed to provide incentives to families to utilize the library through its educative and information functions, and its policies were explicitly or implicitly designed to alter as well as model appropriate behavior. Beilke and Sciara's discussion of the 1983 National Commission on Libraries and Information Science Report on library services for multicultural people illustrates these assumptions about the influence of libraries. They note that, among the premises underlying the goals of the library-in-society, "libraries play an important and unique role in the integration of cultural differences within the community" and "all libraries can assist cultural minorities ... to become equal participants in society through access to information."[64]

These policy goals have been re-articulated by libraries during the last two decades, but with a significantly different emphasis that reflects the incorporation of two major philosophical changes that infuse society. The first change has expanded the original missions of the library as a conveyer and preserver of culture and premier institution for learning the language of the culture into a social services delivery system, while at the same time asserting that the programs are designed to improve literacy skills.[65] Thus, for example, parents need to be involved in educating their children, parenting skills need to be learned, and libraries should provide services that improve parent-child relationships.[66] The large number of articles about services to Hispanic, Latino, and other minority children reviewed have convinced me that the libraries truly believe that they could deliver successful literacy or language-training programs if they coupled them with programs that addressed the social and economic needs of the family unit. The result, however, has been that people who were once patrons became clients and customers for a host of services which diluted the original mission and function of the library and were also inadequately funded to respond to the central patron need, learning the language.[67] Like other social institutions, such as schools and hospitals, libraries adopted a social service model, and attempted to respond to serious social problems that they were unequipped to handle.

Revisionist history of the philosophic origins and mission of the library coupled with the Great Society rhetoric of liberalism may have contributed to subverting the essence of the library, its mission as preserver and transmitter of culture. Revisionist historians taught us that the public library was a purveyor of the culture and values of the power elite, and this was a "bad thing." The Great Society decade set in motion a radical transformation of the concept of responsibility, from the individual to the society. The burden of upward mobility and personal responsibility was shifted to the society and its institutions. Thus, hardships normally experienced by immigrant and minority groups were rationalized by social norms and values that contributed to justifying dependency and reduced personal initiative.

The ideological tenets of the Great Society also infused the American society with a particular version of what the "melting pot" should look like. A host of concepts like "multiculturalism" and "diversity" became translated into programmatic initiatives that, in practice, implemented an ideology which rejected the values of the dominant culture and everything that was implied by this vocabulary. The consequences are shown in the evidence presented in Part Two. Institutions collaborated in reinforcing the myth and the politically correct view: that to learn the values and norms of the dominant culture was to lose one's own culture and identity. It was dried crumbs, thrown at the unwashed masses, and the strategy was remarkably successful. The poor and the uneducated remained dysfunctional and marginal and could be ignored without retribution by political elites operating in the legislative arena.

Still, I could be convinced that library programs do make a difference, if evidence existed. Promoting and setting standards for literacy are admirable goals of our profession, but they are not the same thing as demonstrating that promotion and standards-setting work. It is not persuasive evidence to cite 20 public libraries where five students who attended a literacy program graduated to become teachers. (Five of how many? Over what length of time?) Or that the writings of three students were published in a collection of writings. Nowhere in my search of the research literature or government record-keeping systems, however, could I find evidence. Government record keeping systems on library services, financing, and expenditures contain no detailed information on specific programs for literacy or other services designed to improve understanding of library services for the Hispanic and Latino communities. There are two tables on literacy in the widely distributed *Condition of Education 1998* published by the U.S. Department of Education. To persuade policy makers and legislators that libraries make a difference requires more than faith in the rightness of a cause. I believe that we must reassess the mission of the library. We must ask whether it is appropriate for the library to be a social service agency. We must make hard and targeted choices about which library services to support. We must carefully evaluate the revisionist story of the library, to make sure that even if the story "got it right," the story line does not sidetrack the profession to lose sight of the *razón de ser* for the library. We need institutions in our society that embody its culture and its language. To be a conveyor of American culture and democratic values seems to me, the critical philosophical *razón de ser*. How is this to be accomplished by judicious choices for library services, so that our Hispanic and Latino youth are integrated in our society? remains the million dollar question.

We have bought and sold hook-line-and-sinker the myth that to learn English is to lose one's culture and identity. This is just nonsense. The large body of ethnographic and sociological research shows that generation after generation, the young and the old, do not lose their ethnic identity. They make choices about whether to be "Polish," "Italian," "Irish," or *Puerto Riqueño*.[68] We would not have the richly textured mosaic of the United States if it were true that to learn the values of the dominant culture meant a loss of personal and social identity. Coupled with instances of documented failure of bilingual education and statistical evidence that very large numbers of our Hispanic and Latino young people are not staying in school or learning English, it is time to assess whether libraries can continue to invest in services that reinforce the primary language of the home, with the ostensible goal of promoting literacy. It hasn't worked.

We are running out of time. Whereas immigrant groups who came to this country at the beginning of this century were poor and a very large number of them illiterate, the structure of the economy could accommodate and integrate them. There was work for them to do. But the last two decades have witnessed an economic restructuring of the society. There is no longer a deep reservoir of unskilled jobs that will pay above a minimum wage. The strength of the labor union movement, essential to protect workers and ensure a living wage, has greatly diminished. Today's minimum wage does not pull its recipients out of poverty. The secret lies in achieving a skill level commensurate with the economic restructuring. This means staying in school, learning English — and learning it well. It is the only way to achieve economic self-sufficiency.

To make the hard decisions, to be strategic, requires evidence. The library profession must document and systematically assess whether programs directed to our Hispanic and Latino youth are accomplishing their objectives. The ALA's 21st-century initiative on literacy is a critical first step. Among the valuable materials that have been written for the library profession are introductions to program evaluation and needs assessment for gathering information that have been published by the American Library Association.[69] The library and government record-keeping systems need to be revised to obtain more detailed data on programmatic initiatives. It is imperative that the library profession join with the research community to conduct systematic program evaluation.

Finally, societal change is not accomplished without political mobilization to increase representation in the municipal, state, and national legislatures and advocacy on behalf of children to make the case that society benefits as a whole when individual groups prosper. The library profession, together with the Hispanic and Latino community, must be a fully engaged participant in the social welfare of our nation and advocates for our children.

Notes

1. The term *Hispanic* is currently used to designate highly diverse population groups whose single unifying characteristic is that they speak Spanish. Recognizing the diversity of this population, *Hispanic* and *Latino* are used to reflect the two primary origins of the Spanish-speaking population.

2. Esther Dyer and Concha Robertson-Kozan, "Hispanics in the U.S.: Implications for Library Service," *School Library Journal*, 29, no. 8 (1983): 27.

3. Patricia F. Beilke and Frank J. Sciara, *Selecting Materials for and about Hispanic and East Asian Children and Young People* (Hamden, Conn.: Library Professional Publications, 1986), p. 5.

4. Robert Haveman and Barbara Wolfe, *Succeeding Generations: On the Effects of Investments in Children* (New York: Russell Sage Foundation, 1994).

5. *Ibid.*, 45–46.

6. Background variables include race, gender, foreign or domestic birthplace of parents, birth position of the child in the family, and whether the child's grandparents were poor. Social (governmental) choices (social investments in children) include education of the child's parents, unemployment rate in local labor

market, receipt of welfare benefits by child's parents, generosity of public welfare benefits in the state, and housing tenure status of the family. Parental choices (parental investments in children) include education, work effort, earnings, occupation, receipt of welfare benefits, urban/suburban/rural and region of location, and number of children. Young adult choices made by children include grade last in school, split off from parent's home, years of education, presence of a teenage nonmarital birth, teenage welfare recipiency.

7. *Ibid.*, 30–32.

8. C. Eugene Steuerle, Edward M. Gramlich, Hugh Heclo, and Demetra Smith Nightingale, *The Government We Deserve* (Washington, D.C.: Urban Institute, 1998).

9. Haveman and Wolfe, op. cit.

10. The statistics presented here are drawn from a variety of sources, the principal ones being the 1990 decennial census and surveys from the Bureau of Labor Statistics (Current Population Surveys), Department of Education (National Assessment of Educational Progress), and Centers for Disease Control (surveys on health).

11. Jeffrey S. Passel and Barry Edmonston, "Immigration and Race: Recent Trends in Immigration to the United States," in Barry Edmonston and Jeffrey S. Passel, eds., *Immigration and Ethnicity: The Integration of America's Newest Arrivals* (Washington, D.C.: Urban Institute Press, 1994), p. 31.

12. However, "almost two-thirds of the 1990 Hispanic population consists of either immigrants who came since 1950 or descendants of those immigrants," according to Passel and Edmonston, 52.

13. This statistic is believed to be an undercount of the actual number of persons of Spanish-speaking origin for a variety of reasons, and is viewed as incorporating what is termed "measurement error." This error has been subject to extensive research over the last two decades which has revealed that "race," "national ancestry," and "ethnicity" are concepts that are treated as semantically identical; that the placement of the "ethnicity" item, which follows the "race" item in all official data-collecting instruments, has created a confusion; and that the meaning of "race" and "ethnicity" is culturally defined.

14. "Hispanic Origin" may include people who have identified themselves as either "white" or "black."

15. More than half classified themselves as "white," about 26 percent as "black," with a very small percentage classifying themselves as "American Indian" or "Asian"; however, more than 7 percent identified themselves of "Other Races." Source is "Hispanic Origin by Race," 1990 US Census Data Database. C90STF3C1 (Summary Level: Nation). *http://www.census.gov/*. The Bureau of the Census employs an imputation or allocation technique to assign race, in instances when there appears to be an inconsistency in self-identification.

16. Frank D. Bean, Jorge Chapa, Ruth R. Berg, and Kathryn A. Sowards, "Educational and Sociodemographic Incorporation among Hispanic Immigrants to the United States," in Edmonston and Passel, pp. 73–95.

17. *Ibid.*, 54.

18. U.S. Bureau of the Census, "Resident Population of the United States: Middle Series Projections, 1995 to 2050, by Sex, Race, and Hispanic Origin, with Median Age." *http://www.census.gov/population/projections/nation:/nsrh/nprh9600.txt; nprh0105.txt; nprh0610.txt; nprh1530.yxt; nprh3550.txt.*

19. The difference of 11.2 years in the median age of the white population is, however, projected to be reduced to 8.9 years by 2050.

20. U.S. Bureau of the Census, "Table P80. Household Income in 1989 (All Households)" and "Table P83. Household Income in 1989 (Households with Householder of Hispanic Origin)," 1990 US Census Data Database. C90STF3C1 (Summary Level: Nation). *http://www.census.gov/*.

21. "Table P114A. Per Capita Income in 1989 by Race (All Persons)" and "P116A. Per Capita Income in 1989 (Persons of Hispanic Origin)," 1990 US Census Data Database. C90STF3C1 (Summary Level: Nation). *http://www.census.gov*.

22. The poverty level is based on money income and excludes noncash benefits. The poverty threshold for a family of four was $16,036 in 1996. The levels shown in the table are derived from the ratio of the family's income to the family's poverty threshold. See "Table ECON1.A. Child Poverty: Percentage of Children under Age 18 Living Below Selected Poverty Levels by Age, Family Structure, Race, and Hispanic Origin, Selected Year 1980–96." *http://www.childstats.gov/.../econla.htm.*

23. *Ibid.*

24. Sources are "Table H8. Tenure (All Households)," "Table H10. Tenure by Race of Householder (All Households)," and "Table H12. Tenure by Race of Householder (Households by

Hispanic origin)," 1990 US Census Data Database, C90STF3C1 (Summary Level: Nation) *http://www.census.gov/*. Percentages rounded down below .5 and rounded up above .5.

25. Federal Interagency Forum on Child and Family Statistics, "Table ECON1.A. Child Poverty: Percentage of Children under Age 18 Living Below Selected Poverty Levels by Age, Family Structure, Race, and Hispanic Origin, Selected Years 1980–96," *http://www.childstats.gov/ac1998/econ1a.htm*.

26. More recent data from the Current Population Surveys indicate that 64 percent of Hispanic children under 18 years live with both parents, but about 27 percent live in female-headed households, 4 percent with fathers-only, and 5 percent with no parent. Federal Interagency Forum on Child and Family Statistics, "Table POP5. Family Structure: Percentage Distribution of Children Under Age 18 by Presence of Parents in Household, Race and Hispanic Origin, Selected Years, 1980–97." *http://www.childstats.gov/ac1998/pop5.htm*.

27. Federal Interagency Forum on Child and Family Statistics, "General Health Status," America's Children: Key National Indicators of Well-Being,1998 (Washington, D.C., 1998), *http://www.childstats.gov/healthtx.htm*.

28. Federal Interagency Forum on Child and Family Statistics, "Table ECON5.A. Access to Health Care: Percentage of Children Under Age 18 Covered by Health Insurance by Type of Insurance, Age, Race, and Hispanic Origin, 1987-96. *http://www.childstats.gov/ac1998/econ5a.htm*.

29. Centers for Disease Control and Prevention, National Center for Health Statistics, National Vital Statistics System. Report of Final Natality Statistics, 1995. Monthly Vital Statistics Report, 45, no. 11, Supp. 1; Births and Deaths: United States, 1996. Monthly Vital Statistics Report, 46, no. 1, 1997, Supp. 2; Health, United States, 1996-97 (Hyattsville, MD: National Center for Health Statistics, 1997).

30. Federal Interagency Forum on Child and Family Statistics, "Table HEALTH5. Child Immunization: Percentage of Children Ages 19 to 35 Months Vaccinated for Selected Diseases by Poverty Status, Race, and Hispanic Origin, 1994–96." *http://www.childstats.gov/ac1998/health5.htm*.

31. Federal Interagency Forum on Child and Family Statistics, "General Health Status," *Ibid. http://www.childstats.gov/healthtx.htm*.

32. Federal Interagency Forum on Child and Family Statistics, "Table HEALTH8. Adolescent Birth Rates by Age, Race, and Hispanic Origin, Selected Years, 1980–96." *http://www.childstats.gov/ac1998/health8.htm*.

33. Urban Institute, "Teen Birth Rate (Births Per 1,000 Females Aged 15–19) by Race/Ethnicity, 1980–1995," *Facts at a Glance* (Washington, D.C.: Author, October 1997). *http://www.childtrends.org/faag97.html*.

34. U. S. Bureau of the Census, "Language Spoken at Home," 1990 US Census Data. Database: C90STF3C1 (Summary Level: Nation). *http://www.census.gov/*.

35. Federal Interagency Forum on Child and Family Statistics, "Table POP4. Difficulty Speaking English: Children Ages 5 to 17 Who Speak a Language Other Than English at Home, and Who Are Reported to Have Difficulty Speaking English by Race and Hispanic Origin, Region, Selected Years, 1979–95." *http://www.childstats.gov/ac1998/pop4.htm*.

36. The Bureau of the Census defines a household as "linguistically isolated" in which no person age 14 years or over speaks only English and no person age 14 years or over speaks a language other than English speaks English "Very well." All the members of a linguistically isolated household are tabulated as linguistically isolated, including members under age 14 years who may speak only English. U.S. Bureau of the Census, 1990 Census Database. Technical Documentation. *http://www.census.gov/*.

37. Federal Interagency Forum on Child and Family Statistics, "Table SPECIAL2. Number and Percentage of Children under Age 6 Participating in Child Care and Early Education Programs on a Regular Basis by Type of Arrangement and Child and Family Characteristics, 1995." *http://www.childstats.gov/ac1998/special2.htm*.

38. Federal Interagency Forum on Child and Family Statistics, "Table ED1. Family Reading: Percentage of Children Ages 3 to 5 Who were Read to Every Day in the Last Week by a Family Member by Child and Family Characteristics, Selected Years, 1993–96." *http://www.cldstate.gov/ac1998/ed1.htm*.

39. Federal Interagency Forum on Child and Family Statistics, "Table ED2B. Early Childhood Education: Percentage of Children Ages 3 to 4 Enrolled in Center-based Programs by Child and Family Characteristics, Selected Years, 1991–96." *http://www.childstats.gov/ac1998/ed2b.htm*.

40. Federal Interagency Forum on Child and Family Statistics, "Education Indicators." *http://www.childstats.gov/ac1998/edtxt.htm*.

41. Federal Interagency Forum on Child and Family Statistics, "Table ED3.A. Mathematics Achievement: Average Scale Scores of Students Ages 9, 13, and 17 by Age and Child and Family Characteristics, Selected Years 1982–96." *http://www.childstats.gov/ac1998/ed3a.htm.*

42. Federal Interagency Forum on Child and Family Statistics, "Table ED3.B. Reading Achievement: Average Scale Scores of Students Ages 9, 13, and 17 by Age and Child and Family Characteristics, Selected Years 1980–96." *http://www.childstats.gov/ac1998/ed3b.htm.*

43. National Center for Education Statistics, The Educational Progress of Hispanic Students (Findings from the Condition of Education 1995) (NCES 95-767) (Washington, D. C.: Author, 1995).

44. Federal Interagency Forum on Child and Family Statistics, "Table ED4. High School Completion: Percentage Completing High School Among 18–24 Year Olds by Method of Completion, Race, and Hispanic Origin, Selected Years 1980-96." *http://www.childstats.gov/ac1998/ed4.htm.*

45. William G. Secada, Rudolfo Chavez-Chavez, Eugene Garcia, Cipriano Muñoz, Jeannie Oakes, Isaura Santiago-Santiago, and Robert Slavin, *No More Excuses: The Final Report of the Hispanic Dropout Project* (Washington, D.C.: National Center for Education Statistics, 1998).

46. Federal Interagency Forum on Child and Family Statistics, "Table ED6. Higher Education: Percentage of High School Graduates Ages 25 to 29 Attaining Higher Degrees by Highest Degree Attained, Race, and Hispanic Origin, Selected Years 1980–97." *Http://www.childstats.gov/ed6.htm.*

47. Federal Interagency Forum on Child and Family Statistics, "Table ED5. Youth Neither Enrolled in School Nor Working: Percentage of Youth Ages 16 to 19 Who Are Neither Enrolled in School nor Working by Gender, Race, Hispanic Origin, and Age, Selected Years, 1985–97." *http://www.childstats.gov/ac1998/ed5.htm.*

48. William H. Sewell, Robert M. Hauser, and David L. Featherman, eds., *Schooling and Achievement in American Society* (New York: Academic Press, 1976); Robert M. Hauser and David L. Featherman, *Occupations and Social Mobility in the United States* (Madison, Wisc.: University of Wisconsin Press, 1976); Robert M. Hauser and David L. Featherman, *The Process of Stratification: Trends and Analyses* (New York: Academic Press, 1977); David L. Featherman and Robert M. Hauser, *Opportunity and Change* (New York: Academic Press, 1978); Robert M. Hauser, Brett V. Brown, and William R. Prosser, eds., *Indicators of Children's Well-Being* (New York: Russell Sage Foundation, 1997); and Kirsten K. West, Robert M. Hauser, and Terri M. Scanlan, eds., *Longitudinal Surveys of Children* (Washington, D.C.: National Academy Press, 1998).

49. However, we lack extensive data on how neighborhood characteristics influence outcomes.

50. Haveman and Wolfe.

51. *Ibid.*

52. *Ibid.*, 70.

53. *Ibid.*

54. Frank D Bean, Jorge Chapa, Ruth R. Berg, and Kathryn A. Sowards, "Educational and Sociodemographic Incorporation Among Hispanic Immigrants to the United States," in Edmonston and Passell, op. cit.

55. *Ibid.* The generational status of children and adults is also related to various educational outcomes, and its effect is most visible in the educational and occupational differences of parents and children and between immigrants and the native born. For a recent report, see National Center for Education Statistics, Generational Status and Educational Outcomes Among Asian and Hispanic 1988 Eighth Graders (NCES 1999-020) (U.S. Department of Education, 1998).

56. There is a body of research that examines the effects of discrimination on educational and economic opportunity. A series of exchanges on this issue, published as letters to the editor, are illuminating. See "Race Discrimination Furthers Income Inequality" *New York Times*, February 23, 1998, A18.

57. Recent evidence about the effects of affirmative action programs for admission to higher education do, however, suggests rather strongly that eliminating such programs immediately and negatively affects access by minority groups, including Latinos and African-Americans.

58. President's Advisory Commission on Educational Excellence for Hispanic Americans, *Our Nation on the Fault Line: Hispanic American Education* (Washington, D. C.: Department of Education, 1996).

59. Department of Education, "Table 52-2: Public School Expenditures Per Pupil (in 1996 Constant Dollars), by Function and Selected District Characteristics: School Year 1992-93," *Condition of Education 1997* (Washington, D.C.: Author, 1998).

60. *Ibid.*

61. James Traub, "The Bilingual Barrier, *New York Times Magazine*, January 31, 1999, 32–35; Don Terry, "The Reply, It Turned Out, Was Bilingual: No," *New York Times*, June 5, 1998, A10; Frank Bruni, "Bilingual Education Battle Splits Santa Barbara," *New York Times*, May 22, 1998, A12; "What Shall We Ask of Immigrants" (Letters to the Editor), *New York Times*, May 31, 1998, 16; Jorge Amselle, "The Bilingual Blunder" (Op-Ed), *New York Times*, May 6, 1998, A29; Douglas Lasken, "It's Time to Abandon Bilingual Education" (Op-Ed), *New York Times*, January 13, 1998.

62. Todd S. Purdum, "California G.O.P. Faces a Crisis as Hispanic Voters Turn Away," *New York Times*, December 9, 1998, A1, A6.

63. J. H. Shera, *Sociological Foundations of Librarianship* (New York: Asia, 1970.

64. National Commission on Libraries and Information Science, *Report of the Task Force on Library and Information Services to Cultural Minorities* (Washington, D. C.: Author, 1983). Patricia F. Beilke and Frank J. Sciara, *Selecting Materials for and about Hispanic and East Asian Children and Young People* (Hamden, Conn.: Shoe String, 1986), p. 7.

65. Louise Yarian Zwick and Oralia Garza de Cortés, "Library Programs for Hispanic Children," *Texas Libraries* 50 (Spring 1989): 12–16; Kathleen de la Peña McCook and Paula Geist, "Hispanic Library Services in South Florida," *Public Libraries* 34 (January/February 1995): 34–37; D. Bryan Stansfield, "Serving Hispanic Persons: The Cross-Cultural Border Library Experience at Fabens," *RQ* 27 (1988): 547–561; Amado Alvarez, "Denver Public Library Central Branch," *Colorado Libraries* 17 (1991): 12–13.

66. Denise R. Fisher, "Families Reading Together: Sharing the Joy," *Texas Library Journal* 66 (Fall 1990): 84–88. Pam Carlson, "'Reading Can Give You a Dream," in Karen M. Venturella, ed., *Poor People and Library Services* (Jefferson, N.C.: McFarland 1998).

67. Evidence to support my assertion is only anecdotal, but my three years living in New York City suggest that the demand for these programs is so high that one to two year waits are not uncommon in certain areas of the city.

68. Mary Waters, *Ethnic options: Choosing Identities in America*. (Berkeley, Calif.: University of California Press, 1990).

69. American Library Association, "Evaluation of Family Literacy Programs" and "Needs Assessment Gathering Information for Decision Making." *http://www.ala.org/literacy/facts/eval.html; /.../needs.htm.*

Services to Young Adults in Puerto Rico

Milagros Otero Guzman

Youth are a significant group in the community characterized by differences in attitudes, behavior, interests and other factors related to the physiological changes and stages of development as they move from childhood to adolescence. Young adults are in transition, no longer children, yet not adults. This causes them to experience fear, confusion and insecurity, and so serving them represents a great opportunity and a challenge for public library professionals offering services directed at satisfying their special needs.

According to experts in the field, services for young adults in Puerto Rican libraries are predominantly reference services and activities that are generally not successful at catching the interest of young adults. Some Puerto Rican Department of Education functionaries mention that the majority of staff working in Puerto Rican public libraries do not have the academic preparation and experience required, which affects the services offered. It is important to explore what Puerto Rican public libraries are actually doing for young adults to plan and improve services. The research undertaken focuses on this area.

In Puerto Rico there are three types of public libraries: community libraries (sustained by members of a local community, directed by a citizen board), Department of Education libraries (receiving funds and directed by this agency) and municipality libraries (receiving municipal funds, with employees appointed by the mayor). There are differences among these libraries in terms of services, personnel, collections, equipment and schedules of activities.

The total number of public libraries in Puerto Rico is 141, including 127 public libraries under the direction of the Department of Education, nine municipal libraries and five community libraries. The research sample selected represented 20 percent of the total amount of each type of library. The random sample consisted of 13 Department of Education libraries located in municipalities receiving state and federal funds, two municipal libraries and one community library.

The study employed three techniques to compile data: interview, direct observation and document analysis. The interview technique was used to identify the academic level of library personnel, services offered to

Editor's Note: This summary is based on the author's thesis, "Servicios bibliotecarios para jóvenes en las bibliotecas públicas puertorriqueñas" (Rio Piedras, Puerto Rico: Universidad de Puerto Rico, 1998), in which complete data may be found.

young adults, and young adult needs and interests in these services (from the standpoint of the librarian). In each library the librarian or person in charge was interviewed. The interview technique was also used to explore the opinions of library science professionals and functionaries of the Department of Education with regard to library services for young adults, personnel issues and improving services to youth in Puerto Rico. Three professionals were interviewed.[1]

Direct observation was used to describe library facilities, materials, equipment, and collections for young adults; document analysis, to examine collection development policies, yearly plans, procedures manuals and promotional materials.

Interviews with Library Personnel

Librarians were asked questions about their academic preparation, library services offered to youth and the frequency of offerings, their perception of the importance of services to young adults, their perception of young adults' interest levels in the various services offered, factors that affect young adult services, and library hours. The responses are summarized below.

Academic Preparation

Only one (6 percent) of the public librarians in the sample holds a master's degree in library science. Fifty percent (8) hold a bachelors degree. Three librarians held a bachelor's in elementary education.

Library Services Offered to Young Adults

When asked to identify library services offered for youth, only a few services were consistently cited. Only "Conferences on Young Adults' Preferred Topics" was offered by more than 25 percent of the libraries (31 percent). The other types of services were offered by less than 20 percent of the libraries. Services most offered specifically for young adults were conferences on young adults' preferred topics, reading programs (19 percent) and academic services such as tutorials, high school preparation tests and "Arco" programs (19 percent). Reference service and help with using library resources are the services most frequently offered, but these were services offered to the public at large, not specifically for young adults. Eighty-eight percent of the libraries never offer games or talent contests, and 69 percent never offer help with using computers. In addition, 50 percent never offer reading programs, considered one of the basic important services in public libraries. Half of the libraries holding conferences on young adults' preferred topics offer them only once every six months or once a year.

Importance of Library Services and Interest of Young Adults Toward Library Services

Services considered more important by librarians interviewed are reference services, help with using library resources and conferences on young adults' preferred topics. Less than 20 percent consider reading programs a "very important" service. According to the librarians, the most interesting services to young adults are reference services, help with using library resources, and cultural programs. It is curious that conferences on young adults' preferred topics, considered "very important" or "important" for 82 percent of librarians, are considered by these same librarians to be of little interest to young adults (only 25 percent, it is believed, find the conferences "very interesting").

Factors That Affect the Offering of Young Adult Services

The majority of the librarians interviewed rate administrative support (75 percent), budget (69 percent) and library personnel (63 percent) as the three most important factors which affect (in a negative way) library services offered to youth. Equipment and materials and physical facilities are also considered "very important" by half of the librarians interviewed. Experts in the field also express opinions about these same factors.

Puerto Rican Public Libraries' Hours

The majority (69 percent) of public libraries operate from 8:00 A.M. to 4:30 P.M. from Monday to Thursday. Only 2 (12 percent) of the libraries open on Saturdays, only 1 (6 percent) opens on Sundays. Based on observations, library facilities were generally small. Materials for young adults were on labeled shelves. Only one of the libraries had an area dedicated specifically to youth.

Collection Development Policies

The study intended to examine collection development policies, procedures manuals and annual reports in relation to young adults services. The Department of Education has the responsibility of developing the collection and preparing the procedures manuals for all their libraries. Reports were found in all the libraries and included statistical information such as public served, book circulation and activities held each month.

According to the experts interviewed, library services to young adults in public libraries represent an unexplored area in Puerto Rico. Dr. Figueras noted that this is because in Puerto Rico the preparation for specialists in library services to youth does not exist. The emphasis has been on children's services. This lamentable fact is reflected in the library collections and in the services offered: except for services to children, the majority of the activities in which young adults participate are oriented toward the general public. Young adults between 13–16 years old do not feel comfortable in a children's room and have no interest in children's collections. Neither do many adult books interest them. It is precisely this group which needs a different and separate space. Unfortunately, in Puerto Rico there is little regard for the necessity of a young adult area. According to the experts, the strongest respect for library services to youth is manifested in the activities of the Carnegie Public Library of San Juan and the Dorado Community Library. These two libraries have begun to offer services and activities specifically oriented to youth and have demonstrated a clear interest in serving this group. One other facility, the public library under construction in Bayamón, consulted a library and information science professional (Dr. Consuelo Figueras) regarding its design. This library will be the only Puerto Rican public library up to now to have a specific room for serving young adults. It is to be hoped the Bayamón library will stimulate interest in the creation of space, services and appropriate activities specifically directed at this age group.

The experts suggest that the system of public libraries be separate from the Department of Education. This, they believe, would be the best strategy to improve library services to youth. The next step would be to establish community councils or boards to administer local public libraries.

Experts also agree that public library personnel should be encouraged to grow professionally, and they suggest that graduate schools of library and information science in Puerto Rico, in an effort to upgrade the quality of library personnel, offer courses and develop certificate programs for public library staff.

Concluding Remarks

On the basis of the data collected, it can be concluded that there is a great need for library improvement in services specifically aimed at young adults. The three experts interviewed agree that the academic preparation for specialists in youth services is lacking, as is an awareness of the need for library facilities to serve them. The majority of the personnel working in public libraries lack an adequate preparation in the field. Factors such as a lack of administrative support, insufficient budget, and shortage of library personnel, equipment and materials limit the offering of library services to young adults. The experts consulted proposed separating public libraries from the Department of Education, integrating them in the communities and seeking funding from the commercial sector in hopes of providing better services.

The separation of public libraries from the Department of Education is already happening, with responsibilities for future library development being assigned to municipalities. This change has important implications for the provision of library services to the youth in all Puerto Rican public libraries.

The Dorado Public Community Library is the only one in this study to offer more than one library service on a frequent and regular basis to young adults. Of the rest of the libraries surveyed, few directed services specifically to young adults, and even then conducted them only once a year (for National Library Week). From this study it can be concluded that library services to young adults are more frequent and varied in the fewer community and municipal public libraries in Puerto Rico which receive more administrative support, have better physical facilities and equipment and employ more library personnel.

Based on observations of physical facilities and examination of documents, it may also be concluded that the majority of the public libraries under the Department of Education have an inadequate infrastructure to offer services directed specifically for young adults; they lack the equipment, facilities, tools, policies, and procedures needed for the planning of these services.

Based on these conclusions, the study recommends that

(1) the Department of Education in Puerto Rico provide training for public library personnel including workshops and seminars on improving library services to youth

(2) Library schools include courses in their curricula to prepare new professionals for serving young adults in public libraries and offer continuing education activities to strengthen the knowledge and skills of people already working in this field

(3) The Department of Education encourage, promote, and enforce an upgrade in the academic qualifications required for public librarian positions

Note

1. Dr. Consuelo Figueras, director of the Graduate School of Library and Information Science, University of Puerto Rico, Río Piedras; Mrs. Gladys Gallardo, Department of Education public libraries supervisor; and Mrs. Suzette M. Montaner, Carnegie Public Library (San Juan) children and young adult supervisor.

For Further Reading

American Library Association. *The Public Library Plans for the Teen Age*. Chicago, Ill.: American Library Association, 1948.

Baldwin, Liz. "It All Started in the Summer." *Journal of Youth Services in Libraries* 9, 3 (Spring 1996): 250–251.

Busha, C.H., and S.P. Harter. *Research Methods in Librarianship: Techniques and Interpretation*. New York: Academic Press, 1980.

Doll, Carol A. "Smart Training, Smart Learning: The role of Cooperative Learning in Training for Youth Services." *Journal of Youth Services in Libraries* 10, 2 (Winter 1997): 183–187.

Edmonds, Diana J. *Public Library Services for Children and Young People: A Statistical Survey*. London: British Library Research and Development Department, 1990.

Hannigan, Jane Ann. "A Feminist Analysis of the Voices of Advocacy in Young Adult Services." *Library Trends* 44, 4 (Spring 1996): 851–874.

Higgings, Susan. "Should Public Libraries Hire Young Adult Specialists?" *Journal of Youth Services in Libraries* 7, 4 (Summer 1994): 382–391.

Jones, Patrick. *Connecting Young Adults and Libraries: a How-To-Do-It Manual*. New York: Neal Schuman Publishers, 1992.

Jones, Patrick. "Against All Odds : Creative Support for Serving Young Adults in Public Libraries." *Journal of Youth Services in Libraries* 8, 3 (Spring 1995): 233–240.

Lugo Carrasco, Francisca. "Estudio descriptivo de percepciones que poseen los bibliotecarios escolares y maestros puertorriqueños sobre los servicios para jóvenes que se ofrecen en las bibliotecas escolares del nivel superior en P.R." *M.L.S. Escuela Graduada de Bibliotecología y Ciencia de la Información, Universidad de Puerto Rico*, 1995.

Sprince, Leila, J. "Whose Teen Advisory Board Is This, Anyway?" *Journal of Youth Services in Libraries* 9, 3 (Spring 1996): 247–250.

Wemett, Lisa C. "Librarians as Advocates for Young Adults." *Journal of Youth Services in Libraries* 10, 2 (Winter 1997): 168–172.

Wood, Joan M. "Interagency Cooperation: Benefits of Intergenerational Programming." *Journal of Youth Services in Libraries* 9, 3 (Spring 1996): 237–241.

Measuring In-Library Usage

Dean K. Jue

A common public library problem is how to measure the value of library service to a community. This becomes an even greater problem when a library system has multiple branch outlets and the system director has to allocate the available library funding among the multiple outlets in a manner that will maximize library service and value to all residents of the library system service area.

Many attempts to allocate library funding have focused on library circulation. The assumption is that the more library material being circulated by a particular outlet, the better that outlet is serving its users. It is reasoned, therefore, that such library outlets should receive more funding than those with lower material circulation rates.

Recent research has revealed problems with the emphasis on material circulation for measuring library services and determining library outlet funding allocations.[1] This problem has been exacerbated by increasing competition for a tight local government budget, the source for about 80 percent of most library systems' funding.[2]

Several researchers note that material circulation is lower in public library outlets serving lower income populations, minority populations and recent immigrants to the U.S. than in library outlets serving more traditional user populations. However, in-library usage in the outlets serving nontraditional populations may be higher on a per capita basis.[3]

Library outlets serving majority-minority communities (those in which a minority group outnumber white, non–Hispanics), some of which are Hispanic, usually fall into the category of outlets serving nontraditional library users. Especially in the U.S. border states, these communities may have high numbers of recent immigrants or migrant workers. To help public libraries serving large numbers of Hispanics and other groups of minorities provide better library services to their user population, better measures of in-library usage within these libraries must be employed.

Unfortunately, most efforts to collect data on in-library usage have been sporadic and not collected in a standardized form, like materials circulation. This is because the collection of in-library use data has been harder to automate. One library system may collect the data one way and another library system may collect the same set of data another way in a less detailed manner.

The net consequence of this lack of protocol has been the continued reliance upon standardized and automated materials circulation as the only widely accepted measure of library usage and, ultimately, funding. Such a system is analogous to McDonald's counting only the number of hamburgers sold through the drive-through (i.e., library circulation) while ignoring the number of hamburgers consumed in the restaurant (i.e., in-library usage) when the corporation is evaluating the effectiveness of each restaurant. Yet this is what the vast majority of library systems are doing today.

The Start of a Solution

Christie Koontz and Dean Jue of Florida State University (FSU) realized the need for a uniform and better (especially for the more non-traditional library markets) method to collect in-library usage data. In September of 1996, they received a three-year grant from the U.S. Department of Education (DOE) to study in-library material usage and adult life-long educational needs in majority-minority markets throughout the U.S. The majority-minority markets in this study included African-Americans, American Indians, Asians, Hispanics, and low-income populations.

The first procedure was to identify where high numbers of minorities or low-income individuals resided in close proximity to public libraries. The 1993 Federal-State Cooperative System (FSCS) database of public library outlets throughout the U.S. was geocoded (i.e., assigned latitude and longitude values) based on the street addresses of each outlet. These geocoded library outlets were then imported into a geographic information system (GIS) software product and overlaid on a digital map of the census tracts of the U.S. constructed from U.S. Bureau of the Census digital TIGER files. Because each census tract had the racial, cultural and income characteristics associated with it, the GIS could be used to determine, for example, which public library outlets were located within a mile of a census tract that had a majority of its residents of Hispanic origin. This query found a total of 923 public library outlets out of a total of 15,718 outlets that fit this criterion.

A stratified sample of 400 public library outlets was randomly selected throughout the U.S. The library system directors for each of the 400 selected library outlets were sent a letter informing them of the U.S. DOE/FSU study and asking for their participation. For those who indicated a willingness to participate, a survey was sent to obtain some baseline information for the participating outlets. Part of the baseline information requested was an indication of the primary type of non-traditional users that each outlet served. Based on the information provided by the system directors, 37 library outlets out of a total of 95 outlets participating in this study served a large number of Hispanics. It was possible for a library system director to identify more than one large group of non-traditional users by an individual outlet. A list of the Hispanic outlets participating in this DOE/FSU study is provided in Table 1.

State	**Library System**	**Branch**
Arizona	Maricopa County LD	Aguila Library
Arizona	Tucson-Pima PL	Arivaca Library
California	County of Los Angeles PL	East Los Angeles
California	County of Los Angeles PL	City Terrace Library
California	County of Los Angeles PL	El Camino Real

State	Library System	Branch
California	County of Los Angeles PL	Anthony Quinn
California	Fresno County PL	San Joaquin
California	Fresno County PL	Selma
California	Fresno County PL	Sanger Branch
California	Huntington Beach Lib	Oak View Branch
California	Oakland PL	Cesar E. Chavez Branch
California	Oakland PL	Brookfield Branch
California	Oakland PL	Asian Branch
California	Oakland PL	Elmhurst Branch
California	San Benito County Free Lib	San Benito County Free Lib
California	San Jose PL	Hillview Library
California	San Jose PL	Seventrees Library
Colorado	Denver PL	Valdez-Perry Branch
Colorado	Denver PL	Byers Branch
Florida	Palm Beach County LS	Belle Glade Branch
Illinois	Chicago PL	Rudy Lozano Branch
Illinois	Chicago PL	The Richard J Daley Branch
Illinois	Chicago PL	Humboldt Park Branch
Illinois	Chicago PL	South Chicago Branch
Illinois	Chicago PL	Uptown Branch
Illinois	Chicago PL	Bezazian Branch
Massachusetts	New Bedford Free PL	Howland-Green Branch
New Jersey	New Brunswick Free PL	New Brunswick Free PL
New Mexico	Bloomfield Community Lib	Bloomfield Community Lib
New Mexico	Mother Whiteside Memorial Lib	Mother Whiteside Memorial Lib
New Mexico	Socorro PL	Socorro PL
New York	Queens Borough PL	Queensbridge Branch
New York	Queens Borough PL	Court Square Branch
Pennsylvania	The Free Library of Philadelphia	Logan Branch
Texas	San Antonio PL	McCreless Branch

Table 1. List of Participating Libraries Serving Hispanics

To standardize the collection of in-library performance measures, a hand-held portable bar code scanner was pre-programmed by FSU staff for each library system that participated in the study. Using the bar code scanner helped ensure consistency of data collection because the answers to all questions were pre-defined as bar codes. With practice, data input using the scanner was quick and accurate. Also, the collected data were stored in the scanner until the data could be uploaded to a computer for importing into a database for further analysis, alleviating the need for manual entry of the data.

The three areas for which in-library use data were collected were in-library materials usage (material used in the library but not checked out), library assistance (including reference questions, help writing resumes, and so forth), and in-library activities (a sampling of what users are actually doing in the library on an hourly basis). Tables 2 through 4 provide a list of the types of information collected within the three data areas. The collected data were forwarded to FSU staff. The data were then summarized and returned on a quarterly basis back to each individual collecting library outlet.

1. Material Format (e.g., book, newspaper)
2. Quantity
3. Language of Material
4. Material Status: Can it be checked out
5. Material Type: Age Level of Material
6. Material Classification: Dewey Decimal/LC

Table 2. In-Library Material Use Data

1. Transaction Type (e.g., by phone, in person)
2. Age of Library User
3. Assistance Subject Area
4. Time to Answer Question

Table 3. Library Assistance Data

1. Library Location
2. User Activity
3. Computer Software Used (if applicable)
4. No. of Users in Activity
5. Age of User(s)

Table 4. Library User Activity Data

Summary of the Results from Libraries Serving Hispanics

This section summarizes the preliminary results for the third quarter of data collection for 1998. The remaining data will be published later through the U.S. Department of Education. Throughout this article, the term "Hispanic library" will refer to the libraries listed in Table 1 that have identified themselves as serving a significant number of Hispanics. The term "non–Hispanic library" will refer to all the other libraries participating in this study that did not identify themselves as serving a significant number of Hispanics and encompass library outlets serving significant numbers of either African-Americans, Asian-Americans, American Indians, low income and/or a multiculturally diverse population.

In-Library Material Usage

In this study's libraries, the majority of materials used within a library was capable of being circulated. Over 80 percent of materials used in Hispanic libraries, for instance, could be checked out. This percentage is higher than for non–Hispanic libraries, where just over 67 percent of materials could be checked out.

Almost 42 percent of the materials used in Hispanic libraries, were oriented toward adults while over 61 percent of the in-library materials in non–Hispanic libraries were written for adults. Over 50 percent of the library materials used within Hispanic libraries were aimed at pre-school and juvenile users, whereas the corresponding percentage in non–Hispanic libraries was less than one-third of the materials.

	Hispanic Libraries	Non-Hispanic Libraries	All Libraries
Can Be Circulated	14325 (81.35 %)	12272 (67.32 %)	26597 (74.21%)
Cannot Be Circulated	3284 (18.65 %)	5957 (32.68 %)	9241 (25.79%)
TOTAL	17609	18229	35838

Table 5. Circulation Status of In-Library Materials

	Hispanic Libraries	Non-Hispanic Libraries	All Libraries
Easy	3918 (22.25%)	2084 (11.43%)	6002 (16.75%)
Juvenile	5532 (31.42%)	3855 (21.15%)	9387 (26.19%)
Young Adult	717 (4.07%)	987 (5.41%)	1704 (4.75%)
Adult	7390 (41.97%)	11173 (61.29 %)	18563 (51.80%)
Blind/Handicapped	20 (0.11%)	2 (0.01%)	22 (0.06%)
Large Print	32 (0.18%)	128 (0.70%)	160 (0.45%)
TOTAL	17609	18229	35838

Table 6. Intended Audience for In-Library Materials

As might be expected, materials written in Spanish constituted almost 14 percent of materials used within the library versus less than one percent for non-Hispanic libraries.

	Hispanic Libraries	Non-Hispanic Libraries	All Libraries
English	14794 (84.01%)	17768 (97.47%)	32562 (90.68%)
Spanish	2459 (13.96%)	21 (0.12%)	2480 (6.92%)
Other Languages	356 (2.03%)	440 (2.41%)	796 (2.40%)
TOTAL	17609	18229	35838

Table 7. Language of In-Library Materials.

Regardless of the library type, approximately 50 percent of in-library material usage were classified books and 20 percent were non-classified books, while magazines made up about 12 percent of the materials used within the library. Two format categories in which Hispanic libraries were noticeably lower than non-Hispanic libraries were videos (2.04 percent versus 6.86 percent) and newspapers (4.02 percent versus 7.53 percent)

	Hispanic Libraries	Non–Hispanic Libraries	All Libraries
Books, Classified	9225 (52.39%)	8768 (48.10%)	17993 (50.21%)
Books, Non-classified	4204 (23.87%)	2917 (16.00%)	7121 (19.87%)
Magazines	2316 (13.15%)	2238 (12.28%)	4554 (12.71%)
Newspapers	708 (4.02%)	1373 (7.53%)	2081 (5.81%)
Video	360 (2.04%)	1251 (6.86%)	1611 (4.50%)
Other Formats	796 (4.53%)	1682 (9.23%)	2478 (6.90%)
TOTALS	17609	18229	35838

Table 8. Format of In-Library Materials

There were few differences between Hispanic libraries and non–Hispanic libraries relative to the subject material used within in the library when the intended audience of the library material is not considered. Just over 26 percent of in-library materials used were fiction. Over 35 percent of the materials were not classfied (e.g., current magazines, newspapers). About 38 percent of materials used within the library had either Dewey Decimal or the Library of Congress classification system assigned to them. There were only two subject categories in which there was more than one percentage point difference between Hispanic libraries and non–Hispanic libraries. These categories were natural science on the one hand, mathematics and technology on the other. In both instances, usage of these subject materials was higher within Hispanic libraries.

	Hispanic Libraries	Non–Hispanic Libraries	All Libraries
Fiction	5052 (28.7%)	4332 (23.8%)	9384 (26.2%)
Not Classified	5797 (32.9%)	6804 (37.3%)	12601 (35.2%)
Natural Science/Math	1151 (6.5%)	568 (3.1%)	1719 (4.8%)
Technology	1051 (6.0%)	759 (4.2%)	1810 (5.0%)
Other Classified	4558 (25.9%)	5766 (31.6%)	10324 (28.8%)
TOTALS	17609	18229	35838

Table 9. In-Library Material Usage by Subject.

The above trends generally held even when the intended audience of the material was considered (i.e., whether the material was easy, juvenile, young adult, or adult).

Library Assistance

There were several notable differences in the types of library assistance provided between Hispanic libraries and non–Hispanic libraries. Computer usage assistance is about 15 percent for all the libraries in this study. However, education and homework assistance is noticeably higher within Hispanic libraries than for the non–Hispanic libraries. In contrast, business-financial, genealogical, legal, and local community information is noticeably higher within non–Hispanic libraries than Hispanic libraries in this study.

The above pattern of library assistance held throughout the age groups within the study. Notable exceptions within the young adult age category: (1) non–Hispanic youths were three times more likely to ask for assistance with science projects than Hispanic youths (2.11 percent versus 0.76 percent), and (2) Hispanic youths were twice as likely to ask for library assistance with leisure and entertainment than non–Hispanic youths (12.1 percent versus 6.6 percent).

	Hispanic Libraries	Non–Hispanic Libraries	All Libraries
Business/Financial	77 (1.2%)	265 (3.5%)	342 (2.6%)
Computer Usage	1016 (16.3%)	1161 (15.1%)	2177 (15.6%)
Education/Homework	965 (15.5%)	654 (8.5%)	1619 (11.6%)
Geneaology	38 (0.6%)	201 (2.6%)	239 (1.7%)
Legal	71 (1.1%)	158 (2.1%)	229 (1.6%)
Local Community Info	100 (1.6%)	280 (3.6%)	380 (2.7%)
Other	3980 (63.7%)	4967 (64.6%)	8947 (64.2%)
TOTAL	6247	7686	13933

Table 10. Number of Library Assistance Instances within Libraries.

In-Library Activities

The types of user activities within the libraries in this study reflected the pattern observed in library assistance. Ignoring age differences, non–Hispanic library users are twice as likely to be at the reference desk, eight times as likely to be doing genealogical research, seven times as likely to be working on their resume, twice as likely to be using the copying machine, and 15 times as likely to be using the microfilm or microfiche reader relative to the Hispanic library users. Hispanic library users are 1.5 times as likely to be reading or writing and over four times as likely to be engaged in tutoring activites relative to non–Hispanic users.

For this study, when patrons are using

	Hispanic Libraries	Non-Hispanic Libraries	All Libraries
At Reference Desk	284 (1.4%)	783 (3.3%)	1067 (2.4%)
Genealogy Research	10 (0.1%)	203 (0.9%)	213 (0.5%)
Programs or Tours	1032 (5.1%)	1626 (6.8%)	2658 (6.0%)
Reading/Writing	4894 (24.2%)	3739 (15.7%)	8633 (19.6%)
Resume Writing	5 (0.1%)	182 (0.8%)	187 (0.4%)
Tutoring	396 (1.9%)	88 (0.4%)	484 (1.1%)
Using Copier	335 (1.6%)	717 (3.0%)	1052 (2.4%)
Using Microfilm/fiche	15 (0.1%)	353 (1.5%)	368 (.8%)
Other Activities	13248 (65.5%)	16085 (67.6%)	29333 (66.8%)
TOTAL	20219	23776	43995

Table 11. User Activities within the Libraries.

computer software, Hispanic library users are more likely to be using educational software, the Internet, and online catalog than are non–Hispanic library users. Non–Hispanic library users are more likely to be using online databases and spreadsheet and word processing software. These results have not been adjusted for the availability of these software types among the libraries. For example, the higher Internet usage within Hispanic libraries may simply be that more Hispanic libraries in this study have Internet availability than the non–Hispanic libraries.

	Hispanic Libraries	Non-Hispanic Libraries	All Libraries
Educational Software	363 (13.0%)	340 (8.7%)	703 (10.5%)
Internet/E-Mail	1168 (41.8%)	1363 (34.8%)	2531 (37.7%)
Online Catalog	750 (26.8%)	423 (10.8%)	1173 (17.5%)
Online Databases	56 (2.0%)	267 (6.8%)	323 (4.8%)
Spreadsheets	1 (0.1%)	44 (1.1%)	45 (0.7%)
Word Processing	136 (4.9%)	1022 (26.1%)	1158 (17.3%)
Other	320 (11.4%)	456 (11.7%)	776 (11.5%)
TOTAL	2794	3915	6709

Table 12. Computer Software Usage in Libraries.

Some of the user activity discrepancies observed may be the result of age group differences between Hispanic and non–Hispanic libraries. A comparison of the estimated age category of the individual users shows there is a higher percentage of juvenile users in the Hispanic libraries in this study as compared to a higher percentage of elders in the non–Hispanic libraries.

There was little difference among young adult library users between Hispanic and non–Hispanic libraries. In both library types, the predominant uses were computer use, reading and writing, browsing, and schoolwork, in that order for young adults.

	Hispanic Libraries	Non–Hispanic Libraries	All Libraries
Pre-School	1079 (5.3%)	1425 (6.0%)	2504 (5.7%)
Juvenile (KG–6th)	7003 (34.6%)	5487 (23.1%)	12490 (28.4%)
Young Adult (7th–12th)	2814 (14.0%)	4453 (18.7%)	7267 (16.5%)
Adult	8674 (42.9%)	10964 (46.1%)	19638 (44.6%)
Elder	539 (2.7%)	1300 (5.5%)	1839 (4.2%)
Unknown	110 (0.5%)	147 (0.6%)	257 (0.6%)
TOTAL	20219	23776	43995

Table 13. Age Category of Library Users.

Analysis of the Results

The results presented are sampled numeric counts for one quarter of a calendar year for a year-long study and do not encompass all the data that will be published in the final report presented to the U.S. Department of Education in August of 1999. The purpose of this study was to collect a nationwide "snapshot" of in-library usage among a large diversity of library branches serving primarily minority or low-income populations rather than to strive for statistical significance. This "snapshot," of course, is not yet complete.

Because the above results are for just one quarter, it is inappropriate to over-analyze the above observations. Several trends can be inferred and may bear further analysis. It appears, for instance, that Hispanic libraries serve a younger population than the non–Hispanic libraries in this study. This can be seen in the higher percentage of in-library materials used that are written for pre-school or juvenile populations as well as in the actual hourly tally of library users as part of this study. Non-Hispanic libraries serve a higher percentage of adult or elderly population.

The data also indicate that library users in Hispanic libraries are eager consumers of library materials written in the Spanish or Portugese languages. It is interesting to note that newspaper and video usage within the library is lower for Hispanic libraries than for non–Hispanic libraries. Whether this may partially result from a lack of such materials in the Hispanic languages bears further investigation.

Library assistance and library use within the libraries in this study partially reflect the differences in the age of the population served. Hispanic libraries have higher instances of library assistance involving education and homework than non-Hispanic libraries, as well as use of the library for tutoring. Non–Hispanic libraries have more assistance of users for business and financial questions, genealogy research, résumé writing and legal issues — activities more popular among adult library users.

Implications of the Results for Library Outlets Serving Non-Traditional Populations

The above results confirm one of the major tenets motivating this research project: library use data need to be collected and maintained at the branch level of detail rather than be aggregated into a "library system" or state level of detail.

This research project focused only on non-traditional library user populations. Even so, it is obvious that when library use data are combined across all non-traditional libraries (i.e., the right-hand column in all the above tables), significant pieces of library user information are lost. For example, the greater in-library usage of natural science, mathematics, and technology books in Hispanic libraries or the larger percentage of library users engaged in résumé writing in non–Hispanic libraries would not have been identified.

Consider a situation where a library branch serves primarily a non-traditional library user population within a larger library system with several library branches. Even if library usage data are being collected at all the branches, the unique needs and library usages of the non-traditional population will be lost if the library data are aggregated to a system-wide level for reporting purposes.

When data are aggregated, this additional information is lost. The additional data could improve the ability to justify new funding for improving library services to the non-traditional library user populations such as new immigrants and pockets of ethnic or cultural minorities.

Summary and Conclusion

This U.S. Department of Education-funded project focuses on in-library usage for library outlets serving primarily majority-minority and low income populations. Using bar code sheets and a hand-held bar code scanner, a standardized methodology was developed to collect in-library usage among approximately 100 library outlets nationwide.

There were library usage differences between library outlets serving Hispanic populations and those serving non–Hispanic populations. In general, libraries serving Hispanic populations had a larger juvenile population and this difference was reflected in the types of materials used and in the library activities.

Library data collected at an outlet should not be aggregated with other library outlets, especially if the collected data represent a small group of library users, because doing so dilutes the data, hindering the improvement of library services to these users.

Notes

1. Christine M. Koontz, "Market-Based Modelling for Public Library Facility Location and Use Forceasting," unpublished doctoral dissertation, Florida State University (Tallahassee, Fla., 1990): pp. 319–326.

2. National Center for Educational Statistics, *Public Libraries in the U.S.: Fiscal Year 1994* (Office of Educational Research, U.S. Department of Education. NCES Publication 97–418, May 1997): p. iii.

3. Christine M. Koontz, *Library Facility Siting and Location Handbook* (Westport, Conn.: Greenwood, 1997): pp. 130–139.

Planning School Library Media Services: Resources

Patricia F. Beilke

To develop school library media services for multicultural populations, basic principles should be followed during the preplanning and planning stages. Many concerns need to be addressed when cultural considerations receive high priority. Hispanic children share some similar cultural characteristics, however, there are cultural differences among Mexican Americans, Puerto Ricans, Cuban Americans, as well as Hispanic Americans from Central and South American countries and Spain. Within each culture, there are additional differences. Some of the differences include the following variations: socio-economic status, geographic influences, educational experiences, recency within the United States, language preferences, reading abilities, and strength of cultural ties to home communities in other countries as well as other regions of the United States. Both general and cultural concerns related to the planning of school library media services are addressed in this article.

Leadership is needed to plan school library media programs that provide user services and assure access to information: 1) From a wide variety of sources; 2) By learning many ways of understanding the organization and content of the information; 3) Through the experiences of organizing information into meaningful messages. Examples of the messages may include the following: written works with correct bibliographic citations for the sources of information, audiovisual presentations, activities which involve development of internet links, and oral reports.

Guideline No. 1: Those Influenced by School Library Media Center Services Should Be Represented in Planning and Evaluation

Development of the Vision

This is central to the work of the school library media specialist in collaborating with administrators and teachers to improve the learning of students. Useful sources for the school library media specialist to consult include:

- Patricia Senn Breivik and J. A. Senn, *Information Literary: Educating Children for the 21st Century*, 2nd ed. (Washington,

D.C.: NEA Professional Library, National Education Association, 1998).

This easily read book, enhanced with touches of humor, discusses many ways in which children need to become information literate. In addition, there is an excellent annotated bibliography. It includes writings of Michael B. Eisenberg which provide practical advice about teaching students how to become effective information users. Many library media specialists find the "Big Six Skills Approach" useful in working with their students. Also, the bibliography cites *Bookpeople: A Multicultural Album* by Sharron L. McMeel which provides practical ideas for integrating literature and multicultural activities to help children develop knowledge of and appreciation for many heritages and cultures. An annotated list of Information Literacy Sites on the Worldwide Web is given.

• American Association of School Librarians and Association for Educational Communications and Technology, *Information Power: Building Partnerships for Learning* (Chicago: American Library Association; and Washington, D.C.: Association for Educational Communications and Technology, 1998.)

• American Association of School Librarians and Association for Educational Communications and Technology, *Information Power: Guidelines for School Library Media Programs* (Chicago: American Library Association 1988).

These two professional guidelines are important to examine the teaching learning process.

• Marie F. Zielinska with Francis T. Kirkwood, *Multicultural Librarianship: An International Handbook*, IFLA Publications 59, edited for the International Federation of Library Associations and Institutions, Section on Library Services to Multicultural Populations (New York: K. G. Saur, 1992).

For attention to cultural needs in the planning process, consult chapters in this work. Barriers to use of information, budgets, space requirements, staffing, resource sharing, acquisitions, determining who shall select materials, problems of circulating minority-language materials, and the marketing approach to the promotion of services are some topics addressed. Although writers constantly refer to public libraries, there are many items of information, especially those concerned with possible attitudes and previous experiences of potential users which school library media specialists will find useful. The importance of educating library personnel to provide services to leaders of cultural groups is emphasized.

Gain Support for the Vision

The support of the principal is one of the most important factors in the development of an excellent school library media center. School library media specialists who seek to develop new media centers and improve old ones must enlist the support of their administrators. The following sources are particularly useful.

• David V. Loertscher, *Reinvent Your School's Library in the Age of Technology: A Guide for Principals and Superintendents* (San Jose, Calif.: Hi Willow, 1998).

• American Association of School Librarians and Association for Educational Communications and Technology, *Information Literacy Standards for Student Learning* (Chicago: American Library Association, 1998).

School library media specialists can

provide busy administrators Loertscher's *Reinvent Your School's Library in the Age of Technology: A Guide for Principals and Superintendents.* The American Association of School Librarians suggests that library media specialists provide principals copies of *Information Literacy Standards for Student Learning,* a title which addresses how to evaluate student learning and which is an abbreviated version of *Information Power: Building Partnerships for Learning.*

What are advisable ways of planning school library media programs? How can a media specialist develop a mission statement for a school library media program and work with administrators and teachers to identify objectives for each library media program goal? Examination of written documents which frequently exist in school districts is advocated.

1. Review the philosophy of the school district or corporation concerning its approach to education? What are the goals and objectives stated for the educational program?

2. Review the written philosophy of the educational program at the school. What are the goals and objectives of its educational program?

3. After examination of these documents, it may be useful to confer with the principal about the content of current curricular thrusts, future curricular plans, and the establishment of an advisory committee or committees of teachers and parents.

One middle school principal in Gas City, Indiana, worked with his media specialist and over a period of years managed to rotate all faculty as members of the library advisory committee. The media specialist noted that the advisory committee had helped indicate where major allocations of the library budget should be placed. In addition, each faculty member became aware of the challenges faced by the media specialist in managing the services.

Guideline No. 2: A Written Statement of Philosophy Needs to Be Established by Advisory Committees, Rewritten, and Reviewed Again by the Committees and the Principal

A policy manual needs to be written which has sections about the community and school, user population characteristics, user services, library media personnel, collections, facilities, budgets, and services, as well as procedures for planning and evaluation.

Betty J. Morris with John T. Gillespie and Diana L. Spirt, *Administering the School Library Media Center,* 3rd ed. (New Providence, N.J. : Bowker, 1992).

Betty J. Morris, John T. Gillespie and Diana L. Spirt write of the proactive leadership role library media specialists need to take. They list functions and provide checklists for school library media specialist roles and responsibilities, cooperative program planning, a self-evaluation form, and job evaluations for school library media specialists and the clerical staff. They provide valuable checklists for assessing areas of the school library media program which are doing well in addition to those for aspects of the program which need improvement.

To learn how services of school library media services can be improved, media specialists can take the following actions:

1. Visit lively prototype programs and

help arrange visits of administrators, key teachers, and school board members to these programs.

2. With the principal's permission, contact the office of the state school library media supervisor and invite a consultant to visit and provide advice.

3. Organize focus group meetings with parents and teachers to learn what improvements users desire.

One elementary school principal in Wichita, Kansas, scheduled and attended evening meetings with parents and teachers. They were organized into small groups, which convened concurrently. They planned the conversion of a former cafeteria area into a school library media center.

Responding to Cultural and Technological Needs

It is important to include members of the cultural communities on advisory committees or as consultants. These community members will be able to answer questions about cultural traditions and language barriers, advise about authenticity of materials under consideration for selection and may be aware of special cultural needs and interests. Some schools employ paid aides to be liaisons between parents and school personnel. Many school administrators organize formal and informal outreach strategies designed to identify and seek the guidance which can be provided by community leaders.

Parent participation in the school lives of their children, library media programming (planning of activities designed to promote information literacy), and inservice for all school personnel are needed to add the cultural emphasis desired by many school communities.

Guideline No. 3: Children Learn More Effectively When Expectations of Parents and School Personnel Are the Same

The following sources provide valuable information on encouraging parent participation and facilitating parent-staff cooperation:

- Siobhan Nicolau, et al., *Dear Parents: In the United States ... It's Our School Too*; Eric ED325 541 Nicolau, Siobhan and Carmen Lydia Ramos, *You're a Parent ... You're a Teacher Too, Join the Education Team* (New York: Hispanic Policy Development Project, 1990). ERIC, ED 335173.
- Virginia Vogel Zanger, et al., eds., *Classroom Activities for Cross-Cultural Learning* (Boston, Mass.: Boston District Five Teacher Center, 1990), ERIC, ED 320 423.

Guideline No. 4: Children, Whether Hispanic or of Other Cultures, Need to Learn About Their Own and Others' Cultures

The following sources include ideas for programming that apply to both public and school libraries.

• Adela Artola Allen, "Library Services for Hispanic Young Adults," *Library Trends* 37 (Summer 1988): 80–105.

• Oralia Garza de Cortés, comp., *Program Planning and Services for Children: A Select Bibliography.* Presented at Hispanic Library Education, The Second National Institute: "Latino Populations and the Public Library," Austin, Texas, November 12–15, 1995 (San Antonio, Texas: Central Children's Department, San Antonio Public Library, 1995).

• Kathy Escamilla, *Integrating Mexican-American History and Culture Into the Social Studies Classroom,* Clearinghouse on Rural Education and Small Schools. Digest EDO-RC-92-5. Charleston, West Virginia: ERIC/Cress, Appalachia Educational Laboratory, P. O. Box 1348, September 1992. ERIC, ED 348 200.

• Janice N. Harrington, *Multiculturalism in Library Programming for Children,* ALSC Program Support Publications. Evelyn Walker, series editor (Chicago: American Library Association, 1994).

• Lori S. Mestre and Sonia Nieto, "Puerto Rican Children's Literature and Culture in the Public Library," *Multicultural Review* 5 (June 1996): 26–39.

• Laurie Olsen and Carol Dowell, *Bridges: Promising Programs for the Education of Immigrant Children,* A Publication of the California Tomorrow Immigrant Students Project (Los Angeles: California Tomorrow, 1989), ERIC, ED 314 544.

• Patricia L. Roberts and Nancy Lee Cecil. "Extended Activity Unit: Grades K–3 and Extended Activity Unit: Grades 4–8," in Patricia L. Roberts and Nancy Lee Cecil, eds., *Developing Multicultural Awareness Through Children's Literature: A Guide for Teachers and Librarians, Grades K-8* (Jefferson, N.C.: McFarland, 1993).

• Rhea Joyce Rubin, *Intergenerational Programming: A-How-to-Do-It-Manual for Librarians,* How-to-Do-It-Manuals for Libraries No. 36 (New York: Neal-Schuman, 1993).

• E. Dollie Wolverton, "Multicultural Principles for Head Start Programs," in Lynette Young Overby, Ann Richardson, Lillian S. Hasko, and Luke Kalich, eds. *Early Childhood Creative Arts: Proceedings of the International Early Childhood Creative Arts Conference, Los Angeles, California, December 6–9, 1990* (Reston, Va.: National Dance Association, an association of the American Alliance for Health, Physical Education, Recreation and Dance, 1991).

Guideline No. 5: Teachers and Other School Personnel Need to Engage in Inservice Activities Related to Cultures

Consult the following valuable sources for ideas on culture-specific activity planning:

• J. A. Banks, ed., *Teaching Strategies for Ethnic Studies,* 4th ed. (Needham Heights, Mass.: Allyn and Bacon, 1987).

• Oralia Garza de Cortés, "Behind the Golden Door: The Latino Immigrant Child in Literature and Films for Children," *MultiCultural Review* 4 (June 1995): 24–27, 59.

• Carl A. Grant, ed., *Educating for Diversity: An Anthology of Multicultural Voices,* Sponsored by Association of Teacher Educators (Needham Heights, Mass.: Allyn and Bacon, 1995).

• Cristina Igoa, *The Inner World of the Immigrant Child* (New York: St. Martin's, 1995).

• William Watson Purkey and Paula Helen Stanley, *Invitational Teaching, Learning, and Living* (Washington, D.C.: National Education Association, 1991).

• Christine E. Sleeter, ed., *Empowerment through Multicultural Education.* (Albany: State University of New York, 1991).

• Rose Mary Flores Story, "Understanding and Appreciating the Unique Needs of Mexican Americans," in Kathy Howard Latrobe and Mildred Knight Laughlin, eds., *Multicultural Aspects of Library Media Programs* (Englewood, Colo.: Libraries Unlimited, 1992), pp. 45–53.

Conclusion

This article has indicated resources for planning which relate to general principles for media specialists and which also indicate principles to be aware of in planning library services for multicultural populations.

In addition, representative indicators of the many existing resources show ways to involve parents in schools, plan activities related to cultures and conduct ongoing in-service programs for school personnel.

Involvement of parents, extended family, and all school personnel can be helpful to many children. While culture-specific materials may be appreciated by those from a given culture, persons living in the United States are part of one another's cultures. In addition to learning how to conduct business in the general society, it is the business of everyone to learn of the cultures of all.

Collection Development: Bibliography

Janice Greenberg

The continual growth of the Hispanic–Latino-American population in the United States creates a unique challenge for the children's librarian without an extended background in the Spanish language or with a lack of familiarity with the diverse Latino-Hispanic cultures from which our young users and potential users come. Often the material is widely dispersed or difficult to find.

This bibliography provides a brief selected list of professional resources in a variety of formats. It is a guide for children's librarians who seek easily identifiable items of quality to support collection-development initiatives or continuing education in the areas of Hispanic-American heritage and literature.

Books

Alire, Camilia, and Orlando Archibeque. *Serving Latino Communities: A How-to-Do-It Manual for Librarians,* no. 80. New York, London: Neal Schuman, 1998.

Assessment of community needs; programs and services for Latinos; funding for services; partnerships with organizations and associations; collection development; outreach and marketing/public relations. Includes a directory of resources; bibliography; and appendices.

Allen, Adela Artola, ed. *Library Services for Hispanic Children: A Guide to Public and School Libraries.* Phoenix: Oryx, 1987.

Consists of articles by various authors which cover three central themes: history and approaches to serving Hispanic children; professional issues related to library services for the Hispanic child; and books, nonprint materials, software and resources. Bibliographies.

Beilke, Patricia F., and Frank J. Sciara. *Selecting Materials for and about Hispanic and East Asian Children and Young People.* Hamden, Conn.: Library Professional Publications, 1986.

Covers the selection of materials in the context of library services; in-service training and staff development; background of Hispanic children and young people in the United States. Specific background readings are provided on Mexican Americans, Puerto Ricans, Cuban Americans, provides a general bibliography.

Haro, Robert. *Developing Library and Information Services for Americans of Hispanic Origin.* Metuchen, N.J.: Scarecrow Press, 1981.

Focuses on library services to Mexican Americans, Puerto Ricans, Cubans, and

"Latinos." Covers historical background. Also includes sociological synopses of each group. Existing library services in Mexico, Puerto Rico, and Cuba are described. Also discusses library services to children of Hispanic origin. Other areas covered are the public library and its relationship to Americans of Hispanic origin, and the evaluation of Hispanic-oriented collections and services. Contains a bibliography and appendices.

Schon, Isabel. *Basic Collection of Children's Books in Spanish.* Metuchen, N.J.: Scarecrow, 1986.

Organized into the following sections: reference, nonfiction, fiction, easy books, and professional books. Categorized by Dewey Decimal System. Includes translations of Spanish titles into English. Contains author, title, and subject indexes.

Schon, Isabel. *Books in Spanish for Children and Young Adults: An Annotated Guide/Libros infantiles y juveniles en espanol: una guía anotada, series nos. I–VI.* Metuchen, N.J.: Scarecrow, 1978–1993.

Organized initially by country, then by subcategories which include fiction and various nonfiction categories. Annotations are of Spanish language, bilingual, and English translations. Each annotation includes a rating ("outstanding," "marginal" or "not recommended") and grade level. Includes translations of Spanish titles into English. Author and title indexes.

Schon, Isabel. *Contemporary Spanish-Speaking Writers and Illustrators for Children and Young Adults: A Biographical Dictionary.* Westport, Conn.: Greenwood, 1994.

Lists over 200 Spanish-speaking authors and illustrators for children and young adults. The appendix categorizes the authors and illustrators by country of birth or citizenship.

Schon, Isabel. *Recommended Books in Spanish for Children and Young Adults, 1991–1995.* Lanham, Md.: Scarecrow, 1997.

Consists of annotated citations for 1,055 Spanish-language books targeted for the ages preschool through high school. Sections include reference, nonfiction, publishers'series, and fiction. Includes translations of Spanish titles into English. Contains title, author and subject indexes, and an appendix.

Wadham, Tim. *Programming with Latino Children's Materials: A How-to-Do-It Manual for Librarians,* no. 89. New York: Neal Schuman, 1999.

Covers Latino children and their culture; Latino children's literature; Latino folklore and folk rhymes; other types of Latino children's literature and art; school and library programs; collection development issues; planning and programming resources (includes on-line resources). Contains annotated bibliographies; general, names, and programming indexes.

Articles

Agosto, Denise. "Bilingual Picture Books: Libros Para Todos." *School Library Journal* 43(August 1997): 38–41.

Discusses the importance of bilingual picture books to a children's collection in the library. Examines several books, including *Say* Hola *to Spanish,* by Susan Middleton Elya, illustrated by Loretta Lopez; *Bread is for Eating,* by David and Phillis Gershator; *Abuelita's Heart,* by Amy Cordorva; *Mi primer libro de dichos/My First Book of Proverbs* by Ralfka González and Ana Ruiz; *Gathering the Sun: An Alphabet in Spanish and English* by Alma Flor Ada; *Isla* by Arthur Dorros, illustrated by Elisa

Kleven; *Fernando's Gift/El regalo de Fernando*, by Douglas Keister; *The Iguana Brothers*, by Tony Johnston and Mark Teague; *Chato's Kitchen*, by Gary Soto, illustrated by Susan Guevara; *The Tale of Rabbit and Coyote*, by Tony Johnston, illustrated by Tomie dePaola; and *Carlos and the Cornfield/Carlos y la milpa de maiz*, by Jan Romero Stevens, illustrated by Jeanne Arnold. The article also specifies several types of programs using these books.

Allen, Adela Artola. "The School Library Media Center and the Promotion of Literature for Hispanic Children." *Library Trends* 41(Winter 1993): 437–461.

Discusses the results of a survey of school library media centers with large percentages of Hispanic children. The primary purpose of the survey was to acquire an awareness of the accessibility of Spanish language children's literature in these schools. Findings covered: "The Schools, The Student Body, Their Language, and the Community"; "School Library Media Specialists and Their Support Staff"; "School Library Media Centers' Holding and Budget"; and "The Book Selection Process." Also covered are "Media Center Events and Activities"; "Positive Trends in Hispanic Children's Literature"; "Negative Trends, Needs, and Concerns Regarding Access to Spanish Children's Literature"; and "Successful Events." Includes recommendations of methods to improve library service to Hispanic children. Especially useful for public school administrators and school library media. Includes tables, a bibliography, and an appendix (School Library Children's Librarians' Survey).

Asch, Stephanie. "Urban Libraries Confront Linguistic Minorities: Programs That Work." In Rebecca Constantino, ed., *Literacy, Access, and Libraries among the Language Minority Population*. Lanham, Md.: Scarecrow, 1998, pp. 69–87.

Examines characteristics of successful library programming targeted to the ESL population in the community. These include grants; ties to the community; outreach; bilingual or bicultural librarians and staff; and bilingual signage and bilingual written documentation geared to the need of the ESL library users. Also profiles five libraries with successful ESL outreach programming.

Bern, Alan. "Selection Tools for Materials in Spanish for Children and Young Adults." *Journal of Youth Services in Libraries* 8 (Fall 1994): 55–67.

Recommends selection tools geared toward newcomers in material selection. These include the Guadalajara Book Fair, commercial vendors, books, retrospective collection tools and journals. Annotations are provided for each entry.

Carlson, Lori Marie. "Translation: A Struggle with Words." *School Library Journal* 41 (June 1995): 40–41.

Examines the art of translating from English into Spanish. Also explores the diversity of the various linguistic and cultural Hispanic communities in the United States. Concludes that a good translation need not be grammatical as long as it is faithful to the culture it deals with. Provides several guidelines for consideration when judging translations.

Chávez, Linda. "Collection Development for the Spanish-Speaking." In Salvador Güereña, ed., *Latino Librarianship: A Handbook for Professionals*. Jefferson, N.C.: McFarland, 1990, pp. 68–87.

Examines how to build the Spanish language collection, methods for book evaluation and selection and acquisition issues. Contains bibliographies, including one on collection-development resources.

Cortés, Oralia Garza de , and Louise Yarian Zwick. "Hispanic Materials and Programs." In Carla D. Hayden, ed., *Venture into Cultures: A Resource Book of Multicultural Materials and Programs.* Chicago: American Library Association, 1992, pp. 81–106.

Consists of a bibliography of recommended fiction and non-fiction Spanish and English books for Hispanic children. Audiovisual materials are also annotated. Includes sample program ideas and several story hours with Hispanic themes. Additional annotated bibliographies cover program resources and professional resources for librarians.

Fournier, Julia, and Cecilia Espinosa. "Tierra Fertil: Making the Soil Rich for Discussion for Young Children in Spanish." In Rebecca Constantino, ed., *Literacy, Access, and Libraries among the Language Minority Population.* Lanham, Md.: Scarecrow, 1998, pp. 174–192.

Discusses books that were used successfully by the authors with their Spanish-as-first-language students in the classroom. Also provides brief annotations of fiction and non-fiction books. Bibliography.

Italiano, Graciela. "Reading Latin America: Issues in the Evaluation of Latino Children's Books in Spanish and English." In *Evaluating Children's Books: A Critical Look: Aesthetic, Social, and Political Aspects of Analyzing and Using Children's Books.* Papers presented at the Allerton Park Institute in Monticello, Illinois, October 25–27 1992, by the University of Illinois, Graduate School of Library and Information Science. Urbana-Champaign, Ill: University of Illinois, Graduate School of Library and Information Science, 1993, pp. 119–132

Discusses problems of language and culture. Evaluates four books: *El sombrero de tio Nacho/Uncle Nacho's Hat,* by Harriet Rohmer, illustrated by Veg Reisberg; *My Aunt Otilia's Spirits/Los espíritus de mi tia Otilia,* by Richard Garcia, illustrated by Robin Cherin and Roger I. Reyes: *Abuela,* by Arthur Dorros, illustrated by Elisa Kleven; and *Diego,* by Jonah Winter, illustrated by Jeanette Winter. Includes a bibliography.

Larson, Jeanette, and Carolina G. Martínez. "*Hispanic_Kids@Library.net: Internet Resources for Latino Youth,*" *Journal of Youth Services in Libraries* 11 (Spring 1998): 243–251.

Explores different motivations for focusing attention on Spanish-language and Hispanic-interest Internet sites on OPACS in the library. Also discusses web sites beneficial to librarians in their work with Hispanic youth. Includes tables, figures, and bibliography.

Lesesne, Teri S., and Sylvia Hall-Ellis. "The Selection, Evaluation, and Integration of Culturally Authentic Texts: A Case for Making the Online Catalog Reflect Parallel Cultures." Paper presented at the Annual Meeting of the International Association of School Librarianship, July 1994. ERIC 374 816.

Discusses criteria for selecting multicultural literature, including accuracy and authenticity, avoidance of stereotypes, and the use of language and dialects. Explores ways to integrate multicultural literature into the curriculum. Also describes the challenge of cataloging multicultural materials, especially those written in Spanish.

Library Services to the Spanish Speaking Committee, RASD, American Library Association. "Developing Collections for the Spanish Speaking." *RQ* 35 (Spring 1996): 330–42.

Pucci, Sandra L. "Supporting Spanish Language Literacy: Latino Children and School and Community Libraries." In Rebecca Constantino, ed., *Literacy, Access, and Libraries among the Language Minority Population.* Lanham, Md.: Scarecrow, 1998, pp. 17–52.

Describes research conducted by the author into the Spanish language free-reading materials collections in elementary school libraries in the Los Angeles metropolitan area. Also reviews prior research conducted in several key areas: "free-reading" and language and literacy development; vocabulary acquisition; children, libraries and access to reading materials; and libraries and Latino children. Additional topics addressed include patterns of elementary school library use, public libraries near the schools, children's reported sources of free-reading materials and the role of the school library in supporting the curriculum. Bibliography.

Rome, Linda. "The Art of Inner-City Librarianship: Reaching Out in Cleveland." *Wilson Library Bulletin* 67 (September 1992): 55–58.

Profiles the South Branch of the Cleveland Public Library. Discusses efforts to serve the new wave of immigrants, safety and discipline issues and programming and outreach. Also describes efforts to increase the Spanish-language collection. Lists sources of Spanish and bilingual language materials.

Trujillo, Roberto G., and Linda Chávez. "Collection Development on the Mexican American Experience." In Salvador Güereña *Latino Librarianship: A Handbook for Professionals.* Jefferson, N.C.: McFarland, 1990, pp. 78–90.

Discusses the Mexican American collection in the public library. Areas covered include: the "core" collection; how to build a collection; bibliographic aids; collection development variables; book selection and evaluation; and acquisition. Contains a bibliography.

Internet Resources

Regents, University of California, CLNet, editor. (n.d.). CLNet [Online]. Available: *http://clnet.ucr.edu/*" [January 30, 1998].

Includes: Library, with links to several children's pages; Research Center, which includes links to folklore sites (*http://clnet.ucr.edu/research/folklore.html);* Education, which includes links to Bilingual Education/ESL; K-12 Resources; and Institutes and Centers.

REFORMA, Bibliotecas para la Gente chapter, editor. (1998). Bibliotecas para la Gente [Online]. Available: *http://clnet.ucr.edu/library/bplg/index.html* [January 30, 1998].

Includes booktalks in Spanish and in English, Spanish storytime ideas, web sites of interest to Latinos and search engines in Spanish and English.

Ramapo Catskill Library System, editor. (1999). LibraryLand [Online]. Available: *http://sunsite.berkeley.edu/LibraryLand/* [1999, January 29].

Includes outreach services for Non-English speakers, outreach organizations and review sources in children's services.

Schon, Isabel, ed. (n.d.). Center for the Study of Books in Spanish for Children and Adolescents [Online]. Available: *http://www.csusm.edu/cwis/campus_centers/csb/english/center.htm* [1999, January 28].

Includes "Recommended Books—a form which enables the user to search by such criteria as grade, country, publisher, subject, author, translator, illustrator, title and review source (from Dr.Schon's publications). Also included are lists of Caldecott and Newbery medal winners translated into Spanish, magazines in Spanish for children and adolescents, and singalongs in Spanish. There is also a page with links to related websites.

Vandergrift, Kay, ed. (1998). Kay E.Vandergrift's Special Interest Page. [Online]. Available: *http://www.scils.rutgers.edu/special/kay/kayhp2.html* [1999, January 28].

Includes "Readings in Children's Literature" (with many multicultural titles); "Children's Literature Web Sites"; "Learning About the Author and Illustrator"; "Gender and Culture in Picture Books"; "Translation and Children's Books"; "Gender and Culture Background Readings"; "Gender and Culture Websites"; "Powerful Hispanic and Latin American Images Revealed in Picture Books"; and book selection tools.

Part VI : For the Future

REFORMITA: A GANG FOR THE NEW MILLENNIUM

Dr. Arnulfo Trejo

Last year the Trejo Foster Foundation for Hispanic Library Education (TFF) became the Clearing House for REFORMITA, is a student club organized for the purpose of lending moral support, particularly to students lacking parental care and guidance. This club endeavors to instill in its members self-confidence, resourcefulness and the motivation to strive for educational opportunities, with the expectation of becoming productive and honorable citizens.

My objective is to acquaint you with this student club and explain why I believe there is a need for such an organization. It is not a secret that our Hispanic neighborhoods have a growing number of school dropouts, many of whom are gang members. With or without gangs, the number of felonies committed by young Latinos is alarming.

Before Christmas, an 18-year-old Hispanic allegedly crashed a party in South Tucson. Not being an invited guest, he was refused a beer and left in anger, saying, "I will be back." He did return; this time he was given a beer but was refused a cigarette — that was all it took to start the fight that ended with three people dead and several wounded.

In another incident, a few days before New Year's eve, three persons were reported killed at another party. According to the police the incident was gang-related.

These are not unique events to Tucson, Arizona. Similar cases are reported in other states as well. It does not take a psychologist to recognize that the rage in these confused young men may be the result of psychological deprivation in their early years. It has been established that an individual's welfare is determined before school age. Alert teachers, with the help of parents, can usually identify at-risk children in elementary school.

Knowing this, I believe that REFORMITA can help alleviate the problem. Since teachers, librarians, and parents are the principal leaders in the student club, they can jointly share the responsibility of recruiting at-risk children to assure that no child needing help is left out. I must stress that this club is not only for these children.

The goal of this club is to empower

Editor's Note: Dr. Arnulfo Trejo, founding President of REFORMA and founder of the Trejo Foster Foundation for Hispanic Library Education, delivered this proposal at the closing session of the Trejo Foster Foundation for Hispanic Library Education Fourth National Institute held in Tampa, Florida, in collaboration with the University of South Florida School of Library and Information Science.

children, especially of low income Hispanic families, with reading and library skills to give them self-confidence, appreciation for academic achievement and respect for family values. While REFORMITA has been established to attract Latino students, let it be said that this club is and should always be open to any pupil regardless of race, color, national origin, physical disability, gender, sexual preference, or age. Unlike the Boy Scouts of America, this club will also welcome all children regardless of their immigration status.

REFORMITA is presently recommended for elementary schools, but once the pilot project is successfully implemented there is no reason why REFORMITA clubs could not be organized in middle and high schools.

Studies verify that Latinos are the least educated of all major ethnic groups in the United States. About 50 percent of Latino students drop out of high school, and only 7 percent of Latinos finish college, compared to 12 percent of blacks and 23 percent of whites.

Illiteracy for the total Hispanic population is reported at 14.7 percent in the 1980 Census. The Mexican-origin population had a rate of 18.5 percent, Puerto Ricans 13.4 percent, Cubans 7.8 percent, while other Latinos had a combined rate of 8.2 percent. Little difference is reported in illiteracy rates between males (16.6 percent) and females (17.7 percent).

Why is it that Johnny Smith has a better chance of going to college than Johnny Martinez? It's not brains; it's simply that Johnny Smith is a better reader. No wonder! His mother probably read to him even before he was born. Moreover, he was introduced to the public library even before he was enrolled in school.

Regretfully Johnny Martinez did not learn about reading until he went to school at age six. More than likely he comes from a home where there are no books and no one reads in the family. His parents, if indeed they have discovered libraries, still think of them as bookstores. Of course, there are exceptions, but the truth is that reading is not part of our Hispanic heritage, which is why many generations of Latinos learned the history of their country from corridos (ballads). When the Spaniards came to what is today Mexico, they brought with them the cross and the sword, but very few books. And those few books were mostly in Latin. Their content was religious and erudite. These books were for learned men of the period — the clergy and men of nobility.

Informative or literary works of any kind were prohibited by the Spanish Inquisition. Not until 1810, when Miguel Hidalgo initiated the War of Independence against Spain, was there a concerted effort to improve the social status of the poor. But even after independence was won from Spain, the education of the masses was a low priority. By 1910 the abuse and neglect of the poor ultimately came to a climax. Porfirio Diaz, who had been president of Mexico for 30 years, was finally removed from office. Mexico then went through a brutal seven-year revolution that devastated the country. There was little or no money for schools. Only the children of the upper class attained education.

When General Lázaro Cárdenas became president of Mexico in 1934, he saw the importance of educating the masses and launched a nationwide literacy program. His philosophy was that anyone who knew how to read and write had the responsibility of teaching someone else. Since that time literacy has improved in Mexico, but it still lags behind in extending literacy to its entire population.

In a survey conducted by the Department of Library, about 15 years ago, to determine the kinds of books that should be included in Mexico's public libraries, it was determined that only 4 percent of the population was able to read novels of the caliber written by Carlos Fuentes. That meant that a very small percentage was able to read scholarly literary works. The survey also showed that most readers were reading novelettes such as *El vaquero* and *El semanal.*

Literacy, however, has improved over the years: UNESCO reports that, for 1995, Mexico's illiteracy has dropped to 10.4 percent. Interestingly, the combined rate for Central America is 24.8 percent (largely this high rate is because Guatemala's illiteracy rate is at 44.4 percent). The illiteracy rate for South America is recorded at 8.6 percent. Argentina has an eviable percentage 3.8 percent.

It is a fact that more Hispanics are reading today both in this country and in Latin America. But you can see why Johnny Martinez does not read as well as Johnny Smith. It has been a rocky road that we have traveled to get to where we are today. For the most part, our grandparents, and in some cases our parents, never discovered the power of the printed word or the importance of books and libraries. But let us not feel sorry for them: their lives demanded more practical concerns, and they could boast an uncommon strength of spirit. Their strength, in fact, allowed them to endure political revolutions and the hardships of a country that was struggling to survive.

The Hispanic child is also a victim of our changing society. In the traditional Latino family, the mother stayed home to care for the children and strengthen them with faith in God. Times have changed. Statistics show that there is a definite increase in the number of Hispanic women represented in the American work force, which means that their children end up in day care centers. Since these can be expensive and the earning power of the Hispanic wife is limited, those children do not always get the tender care they so badly need. Then there are the children of the single mother. Their situation is even worse, because in many cases they are left to fend for themselves.

Hopefully these insights may also explain why there is an increase in gang membership, drug addiction and violent crimes in the Latino population. By contrast, the percentage of bilingual, Hispanic librarians is insignificant: I estimate that there are less than 1,000 in a population of 38 million Hispanics. Fortunately, there are non-Hispanic librarians who are willing to work with our people. It becomes obvious that if we want more Hispanic librarians, we will need "to grow" our own through REFORMITA clubs.

For this organization to achieve its goal, funding is required. Someone must undertake the task of writing a proposal for the creation of REFORMITAs throughout the nation, though in truth the project need not be that large. Tucson already has such a student club and the cost was nominal.

Aware of the conditions with which a Hispanic child finds himself or herself faced in school, educators — that includes librarians — must explore ways to help these children overcome the hurdles that prevent them from functioning successfully in mainstream America. First and foremost, teachers and librarians must encourage students to develop partnerships with books and libraries.

So, the count down is on. Let's see how many REFORMITAs we can create. If the kids want to join a gang, I mean a real tough one, let's give them the opportunity to join the best—REFORMITA, the gang for the new millennium.

About the Contributors

Patricia F. Beilke is a professor of Library and Information Science and Secondary Education, Teachers College, Ball State University, Muncie, Indiana and coordinator of Library and Information Science Programs. She has served as chair for the Ethnic Materials and Information Exchange Round Table of the American Library Association and for the Research Committee of the International Association of School Librarianship. She represented IASL for 16 years at meetings of the International Federation of Library Associations and Institutions. She is co-author with Frank J. Sciara of *Selecting Materials For and About Hispanic and East Asian Children and Young People* (Library Professional Publications, 1986) and with Frances Laverne Carroll of *Guidelines for the Planning and Organization of School Library Media Centres* (Unesco, 1978). The revised edition (Unipub, 1982) and a Spanish translation (*Directrices para el planamiento y la organización de mediatecas escolares*, Unesco, 1982) are also available.

James O. Carey is associate director at the School of Library and Information Science, University of South Florida, Tampa, where he teaches computer applications in libraries, instructional technology, and school media management. He currently holds a number of state and national committee responsibilities related to his interests in applications of information literacy and technology in school media services. In addition to his academic work, Dr. Carey has extensive experience in the private sector, serves on a variety of community boards concerned with children's advocacy, and has served as the chief evaluator for numerous federal, state, and local projects.

Oralia Garza de Cortés is a leading advocate of literature and library services for Latino children. A member of REFORMA, she co-founded the Pura Belpré Award as a way to honor and promote more writing and publishing by Latino authors and illustrators. She serves on a national team to launch a national movement to declare April 30th as "Día de los Ninos: Día de los Libros" as a way to focus on the literacy needs of Latino children in the United States, and is the current chair of the Library Services to Spanish Speaking Populations, a Round Table of the Texas Library Association.

Her contributions to the literature of multiculturalism include *Our Family, Our Friends, Our World: An Annotated Guide to Significant Multicultural Books for Children and Teenagers* (R.R. Bowker, 1992); *Venture into Cultures: A Resource Book of Multicultural Materials and Programs* (American Library Association, 1992); and a co-edited chapter in *Multiethnic Literature: Pre–K-12* edited by Violet Harris (Christopher Gordon, 1997).

She was the first Latina elected by the membership to serve on the Board of Directors of ALSC, the Association of Library Services for Children, and the first Latina elected to serve on the Caldecott Committee for the year 2000. In 1996 she received the Leonard Wertheimer Award from the Public Libary Association for outstanding contributions that promote and enhance multilingual librarianship, and in 1997 she received the SALSA Award from the San Antonio Public Library for her work on the committee to develop CATALITA, the Spanish online Kids' Catalog.

Eliza T. Dresang is an associate professor at the Florida State University School of Information Studies, Tallahassee. She is serving a second term on the American Library Association Council and the Board of Directors of the Association for Library Service to Children. She co-directed a 1998 U.S. Department of Education–funded leadership Institute at FSU for school and public librarians. She is the author of *Radical Change: Books for Youth in a Digital Age*

(H.W. Wilson, 1999) and co-author of *Dealing with Censorship in the 21st Century: A Guide for Teachers and Librarians* (forthcoming, Greenwood Press). She has served on the Newbery and Caldecott Award Committees and her teaching interests include the ethnic and cultural information needs of children and young adults.

Lucía M. González is a children's librarian, author, and storyteller at the Miami Dade Public Library System. She chairs the Foreign Languages Committee and "Grupo Colorín-Colorado," a project created to develop system-wide Hispanic children's programs. She has published two books for children and other stories in anthologies. Her first book, *The Bossy Gallito,* was awarded the Pura Belpré Children's Literature Honor Medal in 1996 and was selected for inclusion in the Aesop Accolade List of the American Folklore Society and in the New York Public Library's "100 Recommended Titles for Reading and Sharing." Her second book, *Señor Cat's Romance*, published in 1997, has received excellent reviews in *Horn Book Magazine* and *School Library Journal.* Ms. González was named the Jean Key Gates Distinguished Alumni by the University of South Florida School of Library and Information Science for 1998.

Janice Greenberg is a children's librarian with the Brooklyn Public Library and a member of the library's Juvenile Advisory Committee. She served on the REFORMA Northeast Chapter's Pura Belpré Award Committee for 1998 and compiled the bibliography *Leadership & Participative Management* for the Third National Institute for Hispanic Library Education in 1997. Over the past decade, she has been extremely involved in the needs of special populations, most significantly ESOL and infants, toddlers and preschoolers.

Haydee C. Hodis is the assistant supervisor/children's librarian at the Brightwood/Mason Square Branches, Springfield Library, Springfield, Massachusetts, and a part-time reference librarian at the Central Connecticut State University Library, New Britain. She is a member of the American Library Association, the Ethnic Materials and Information Exchange Round Table, the Connecticut Library Association, REFORMA Northeast Chapter, and the Latino Family Child Care Providers Association, Springfield, Massachusetts. She has been collaborating with Irene Wood, ALA *Booklist* audio visual editor, reviewing Latino and Hispanic nonprint library materials slated to be published by Neal-Schuman. She currently serves on the board of directors of the Hispanic American Library, Springfield, Massachusetts.

Barbara Immroth is a professor at the University of Texas at Austin, Graduate School of Library and Information Science. She is president of Beta Phi Mu, past-president of the Texas Library Association, and the American Library Assocation representative to the International Federation of Library Associations and Institutions Standing Committee on Children's Libraries. She is on the ALA research team for the national assessment of the role of public and school libraries in education reform and is a past president of the Association for Library Services to Children.

Catherine Jasper is librarian in the Arts and Letters Department of the main library of Tampa–Hillsborough County Public Library System and a graduate of the University of South Florida, School of Library and Information Science, where she was president of the USF Student Chapter of the Special Libraries Association. She coordinated the Florida Library History Project, compiling histories of Florida's public libraries and creating a webpage to make them accessible. Before entering library school she taught English as a second language in both Ecuador and the United States. She was co-chair of the Fourth Trejo Foster Foundation Hispanic Library Education Institute in 1999.

Dean K. Jue is a research faculty member at the Florida State University in Tallahassee and co-directs the GeoLib program with Christine M. Koontz. He has a multidisciplinary background that encompasses biology, public policy, computer science, and public libraries. He is a co-chair of the Geographic Information Systems Interest Group of the Library Information and Technology Association. He is one of the principal members of the FSU research team investigating public library usage in library outlets primarily serving minority populations. His research specialty is applying technology such as geographic information systems to help library managers and directors better market their library services.

Kathleen de la Peña McCook is professor at the University of South Florida School of Library and Information Science, Tampa and Coordinator for Community Outreach of the College of Arts and Sciences. She has been president of the Association for Library and Information Science Education; chair of the American Library Association Office for Literacy and Outreach Services Advisory Committee; and editor of *RQ* and *Public Libraries*; and has served on the board of directors of REFORMA. She is a contributing editor of *American Libraries*. Her most recent books are *Women of Color in Librarianship* (ALA, 1998), and *A Librarian at Every Table* (ALA, 2000).

Milagros Otero Guzman is a student at the University of Puerto Rico Graduate School of Library and Information Science, Río Piedras, Puerto Rico. She has been a middle school librarian and an elementary and middle school English teacher. Her article "Red ORACLE Caribbean," was published in *Bibliotemas* in 1996.

Derrie Perez is the interim director of the University of South Florida Tampa Campus Library and an assistant professor at the University of South Florida School of Library and Information Science, Tampa. She has 21 years of community college library experience and held the position of associate vice president for learning resources services for eight years at Hillsborough Community College, also in Tampa. She has been president of the Florida College Center for Library Automation, the Tampa Bay Library Consortium, the National Council of Learning Resources, the Community and Junior College Library Section of Association of College and Research Libraries, and the Tampa Educational Cable Consortium. Currently she serves on the editorial board of *Community College Libraries*, and as a member of several USF strategic planning task forces.

Alice Robbin is an assistant professor in the School of Information Studies at Florida State University. Her research interests include information policy with an emphasis on the political, economic, and social dimensions of access to information; requisites for information infrastructure development and management; and social networks and information and communication flows in complex organizations. She is currently analyzing the political controversy about revising federal statistical policy for classifying racial and ethnic group data. She is a member of the American Society for the Advancement of Science; the American Association for Public Opinion Research; the Association for Computing Machinery; the American Library Association; the Association for Library and Information Science Educators; the American Political Science Association; the American Society of Information Science; the American Sociological Association, and the Information Industry Association.

Judith Rodriguez is supervising project librarian of the Connecting Libraries and Schools Project, New York Public Library. Through this project, she works with Latino parents in the Washington Heights area to introduce them to children's literature through picture-book discussion groups and poetry workshops in Spanish and English. She is a member of the Latin American Authors Committee of NYPL, the YALSA research committee, and the REFORMA Children's Services Committee. She served on the 1997 Pura Belpré Award Committee and received the 1993 Bertha Franklin Feder Award for outstanding librarianship.

Isabel Schon is director of the Center for the Study of Books in Spanish for Children and Adolescents (http://www.csusm.edu/campus_centers/csb/) and a member of the founding faculty member at California State University, San Marcos. Born in Mexico City, Dr. Schon came to the U.S. in 1972 and earned her Ph.D. at the University of Colorado in 1974. She has been a consultant on books in Spanish for young readers and bilingual and bicultural educational materials to schools, libraries and ministries of education in Mexico, Colombia, Guatemala, Argentina, Venezuela, Chile, Spain, Italy, Ecuador, and the United States. She has written 22 books and over 300 articles and chapters in books.

Henrietta M. Smith is a professor emerita on the faculty of the School of Library and Information Science, University of South Florida, Tampa, where she continues to teach in the area of materials for children and young adults. She has served on Newbery, Caldecott, Batchelder, and Wilder award committees and has chaired the Coretta Scott King Task Force and served on the award jury. She edited *The Coretta Scott King Awards Book: From Vision to Reality* (ALA, 1994) and *The Coretta Scott King Awards Book, 1970–1999* (ALA, 1999).

Arnulfo Trejo is the president of the Trejo Foster Foundation for Hispanic Library Education, a professor emeritus of the University of Arizona, and president of Hispanic Books Distributors, Inc. He has worked in libraries and the library community for more than forty years, including positions at the National University of Mexico, University of California at Los Angeles, and California State University. He received the Simón Bolívar Award, Colegio de Bibliotecônomos of Venezuela, in 1970; El Tiradito award from the El Tiradito Foundation in 1973 and 1975; the annual award from the League of Mexican-American Women in 1973; the Rosenzweig Award, Arizona State Library Association, 1976; and the Distinguished Alumni Award, Kent State University School of Library Science. Publications include *Diccionario etimológico del léxico de la delincuencia* ("Etymological Dictionary of the Language of the Underworld") (UTEHA, 1969); *Directory of Spanish-Speaking/Spanish Surnamed Librarians in the United States* (Bureau of School Services, College of Education, University of Arizona, 1973); *Bibliografía Chicana: A Guide to Information Services* (Gale, 1975); *Proceedings of the April 28–29, 1978; Seminario on Library and Information Services for the Spanish-Speaking: A Contribution to the Arizona Pre–White House Conference,* editor and contributor (Graduate Library Institute for Spanish-Speaking Americans, 1978); *The Chicanos: As We See Ourselves* (essays by fourteen Chicano scholars), editor and contributor (University of Arizona Press, 1979). Dr. Trejo is the founding president of REFORMA (in 1971).

Rose V. Treviño is the youth services coordinator for the San Antonio Public Library. She is a member of the Library's puppet troupe and reader's theater troupe and she participates in numerous outreach events. As a member of the Texas Library Association, she serves on the executive board of the children's round table. Also a member of ALA/ALSC, she is presently on the ALSC International Relations Committee as well as on the Newbery 2000 Committee. In addition, she developed a bilingual Born to Read program whose targeted audience is Hispanic teen mothers. A 5½ minute video was produced in English and in Spanish. A bilingual manual was written which includes tips on reading to babies plus Mexican nursery rhymes, songs, and lullabies. This Born to Read program was a 1998 recipient of the John Cotton Dana award.

Tim Wadham is assistant manager of the Pleasant Grove Branch of the Dallas Public Library. He served as a member of the 1998 Newbery Award Committee, and has been both a member and chair of the Association for Library Service to Children Notable Video Review committee. He is the author of *Programming with Latino Children's Materials: A How-to-Do-It Manual* (Neal-Schuman, 1999).

Dana Watson is an assistant professor at Louisiana State University, School of Library and Information Science, Baton Rouge. She is a member of the Readers' Advisory Committee of the Collection Development and Evaluation Section, Reference and User Services Association (a part of the American Library Association) and serves on the editorial board for *Reference and User Services Quarterly*. She is a member of the Association for Library Services to Children, American Association of School Librarians, and the United States Board on Books for Young People. In 1997, she was co-director of a U.S. Department of Education funded program, Multicultural Children's Resources Development Institute.

Sonia Ramírez Wohlmuth is assistant director of the School of Library and Information Science, and an instructor in the Division of Languages and Linguistics at the University of South Florida, Tampa. Through this joint position she is able to follow professional interests in service to Spanish speaking clients and the development of publicly accessible collections of Spanish language materials. She has been professionally active with the local library community in providing Spanish language training for staff members. She continues to pursue research and publishing projects on intercultural communication and Latin American literature.

Elaine Yontz is an assistant professor at the School of Library and Information Science at the University of South Florida, Tampa. She previously worked in cataloging at the George A. Smathers Libraries of the University of Florida in Gainesville. She has been president of the ALA New Members Roundtable.

INDEX